BEFORE
INTIMACY

BEFORE
INTIMACY

Asocial Sexuality in Early Modern England

DANIEL JUAN GIL

UNIVERSITY OF MINNESOTA PRESS

MINNEAPOLIS • LONDON

Material from the Introduction and chapter 1 was originally published as "Before Intimacy: Modernity and Emotion in the Early Modern Discourse of Sexuality," *ELH: English Literary History* 69 (2002): 861–87. A version of chapter 4 originally appeared as "At the Limits of the Social World: Fear and Pride in *Troilus and Cressida*," *Shakespeare Quarterly* 52 (Fall 2001): 336–59.

The rabbit-duck figure that appears in chapter 5 is taken from Ludwig Wittgenstein, *Philosophical Investigations: The German Text, with a Revised English Translation,* third edition, translated by G. E. M. Anscombe (Malden, MA: Blackwell Publishing, 2001). Reprinted with permission.

Published by the University of Minnesota Press
111 Third Avenue South, Suite 290
Minneapolis, MN 55401-2520
http://www.upress.umn.edu

Library of Congress Cataloging-in-Publication Data

Gil, Daniel Juan.
  Before intimacy : asocial sexuality in early modern England / Daniel Juan Gil.
    p. cm.
  Includes bibliographical references and index.
  ISBN 0-8166-4632-5 (acid-free paper) — ISBN 0-8166-4633-3 (pbk. : acid-free paper)
    1. English literature—Early modern, 1500-1700—History and criticism. 2. Sex in literature. 3. Literature and society—England—History—16th century. 4. Literature and society—England—History—17th century. 5. Sex customs—England—History—16th century. 6. Sex customs—England—History—17th century. 7. Man-woman relationships in literature. 8. Intimacy (Psychology) in literature. 9. Sex (Psychology) in literature. 10. Emotions in literature. I. Title.
  PR428.S48G55 2006
  820.9´3538´09031—dc22

                                                           2005021946

Printed in the United States of America on acid-free paper

The University of Minnesota is an equal-opportunity educator and employer.

12 11 10 09 08 07 06   10 9 8 7 6 5 4 3 2 1

CONTENTS

ACKNOWLEDGMENTS

I have benefited in countless ways from the intellectual and personal generosity of colleagues, teachers, and friends. First and foremost, I want to express my heartfelt gratitude to Jonathan Goldberg, who was the best graduate adviser anyone could ask for and who has been a wonderful friend ever since. His relentless intelligence, his suspicion of received wisdom, his hard work, and his boundless generosity are an inspiration to me. Barbara Correll's uncanny brilliance and kindness have been an encouragement for many years. Allen Grossman and John Guillory offered important early guidance. At the University of Oregon I want to thank my colleagues Lisa Freinkel and Ben Saunders, and I am especially grateful to Karen Ford for her unflagging support and her wisdom. George Rowe commented on some of the last drafts with critical rigor and grace, and for this and much else I am grateful to him. I want to thank Gail Kern Paster and the two anonymous readers at *Shakespeare Quarterly* for their invaluable help with the chapter on *Troilus and Cressida* that first appeared in that journal. I also owe an enormous debt to the University of Minnesota Press's two anonymous readers for the care and generosity with which they read the manuscript; this book is immeasurably better because of their work. Thanks are due, as well, to Richard Morrison, my editor, for his interest in the book and for the care with which he guided it through publication, as well as to Nancy Sauro for her expert copyediting.

This book would not have been possible without the friendship of Frances Dickey, Michael Drexler, Julie Kimmel, Kirstin Bucci, and

Frances Sackett. I am also grateful to Rick Keyser, Doug Robertson, and Brian Warren for the benefit of their conversation over many years; they are my School of Night. Finally, I owe more than I can say to Anne Frey, whose formidable intellect has improved every page of this book and whose love and humor have sustained me.

INTRODUCTION

One of the key assumptions of Renaissance studies in recent years has been that sexuality is inextricably intertwined with other registers of early modern social life. Drawing on groundbreaking work by Alan Bray, Jonathan Goldberg, Eve Kosofsky Sedgwick, Bruce R. Smith, and Valerie Traub, critics have shown that early modern sexuality could inhabit a whole range of conventionally social relationships without necessarily bringing attention to itself as sexuality, and Sedgwick's concept of "homosocial desire" is often taken as a shorthand for this situation. The homosocial paradigm has, in fact, had the immensely beneficial effect of highlighting how central sexuality is to a complete understanding of early modern society as a whole.[1] But, as Jeff Nunokawa has warned, this approach has also created a certain methodological blindness to the recognition of sexuality *in itself* as a specific experience that is at least sometimes set apart from the rest of social life.[2] Nunokawa calls for more attention to the historically variable discursive borders that define sexuality as a social domain or node of its own.

Although there have been important efforts to do just this, critics have most frequently attempted to highlight the separateness of sexuality from early modern society by deploying a sex-as-transgression rubric that fastens on early modern accusations of sodomy as ipso facto recognitions of sexuality *in itself*.[3] But, as Alan Bray has shown, when early modern friendships between men are attacked as instances of sodomy, the charge typically arises not from the sheer fact of sexual contact between men but from a failure to respect the conventions of a rank-bound society; acts that might elicit the denunciation of sodomy in one context might well be valorized as signs of friendship in another—for example, if the men involved were both of aristocratic rank.[4] Because it sees a transgressive sexuality only in conjunction with some more general attack on social life, the notion of sodomy inevitably remains within the orbit of a homosocial paradigm that emphasizes the intertwining of the sexual and the social.

Bray suggests another way that sexuality might be singled out as a specific kind of experience separate from the rest of early modern social life, namely, by anticipating modern sexual identities. Thus, he argues that eighteenth-century molly houses highlight male-male sexuality *as such* by spinning it into a kind of nascent gay identity. Critics like Smith, Traub, and Elizabeth Wahl have likewise identified moments when early modern sexuality seems to become aware of itself as a kind of nascent sexual identity.[5] As with all genealogical approaches, however, attempts to locate the roots of modern sexual identities in early modern culture can have the unintended effect of positing the modern identitarian regime as a historically inevitable outcome and occluding other historical possibilities.[6] Moreover, claims about nascent sexual identities in Renaissance culture often end up shading into the sex-as-transgression rubric by fastening on anticipatory developments that transgress against the historically dominant sex-gender system.

The difficulty critics have had in separating sexuality from other aspects of early modern social life highlights the important sociological fact that the early modern sex-gender system lacks the notion of *intimacy*—a special class of *interpersonal relationships* (whether between men, between women, or across gender) in which sexuality has a privileged home.[7] In modern societies, within the context of a private, familial life that is set apart from the rest of social life, sexuality has a policed but nonetheless sanctioned place as a privileged and highly valued experience. This form of private intimacy is richly imagined in eighteenth-century novels like *Pamela,* and reviewing its rise will be one of my concerns in this study. My aim in reviewing the genealogy of intimacy, however, is not to posit it as an inevitable outcome, but to identify early modern alternatives or even rivals to it. In essence, I want to pose the question of whether there is an early modern discourse that frames sexuality as a *special class of interpersonal relations* that, like modern intimacy, is set apart from conventional modes of sociability and the whole bundle of social relations that define society as a whole even if, unlike intimacy, it does not have an institutionalized home in a private, domestic sphere.

I will argue that early modern literary texts do in fact contain a discourse that frames sexuality as a special class of interpersonal relationships, and I will suggest that this literary discourse is built out of the friction and turmoil generated by the conflicted, contested, and uneven emergence of a modern social formation; drawing on this social turmoil, literary texts conceptualize a class of powerful, phenomenologically sexual connections that spring up between people who have in some important way dropped out of the functional dimensions of an early modern society riven by historical change.

In order to specify the early modern social trauma that is at the root of this literary discourse of sexuality, I rely on sophisticated and influential sociological models of the rise of modernity, especially Niklas Luhmann's discussion of the rise of modern intimacy and Norbert Elias's classic analysis of the civilizing process.[8] I use these models to highlight the dead ends, the points of hot friction that the process of modernization inevitably generated, and not to celebrate the triumphal emergence of a modern social formation. My central argument will be that early modern sexuality—conceived as a special class of interpersonal relations—is rooted in the friction generated when a characteristically modern ideal of universal humanity is undercut or abraded by residual elements of a premodern social imaginary that emphasizes inherent identities and quasi-biological differences between persons. In the literary discourse I examine, this abstract sociological contradiction energizes a privileged sexual experience in which people are driven together by the allure of a shared humanity only to be plunged apart at the last moment by a resurgent sense of fundamental, blood-borne difference and almost bodily incompatibility. In early modern literary texts, the bodily incompatibility that is *felt as* the (pleasurable) violation of a hypothetically universal humanity constitutes a sexual intersubjectivity that separates itself from conventionally social modes of interpersonal bonding. In this literary discourse an experience of social breakdown comes to be valued for the way it defines a specifically sexual mode of bonding; when shared humanity is short-circuited, characters are torn out of the functional social world and dropped into a kind of parallel society where the pain of interpersonal breakdown is recast as a pleasurable connection to another body.

In the texts I examine, the positive, felt reality of this abstract, sociologically defined sexuality is captured by powerful, often one-sided emotions like fear, pride, and shame.[9] In describing the role of literary representations of emotions in documenting the experience of early modern sexuality, I draw on recent, vital work on the history of the emotions by Gail Kern Paster and Michael Schoenfeldt as well as philosophical work by Martha Nussbaum; I propose that sixteenth-century literary texts do not treat emotions as signs of deep, inner states or personalities, or as potentially destabilizing humoral imbalances or impurities as a Galenic approach would suggest.[10] Rather, these texts value powerfully corporeal, often depersonalized emotions for the ways they define specific forms of connection between bodies that arise when functional connections between socially legible persons have been foreclosed. To put it another way, the confused state of early modern thinking about the connection between emotions and selves opens the door to using emotions to define sexual limit experiences in which selves are temporarily unmoored from their normal positions in the social world and recoded into an emotional space where they can enter into powerful connections with other, socially unmoored selves.[11] In essence, the emotions represented in literary texts sketch the grammar of a nexus of bodily connections that simply leave early modern social conventions and norms behind. Critics have, in fact, had difficulty seeing this form of emotionally mediated sexual bonding because they have tended to assume that sexuality is either seamlessly congruent with the whole complex welter of early modern social life (as the notion of homosocial desire suggests) or radically transgressive of it (as the notion of sodomy suggests).[12] Departing from the dialectic of social norm and transgression, I describe a sexuality that is neither *social* nor *antisocial* but *asocial* in that it represents a form of emotionally mediated inter-personal bonding that grows out of fundamental contradictions within early modern social life and then leaves those contradictions behind.

One of the most important theoretical influences on my discussion is Leo Bersani's account of sexuality as a beneficent shattering of the self or ego, and part of my aim is to historicize Bersani's powerful model. Drawing on the psychoanalytic work of Jean Laplanche, Bersani argues that sexuality is an "evolutionary conquest" that enables humans to survive the prolonged infancy during which their egos are not well enough fortified to project a continuous sense of selfhood in relation to the outside world.[13] When the human infant is confronted with waves of potentially overwhelming sensory stimulus, it protects itself, so to speak, by learning to take pleasure in self-dissolution, a form of adap-tive pleasure that forms the blueprint for the "adult" sexuality in which a more fully formed and defended ego again gives itself up to the pleasure of being unsettled or shattered. Several critics have identified this account of sexuality as a powerful tool for investigating Renais-sance culture, notably Jeffrey Masten and Cynthia Marshall.[14] And yet, Bersani's assumptions about the self are not the same as those of Renaissance culture insofar as the well-defined, well-defended ego that he assumes as the subject of a pleasurable self-shattering is not some-thing that could be taken for granted *yet* in the early modern era.[15] I essentially transpose Bersani's model of sexuality as a failure of a well-fashioned self into an account of sexuality as a historically conditioned failure of the functional social ties on which selves depend. Seen in this light, early modern sexuality amounts to an adaptive response to the trauma of an emerging modernity; where Bersani's infant must survive early life by learning to take pleasure in the always present threat of ego-dissolution, the literary texts I examine suggest that the unprece-dented historical trauma of the European emergence into modernity could be survived by learning to take a kind of pained pleasure in the threat of social dissolution or social entropy. So seen, the literary dis-course of sexuality I examine in this book, forged at the very moment when the modernity we now inhabit was consolidated, represents a powerful resource for rethinking and reimagining the terms of social life from the ground up, as it were, by focusing our attention on alternatives to the most basic ways people negotiate their experience of others in social life.[16]

The experience of sexuality that I describe here is rooted in the most fundamental sociological pressures of the age, but precisely because it is unsocial or asocial it leaves few marks in conventional historical archives. It is, however, recognized, represented, and theorized by the most self-consciously serious literary texts of the age. By bringing this asocial sexuality into language, literary texts begin to give it a *discursive* home of its own as a special class of interpersonal relations that are set apart from the rest of social life. These texts can therefore act as an archive of the experience that we can recover today; it is, in fact, the *literary* discourse of asocial sexuality that is the immediate object of my analysis here.[17]

If the sexuality that grows out of the historical trauma of early modernity is archived in early modern literature, then this is at least partly because it intersects there with one of the central developments of literary history, the emergence of something like an autonomous literary sphere out of what had previously been a more socially functional courtly culture. Although one source for my notion of an autonomous literary sphere is the complex sociological model of culture proposed by Pierre Bourdieu, I mean by it something quite simple: that artists address readers and other artists according to criteria that apply only to art and not also to other forms of social practice. In this sense, autonomy for the literary field could not yet be taken for granted during the early modern period where the surest path toward cultural prestige lay in simply asserting courtly sophistication, or in delivering art that would testify to the social distinction of its patrons. In sketching the emergence of something like literary autonomy out of this courtly culture, I rely, in part, on Richard Helgerson's important account of the rise of self-consciously serious authors in his *Self-Crowned Laureates*.[18] The rise of "laureates" is obviously an important step in the emergence of literary autonomy, but Helgerson's argument is largely symptomatic; he cites Spenser and Jonson as men who simply declined to frame themselves exclusively as courtly poets and instead asserted a new kind of literary authority for themselves as serious writers. But asserting such a literary authority makes sense only within the context of an already institutionalized literary field, which in turn authorizes specifically literary ambition. In that sense, Helgerson ends up pointing to a hole or a hiatus in literary history; while a later generation of writers could imagine literary autonomy because they inhabited an already existing literary field with a complex, structurally inverted relation to a commercial market for culture, the most self-consciously serious writers of Spenser's generation could define their role as writers only through a kind of theatrical, creative negation of the role of courtly poet, a negation that only makes sense in retrospective literary history.

I will argue that the literary discourse of asocial sexuality both *enacts* and *theorizes* the strange, unrooted, and uprooting ambition that drives writers out of the realm of courtly culture in the absence of any institutionalized alternative: enacts it, insofar as developing an emotional grammar of sexuality allows writers to decline the default task of service to the court; and theorizes it, insofar as an ambition that operates by pushing writers out of any legible career track can itself be experienced as a kind of desire—Spenser, for one, is quite explicit in framing his experience of writing as a species of sexuality.[19] In a sense, therefore, I see the literary discourse of sexuality I examine here as an allegory of writing that provides a set of terms for a cultural practice that is as socially exorbitant and even dysfunctional as the sexuality these texts describe, and here my argument finally circles back to Bersani and his account of high modernist aesthetics as a way of engaging the very pleasures of self-annihilation or self-shattering that define, for him, sexuality.[20] Approaching sixteenth-century literature through the lens of Bersani's comments on sex and literature brings into focus a nexus of an asocial sexuality that arises from the historical trauma of early modernity and a literary ambition that is also, in certain of its ineradicable aspects, exorbitant or dysfunctional, pushing writers away from a very legible courtly mode of cultural politics and into a strangely unreactive or dysfunctional cultural realm that does not yet have a proper name in the early modern context.[21]

This book is organized into an initial theoretical overview in chapter 1, followed by four case studies of major early modern writers. In the first chapter, I offer a sociologically elaborated and historically contextualized version of the argument I sketch in this introduction. In presenting this overview, I examine influential theorists of modern society like Elias and Luhmann, the work of contemporary theorists of sexuality and the emotions like Bersani and Nussbaum, together with early modern theorists, including Edward Reynolds, Ben Jonson, and Robert Burton, to explain how Renaissance writers use emotions to define connections between bodies that spring up when functional connections between socially legible persons have been foreclosed. I end this theoretical overview with a careful analysis of poems by Sir Thomas Wyatt that illustrates how this sociohistorical methodology can be applied in practice to reveal the structural coherence of the discourse of emotionally mediated sexuality that runs through Wyatt's writing.

In the balance of the book I apply this sociological mode of reading in case studies of Sidney, Spenser, and Shakespeare. In chapter 2, I examine the connection between a deviant literary ambition that aims to leave the notion of courtly poetry behind and the literary discourse of asocial, emotionally mediated sexuality by contrasting Sidney's self-consciously courtly sonnet sequence *Astrophil and Stella* with Spenser's curiously professional stance in the *Amoretti*. In chapter 3, I describe how Spenser uses the discourse of civility to calibrate his major epic, *The Faerie Queene,* to systematically explore and catalog the fault lines and breakdowns that plague early modern society and that generate an asocial sexuality that runs beneath the surface of early modern society as we have grown accustomed to seeing it. Finally, in chapters 4 and 5, I use *Troilus and Cressida* and the *Sonnets* to argue that Shakespeare builds on the literary discourse of sexuality that he inherits from Sidney and Spenser to arrive at an unusually precise emotional vocabulary of asocial sexuality (emphasizing pride, fear, and shame) that is aligned with a powerful and still timely account of literary culture as profoundly—and even perversely—indifferent to the needs and anxieties of Renaissance society.

CHAPTER I

The Social Structure
of Passion

One of the central claims of this book is that the sexual intersubjectivity that early modern literary texts describe both anticipates and departs from some of the key assumptions of the modern sexual ideal of intimacy. I begin to decribe this early modern alternative to intimacy, and its historically specific use of emotions, by reviewing Niklas Luhmann's sociological account of the emergence and function of intimacy as a specific *structure of relationship,* tied to the whole system of social relationships, that defines modernity.[1]

One of the hallmarks of modernity, for Luhmann, is a social world organized by impersonal systems such as the economy and party politics, and he argues that these impersonal social systems gradually displace the heritable, relatively local hierarchies of traditional society. As traditional hierarchies wane, people are less and less able to derive a sense of personal identity from their positions within the social world; Luhmann argues that people compensate by deriving a sense of themselves from their particular ways of looking at the world, from their personalities:

> Possessing a name and a place within the social framework in the form
> of general categories such as age, gender, social status and profession no
> longer suffices as a means of both knowing that one's organism exists
> and of self-identification—the basis for one's own life experience and
> action. Rather, individual persons have to find affirmation at the level
> of their respective personality systems, i.e., in the difference between

themselves and their environment and in the manner in which they deal with this difference—as opposed to the way others do.[2]

For Luhmann, the "personality system" that has value precisely because it sets someone apart from others must, somewhat paradoxically, be affirmed by at least one privileged spectator. What he describes as the code of intimacy deals with the paradoxical and characteristically modern task of affirming the lifeworld of an individual as something particular, as something that essentially cannot be communicated or at least cannot be communicated easily. Intimate relationships are designed to mediate between individuals who have disparate experiences of the world and who value these disparate experiences as a source of personal identity. Moreover, because intimacy is charged with communication about personalities that are defined as being noncommunicable and separate from the shared world, Luhmann argues that it seizes on bodily passion to say what cannot be said. He writes, "love solves its own attendant communicative problems in a completely unique manner. To put it paradoxically, love is able to enhance communication by largely doing without communication."[3] Thus, even though modern societies rely more and more on impersonal connections, they also lay the groundwork for increasingly deep personal connections. In the context of a modern form of social life, intimate personal bonds are part of the individual's effort to cultivate a sense of self that does not rely on a stable position within a social hierarchy. At the same time, intimate relations compensate persons for the alienation that comes from exposure to impersonal social systems that are not respecters of persons. As a structure of relationship, therefore, intimacy becomes the hallmark of a modern notion of private life that nourishes a personality that people value as the essence of who they are.

Luhmann's narrative of modernization and the rise of intimacy postdates the sixteenth century, but it seems clear that already in the sixteenth century normative hierarchies are being challenged, and their ability to deliver stable social identities is therefore no longer assured. In fact, in part because of the breakdown of traditional hierarchy and the consequent pressure to seek other supports for personal identity, there are instances of intensely intimate connections that provide compensation for a loss of traditional social identity. Such intimacies occur between men or between women more frequently than they occur between men and women. Unlike the modern intimacy Luhmann describes, however, in the early modern period such relationships are not seen as separate from a public world of impersonal ties. Rather, they are celebrated, under the rubric of friendship, as fundamental pillars of social stability. Alan Bray's analysis of sodomy suggests that such intimacies can, at times, seem profoundly transgressive precisely because the weight of the social world stands on their shoulders.[4] In other words, in the early modern period intimacy is not yet institutionalized as a realm apart from the public world and its status hierarchies, and when an intimate relationship comes to seem dangerous it is the whole social world that is endangered. Even so, early modern friendship may indeed be the precursor to the intimacy Luhmann models. But because Luhmann's narrative is so strongly teleological, leading inexorably toward the modern intimacy that is housed within a private, domestic sphere, it does not allow room for alternatives to modern intimacy that arise during the tumultuous process of modernization.

To describe an early modern *rival* to intimacy, a rival that also defines sexuality as a *structure of relationship* that is set apart from day-to-day social life but which is not yet rooted in a domestic or private sphere, I turn to Norbert Elias's account of modernization, which parallels Luhmann's but leaves room for alternative social formations that, strictly speaking, have no future after the version of modernity we now inhabit coalesces. In *The Civilizing Process*, his monumental study of conduct literature from the Middle Ages to the Enlightenment, Elias connects the rise of modernity to changes in the emotional and psychic life of individuals.[5] For Elias, as for Luhmann, modern societies rely on an unprecedented degree of interconnection between individuals on which the life and safety of each individual depends. Elias writes that in the modern condition every person is embedded in long, seamless webs of social dependency that are not regulated by an external hierarchy.[6] To make these chains of interdependence possible, the instinctual life of every individual has to be dampened. Elias argues that Renaissance conduct manuals encourage a new emphasis on elegant and refined manners that are designed to conceal and disguise the life of the body beneath a veneer of civility. People are encouraged to pay constant attention to the impact their own bodies have on others in order to lubricate the countless interpersonal encounters on which modern social life depends. To use one of Elias's most forceful slogans, the civilizing process makes modern social life possible by lowering the threshold for feeling shame.

Elias himself sometimes speaks as though he were charting the historical rise of a repressive superego, but his larger sociological argument suggests that he is describing not a *quantitative* reduction of instinctual life but a *qualitative* change in the nature of human ties.[7] I suggest that the self-restraint and highly elaborated manners championed by the early modern project of civility are not only repressive but also signs of a qualitatively new and productive interpersonal ideal, the ideal of a humane relationship that aims to respect some human essence shared by everyone. Given the early modern celebration of hereditary rank, the hypothesis that there is a human core that is shared by everyone and that ought to be respected in all social interactions is anything but obvious. The slow emergence of such an interpersonal ideal can best be grasped in the widening scope of—and changing rationale for—civilized manners. The earliest conduct manuals Elias examines are specifically courtly; they were written for members of an aristocratic elite, and the rules they advocated were not applicable to other people in the social world. But during the Renaissance, the program of good manners and civility was gradually applied to wider and wider segments of the population until it applied, in principle, to everyone. And as the scope of civility expanded, good manners acquired a new rationale: whereas medieval conduct manuals framed manners as a way of looking high-class, Renaissance manuals increasingly frame manners as a way of recognizing and affirming some shared humanity found in everyone. Again and again in Erasmus's *Civility in Boys,* for example, the basic rationale given for adopting good manners is the need to identify with other human beings—and to avoid insulting or embarrassing them—simply because they *are* human beings.[8] Thus, while the

Renaissance project of civility does repress patterns of emotional and bodily life that characterized an older and simpler social world, it also cultivates new emotional experiences (not least, shame) that are calibrated to recognize a human core that Renaissance humanists increasingly hypothesize in all human subjects, and that is the basis of the new social ideal of a humane relationship.

An important part of my argument in this book is that the growing recognition of some human core identity in the Renaissance discourse of civility is in fact a *misrecognition* of a new social reality—a dense, interconnected, mutually dependent social world from which no one and no group can secede.[9] This complex, interconnected social totality is only slowly coming into conscious focus in the early modern period in discourses like political theory and even early statistics.[10] Within the discourse of civility, this new social reality appears in a symptomatic form as the real referent of the universal "humanity" that the discourse of civility hypothesizes and offers as the rationale for good manners.[11] Thus, in the discourse of civility a new social reality—based on competitive social interrelatedness—is recognized, in part, through a new way of conceiving human relationships as defined by the obligation to respect a core human identity shared by all. Needless to say, the inclusive social world that is dimly glimpsed in the discourse of civility is characterized not by a coincidence of interests between all but by competition and struggle between individuals and social groups; for this reason, the terms of fully humane relationships are themselves an object of social struggle. As a contested ideal, the notion of a shared humanity nevertheless amounts to a powerful new way of envisioning social relationships and the social world, a powerful new social imaginary.

This new ideal of a humane relationship and the hypothetical core of humanity that underpins it are important because they act as a goal toward which real behavior is directed. In other words, once the ideal comes into focus, people really do aim for humane relationships, and on an ever-expanding scale. But the new ideal is equally important insofar as it makes it possible to recognize spectacular violations of a shared human core identity. These violations of the emerging ideal of humanity are at the heart of the sexuality I examine in this book.

The most obvious violations of the emerging ideal of shared humanity during the early modern period come from the continuing presence of vestiges of the traditional, aristocratic social framework. It is a
fundamental fact of early modern society that a modern conception of
social life, organized around the ideal of universally shared humanity,
fails to displace an older, and radically less dynamic, conception of the
social world in which relationships are mediated by an inherited status hierarchy that defines blood-borne identities. This traditional social
hierarchy, and the stable social identities it anchors, allows for fierce love
between those bound together by kinship ties and equally fierce hatred
of blood enemies; it also allows for utter indifference toward those
whose social position or class renders them beyond the social horizon,
something that is quite impossible from a standpoint that assumes a
humanity shared by all.[12] Throughout the early modern period, and
throughout the early modern literary texts I examine in this book,
aristocratic bloodlust, unconditional hatred, and social indifference all
collide with the emerging ideal of shared humanity. In essence, it is
a collision of different ways of picturing the social world, a collision of
social imaginaries.

There is another, allied, violation of universal humanity, which paradoxically occurs inside the world brought into existence by the universalizing discourse of civility. Since universal civility has its roots
in the medieval "courtliness" that applied only to the courtly elites,
adopting a veneer of manners is still most advanced at the absolutist
courts of the Renaissance. There the quest for civility is a form of symbolic competition; it aims for a kind of self-fashioning that will elicit
social recognition and respect. At court, manners and civility have a
status effect; they distinguish, and, as such, they are an important field
of contest for courtly elites.[13] By applying the standards of civility to
everyone, humanist conduct manuals paradoxically increased the prestige of the new elites at court who became a kind of civility vanguard.
Indeed, humanist conduct manuals endorse the notion of a courtly
civility vanguard when they identify courtiers around the absolute
monarch as models for good behavior that other social agents ought to
imitate. Thus, even as the discourse of civility tries to civilize everyone

in the name of respecting the core of humanity shared by all, it also makes civilized and refined behavior into a powerful guarantor of the superior social status of the courtly elite. Moreover, the discourse of civility often folds this cultural distinction back on the terms of the premodern social imaginary by treating different degrees of acculturation as though they were borne by different degrees of aristocratic blood. Much of elite court culture is, in fact, oriented toward the paradoxical project of *acting wellborn;* good behavior and personal refinement are framed merely as *expressions* of an aristocratic status that resides not in cultural or symbolic achievements but in aristocratic blood. At such moments, the project of civility and good manners is used to disavow any universal social life or universal humanity in favor of reasserting fundamental, biological differences between persons.[14] In practice, therefore, the discourse of civility oscillates between providing potentially universal terms for social interactions rooted in a hypothetically shared humanity and redefining the insuperable, quasi-heritable differences between people that are pegged to an aristocratic social imaginary.[15]

During the early modern period, friction between these incompatible social imaginaries and the different norms of sociability that characterize them defines a massive and recurring crisis in which the very possibility of establishing functional social ties seems threatened. But it is precisely this massive social crisis that energizes the special class of sexual intersubjectivity that I examine. The conflict between modern and premodern social forms opens a phenomenological experience of sexuality triggered when characters are pulled together by the gravity of a hypothetically shared humanity only to be actively repelled from one another, like negatively charged particles, because of a sudden resurgence of hereditary difference defined by a premodern social imaginary. At such moments, incompatible social imaginaries fuse to generate a structure of relationship that is premised on an almost physical sense of repulsion or incompatibility; my central argument is that bodily incompatibility that is *felt as* the (pleasurable) violation of a hypothetically universal humanity defines a sexual intersubjectivity that is set apart from other, conventionally social relationships.[16] The sexual intensity attained by short-circuiting humanity or by catastrophically undermining the terms of humane ties places those who experience it in a social bubble, neither part of a conflicted social world nor fundamentally separate from it. Like the modern intimacy that Luhmann describes, the sexual intersubjectivity defined by the violation of a hypothetical humanity defines a place apart from the social world in which sexuality can flourish. But unlike intimacy, the experience of characters caught in the attraction/repulsion loop of early modern sexuality is not institutionalized in a private, domestic realm, nor does it affirm the rich, human personhood that flourishes within an institutionalized private sphere. Quite the opposite, in fact; the early modern discourse of sexuality I examine celebrates sexuality as a way of violating an increasingly prestigious social norm of universal humanity that compels respect for all persons.

One way of clarifying the nature of this historically rooted sexuality is by comparing it with Leo Bersani's powerful account of sexuality as a pleasurable shattering of the ego or the self.[17] Though there have been important efforts to apply Bersani's model to the early modern context, his assumption of a stable, well-defined self that is pleasurably shattered by sexuality seems anachronistic in a context where self-fashioning is still very much on the cultural agenda.[18] But some of Bersani's own formulations suggest a way of historicizing his account by transposing the notion of sexuality as a failure of a self into an account of sexuality as a failure of certain kinds of social relationships. Discussing Freud's early *Three Essays on Sexuality*, for example, Bersani suggests that Freud's account of the self arriving at "natural" "post-Oedipal" relations is troubled by a speculation about a form of desire that shatters the psychic structures that are necessary for any relationship whatsoever:

> [O]n the one hand Freud outlines a normative sexual development that finds its natural goal in the post-Oedipal, genitally centered desire for someone of the opposite sex, while on the other hand he suggests not only the irrelevance of the object in sexuality but also, and even more radically, a shattering of the psychic structures that are the precondition for the very establishment of a relation to others.[19]

Obviously, the implied notion that oedipal relationships are the blue-prints for all social relationships is quite wrong in the early modern context, yet the notion that sexuality operates by disrupting the conditions of a "relation to others" opens the door to a more historically rooted conception. In his political writings, in fact, Bersani celebrates sexuality's ability to suspend not timeless oedipal relations but historically conditioned social ideals and norms. In his important 1987 essay on the AIDS crisis, for example, Bersani offers an ironic endorsement of Catherine MacKinnon and Andrea Dworkin's critique of pornography because "their indictment of sex—their refusal to prettify it, to romanticize it, to maintain that fucking has anything to do with community or love—has had the immensely desirable effect of publicizing, of lucidly laying out for us, the inestimable value of sex as—at least in certain of its ineradicable aspects—anticommunal, antiegalitarian, anti-nurturing, antiloving."[20] I transpose this claim that sexuality disrupts the norms of functional social relationships into the historically specific early modern conflict between competing social imaginaries. One of Bersani's most remarkable slogans is that sexuality is "socially dysfunctional in that it brings people together only to plunge them into a self-shattering and solipsistic *jouissance* that drives them apart."[21] I historicize this slogan by claiming that early modern sexuality arises when characters are driven together by the emerging modern theory of a universally shared humanity only to be driven apart at the last moment by the sudden (and, again, historically rooted) resurgence of a sense of essential, blood-borne difference between persons.[22] This formulation opens a path away from a transhistorical theory of sexuality rooted in a transhistorical theory of the psyche (such as the Freudianism that Bersani continues to use as a basic explanatory framework, even as he performs virtuoso deconstructions of key texts by Freud) and toward a fully *social* account of sexuality rooted in nothing but the dark energy generated by historical contradictions and conflicts between competing structures of relationship.

A key part of this historically rooted experience of sexuality is its historically specific engagement of the emotions. If early modern sexuality emerges as a special class of relationships whose distinctive relational structure is determined by the conflict between competing ways of imagining social life, then literary texts *graph* this distinctively sexual relational structure by means of a very particular discourse of the emotions. In the context of the literary discourse of asocial sexuality, early modern writers treat emotions neither as states of a deep, personal psychology, as modern cognitive psychologists do, nor as humoral imbalances that trigger disease, as many early modern thinkers still did. Instead, these writers take advantage of early modern uncertainty about the connection between passions and selves in order to treat the passions as a sort of parallel form of social glue; for these writers, emotions define bodily states that open connections to other, emotionally inflamed bodies that arise when functionally social ties between socially legible persons have been foreclosed. In short, the powerful, corporeal emotions that run through early modern literary texts outline the grammar of a nexus of sexual ties that cannot be described in any social discourse precisely because they are born of the friction between competing social discourses.

The innovative way early modern literary texts use emotions is easiest to see when it is contrasted with some of the basic assumptions that characterize modern thinking about the emotions. Martha Nussbaum's *Upheavals of Thought: The Intelligence of Emotions* is useful in this regard because it captures much of a modern consensus about the emotions.[23] As the subtitle of Nussbaum's book implies, hers is a cognitive approach to the emotions: she sees emotions as possessing a kind of intelligence, as a sort of parallel-thinking system that enables an individual to care about many different things in many different ways. For her, emotions are judgments about what things and people in the world are important to the self; the emotions enshrine a personality, a particular worldview, so much so that to change the emotional life is to change the personality and vice versa.[24] But even as the emotions define an irreducible personality that is distinct from others, they also go forth from the individual to affirm responsibility for other persons (and even for certain animals). In fact, for Nussbaum, the primary goal of education should be to build in the individual an emotional life that maximizes the emotional identification between self and others. Nussbaum's account thus illustrates the paradoxical task that emotions are called on to perform within a modern cognitive framework: emotions are valued both because they define a singular and irreducible personality and because they provide a bridge between disparate individuals. It is a framework that fits perfectly into Luhmann's account of romantic intimacy.

While many of Nussbaum's assumptions about the self and personality are quite foreign to the early modern context, some aspects of her account are anticipated by early modern writers. For example, in *A Treatise of the Passions and Faculties of the Soule* (1640), Edward Reynolds develops the view that emotions define an individual identity, and he views controlling and managing the emotions as the key to controlling individual behavior.[25] For Reynolds, to mold the emotions is to mold the individual and his or her most fundamental ways of responding to the world, and he believes that the goal of education should be to hard-wire a Puritan sociability into the individual subject in just the way that Nussbaum believes education should hard-wire a liberal sociability. Despite his emphasis on the possibility of molding the emotional life, however, Reynold's text is suffused with moments in which emotions that are endowed with a recalcitrant, alien power invade the well-constituted, Puritan subject. Reynolds interprets these emotional outbreaks as moments in which God (or Satan) breaks directly into the individual consciousness. In fact, however, these alien emotions emanate from another *discursive* world, the world of generic Galenism that still informs much early modern thinking on emotions.[26] This generic Galenism interprets emotions not as components of a psychology that define an individual but as humoral imbalances that can be modified more readily by diet, drugs, and purges than by mental work.[27]

The view of emotions as states of the body is an important and widely shared bias in the early modern period, but it has given rise to some misconceptions about how the early modern approach to emotional life differs from the modern. To some extent, for instance, the early modern refusal of a sharp distinction between thought and body recurs in Nussbaum's account of emotions as a sort of corporeal thinking.[28]

The most important consequence of the Galenic bias in early modern culture is how emotions are valued or what information about the self and the world they are asked to provide. Unlike modern cognitive theorists, early modern writers typically did not value the emotions for the personality or worldview that they supposedly embodied. In early modern thinking on the humors, the category of personality is largely replaced by the notion of recurring dispositions, as it is in Galen, who posits four humors and nine basic personal dispositions corresponding to various combinations of these humors. To a considerable extent, early modern thinkers viewed emotions as constituting a finite set of body-mind types that could be readily classed. And rather than valuing humoral dispositions as a source of individuality or personal identity, early modern thinkers typically couple the theory of recurring humoral dispositions with a normative account that values a kind of stoical balance and emotional neutrality. Texts like Robert Burton's *Anatomy of Melancholy* (1621) and Ben Jonson's humoral comedies (I am thinking specifically here of *Every Man In His Humor* [1598]) imply that to whatever extent humors do ossify (or worse: are actively shaped) into something resembling a personal disposition (what Burton calls a "habit"), to that extent the individual is sick and in need of a cure. Drawing on deep reservoirs of stoicism in Renaissance culture, the goal of both Burton's disquisition and Jonson's comedies is to restore a balanced, neutral disposition that looks a lot like the absence of any personality whatsoever.[29] What is importantly true of Burton and Jonson, though not always true of Reynolds, is that they do not value emotions as signs of a distinct personality. Rather, they tend to view them as recurring bodily patterns that threaten to shift the individual out of the shared social world.

The early modern discourse that couples the theory of recurring humoral dispositions with a normative stoicism opens the door to an emotional counterdiscourse that becomes an important part of the literary discourse of sexuality I examine here. When emotions are conceived as recurring somatic types rather than as private, mental states, they can be used to define bodies that link with (or repulse) other emotionally defined bodies in ways not regulated by social norms. In Jonson's *Every Man In His Humor,* for example, different humoral types can do quite a lot with and to one another, even if what they do seems antisocial. Proud and fearful characters are yoked together in an endless, if sadistic, dance. These humors define connections between bodies that spring up when connections between persons have become temporarily unavailable. And if writers like Burton and Jonson see emotional dispositions (and the interpersonal interactions they generate) as antisocial because they separate people from a social world defined (for them) by norms of moderation and balance, then such dispositions can also be valued precisely on the grounds that they define interpersonal connections that stand outside of the normal frameworks of the social world, that are in some important sense an alternative to the normative interactions on which early modern society depends. The literary discourse of sexuality I examine here seizes on emotions because they can put the body in touch with other bodies in ways that cannot be reduced to intimacy between persons or to any of the norms of social interaction that allegedly govern the social world.

The ability of emotional states to define a grammar of relationships at a somatic, body-to-body level is one reason sixteenth-century literary texts turn to them to describe a sexuality born of friction between incompatible visions of functional social ties. An equally important reason is that they do not seem psychologically inward or hard to see. After all, if emotions are imbalances of humors in the body, then they are visible to a spectator (or at least a trained spectator) in just the way that other facts about the body are. In *The Faerie Queene*, for example, Spenser thinks that physical descriptions of characters in the grip of a powerful emotional experience give full access to the emotional states of these characters; no further information is needed, and there is no deep problem about sharing emotional states with his readers. In the absence of a theory of rich interiorized personality, early modern emotions do not seem especially private or hard to communicate; they are public, and they can therefore be used to define a public matrix of sexual interactions into which emotionally defined bodies can enter. In short, in early modern literary texts, emotions encode the position of characters in an emotional space where the self and others can interact in ways that bypass any available social norms. Rather than seeking to renegotiate a relationship that is at an emotional impasse, the early modern discourse of sexuality I describe celebrates emotions themselves as the basis of a powerful, asocial connection. A perfect example of this sort of interaction comes in the final stanzas of book 4, canto 7, of *The Faerie Queene,* when Arthur reads Timias's terrible depression as ipso facto evidence of love, and interacts with Timias not according to the social norms of master and squire but only by managing Timias's erotic pain.[30] At this moment, Arthur makes use of a sort of X-ray vision that cuts behind the supposed norms of early modern social interaction to reveal circuits of sexual sociability that inhere in powerful emotions that open and close bodies to one another in profoundly extrasocial ways.

One analogue to the X-ray perspective that reveals powerful emotional connections between bodies that go beyond the norms of the social world lies in the sadomasochism that Bersani, for one, sees as revealing the truth of all sexual encounters, even those that appear to be based on mutuality and respect.[31] In sadomasochistic scenes, social codes, often invidious codes of gender or class hierarchy, are used tactically to provoke an emotional charge that also contains a sexual charge. Part of the reason these emotions are erotically charged is that they define relationships—or at least interactions—between people that seem to go beyond the claims of the social world. Judith Butler, among others, has sought to portray sadomasochistic scripts, along with camp parodies, as critical political acts that reveal that social codes are, at bottom, merely performative.[32] Responding to such claims, Bersani rightly notes that camp and sadomasochism are not about political critique but about delivering a sexual charge. The emotional charges generated through sadomasochistic scripts (pride, perhaps, or fear or hatred) deliver an erotic charge despite the self-consciously theatrical way in which they are produced, and these emotional charges define relationships (or nonrelationships) that feel sexual precisely because they cannot be reduced to any functional social terms. Like the luxuriant emotions that are liberated in sadomasochistic scenes, early modern emotions designate not states of psychologically deep individuals but social states that cannot be described in any other way.

Converting the threat of social dissolution into a pleasure that is marked by intense, unsettling emotions is one of the hallmarks of the poetry of Sir Thomas Wyatt. Wyatt's poetry provides a case study of how sociologically informed historicism allows us to treat literary texts as an archive of the felt reality of early modern sexuality. In discussing Wyatt's poetry, I will attend to the complexity that results from including gender in the analysis. While the basic contradiction that opens the door to the early modern experience of sexuality is not gender specific, in practice the contradiction between incompatible terms of social ordering is almost always vectored through gender. In "The Long Love That in My Thought Doth Harbour," for example, the speaker triggers a sexual experience by trying unsuccessfully to renounce the complex social totality of the modern world in favor of a simpler, less ambivalent, and distinctly feudal kind of relationship defined by a traditional hierarchy; at the same time, however, this turn is depicted as a move away from cross-gender relationships to same-sex relationships:

> The long love that in my thought doth harbour
> And in mine heart doth keep his residence
> Into my face presseth with bold pretence
> And therein campeth, spreading his banner.
> She that me learneth to love and suffer
> And will that my trust and lust's negligence
> Be reined by reason, shame, and reverence,
> With his hardiness taketh displeasure.
> Wherewithal unto the heart's forest he fleeth,
> Leaving his enterprise with pain and cry,
> And there him hideth and not appeareth.
> What may I do when my master feareth,
> But in the field with him to live and die?
> For good is the life ending faithfully.[33]

The beloved here teaches ("learneth") Wyatt a new standard of civilized self-restraint that seems to him a constraining of his natural impulses; she wills that his "trust and lust's negligence / Be reined by reason,

shame, and reverence." From Wyatt's standpoint, the standard of restraint championed by the lady represents a commitment to a kind of
sickliness, a loss of power, since with his "hardiness" she "taketh displeasure." The lady's displeasure is specifically directed toward the sexualized "banner" that Wyatt's "long love" spreads on his face. This
banner suggests a blush that, for the lady and apparently for Wyatt, is
not the sign of a self-conscious struggle with forbidden desire (the sort
of thing the lady would evidently endorse), but an act of aggression
akin to a military campaign.

In the sestet Wyatt flees from this perverse (and modern) standard
of civility to seek refuge in the very different bond that connects a
feudal lord and his vassal: "What may I do when my master feareth, /
But in the field with him to live and die?"[34] The lord-vassal bond, with
its unconditional internal loyalty and unchecked, outward aggression,
is presented as a comforting alternative to the disturbingly inhibited,
modern bond proposed by the lady. By moving backward in time, by
fleeing into the arms of his feudal warlord, Wyatt effectively rejects the
terms of the modern, complex social totality associated with the restraint that the lady champions.[35] And yet, it is an escape that remains
within the orbit of the lady's restraint, for insofar as the lord here is only
a metaphor for Wyatt's own desire, the feudal bond that is so comforting *also* maintains, indefinitely, the struggle within the self that the lady
advocates. The master-vassal relationship has been transposed from a real
battlefield onto the psychological battlefield of the "heart's forest" to
which Wyatt flees; war, hereafter, will turn self against self. The moment
a relationship with the other is shattered is also the moment the self
is shattered. And if this double social crisis triggers the luxuriant emotions that flood the speaker's breast where he can take pleasure in them,
it is a pleasure that is inseparable from the painful pressure applied by
the lady and the norms of interpersonal bonding that she projects.

This poem defines an experience of sexuality that seems to yoke
Wyatt and the lady together in ways that depend on an intensified experience of the friction between incompatible accounts of social bonding. Respect for a hypothetically universal core of humanity sponsored
by the lady seems to drive her and Wyatt together toward a relationship

of emotional restraint that is then spectacularly violated by Wyatt's inability to imagine completing the journey. Wyatt and lady are driven together only to be powerfully repelled again by the continuing pressure of archaic social ideals. Far from aiming to resolve the interpersonal impasse, far from trying to reenter the world of functional social ties, Wyatt's poem celebrates the proud and unswerving beloved as the occasion for an endlessly renewed turn away from others and away from the self in order to occupy a place defined only by lavish, emotional suffering.[36]

Here, as in so many of Wyatt's poems, the basic contradiction between a nascent universal social grammar and persistent vestiges of a premodern social vision are vectored through gender. An extreme emphasis on gender difference is, to some extent, a hallmark of Petrarchan poetry generally, and such poetry often seems to be an expression of homosocial desire. In the basic Petrarchan scenario, competing for a beloved can readily become a way of competing with other men.[37] For Wyatt, the struggle to refine the masculine self to make it worthy of the female beloved is, at the same time, a struggle to triumph over other men at court who also seek to display a conspicuous civility. In Wyatt's Petrarch translations—of which "The Long Love" is one—the beloved often embodies, effortlessly, the ethos of the glittering, civilized, cultured, and restrained world of the absolutist court that Wyatt has trouble adopting himself but that other men have presumably adopted without difficulty.[38] But in Wyatt's sonnets, gender difference is pushed to the point where it provokes a beneficent social crisis that opens the door to a sexual experience whose consequences cannot readily be calculated in the register of homosocial competition between men. If Wyatt's poems sometimes reveal the connection between cross-gender courtship and homosocial competition, they more frequently reveal the poet pushing beyond this connection in an attempt to define specifically sexual connections, both with the beloved and with other men that stand outside of a homosocial dynamic. In "Whoso List to Hunt," for example, because the beloved wears a collar that marks her as the king's property, desire for her becomes a way of exploring a desire to displace the king himself:

Whoso list to hunt, I know where is an hind,
But as for me, helas, I may no more.
The vain travail hath wearied me so sore,
I am of them that farthest cometh behind.
Yet may I by no means my wearied mind
Draw from the deer, but as she fleeth afore
Fainting I follow. I leave off therefore
Sithens in a net I seek to hold the wind.
Who list her hunt, I put him out of doubt,
As well as I may spend his time in vain.
And graven with diamonds in letters plain
There is written her fair neck round about:
"Noli me tangere for Caesar's I am,
And wild for to hold though I seem tame."

Here Wyatt plays a dangerous game, announcing a desire to possess a beloved owned by Caesar, even as he ostentatiously declines to compete for her.[39] But discouragement results not so much from the face-to-face encounter with a forbidding master as from the fact that winning over the lady herself is as impossible as the quest is alluring; Wyatt may by no means his "wearied mind / draw from the deer," yet chasing her is as futile as chasing the wind. This economy of an endlessly renewed but endlessly impossible quest suggests that the principle of exclusion operating between Wyatt and the deer is nothing so simple as the worldly power of Henry VIII. The fact that the lady wears a collar marking her as Caesar's property does not seem to rule out others' chasing her. Wyatt hints that he does not expect the readers he is addressing to have any more luck with the deer than he has had, but at the same time he remarks that he is especially bad at hunting deer, being one "of them that farthest cometh behind." The beloved's attractive-repulsive quality is produced by a force that cannot easily be reduced to the turns of male-male homosocial desire.

Far from engaging in red-blooded competition with other men, Wyatt here seems to be developing a kind of compensatory pleasure in announcing what a loser he is, how little threat he is to his male competitors, a move that may also have the effect of depriving his male competitors of the pleasures of vanquishing him insofar as he beats them to the Sunday punch. But the pressures of male-male competition over a lady who is off bounds is absorbed, in this poem and in others, by the lady herself and by the metaphysical problem of catching her. The final line of the poem—in which Wyatt reads on the lady's collar that she is "wild for to hold though I seem tame"—introduces a vocabulary that Wyatt uses throughout his poems to figure the problem of access to women who may be the property of other men. But the wild/tame vocabulary seeks to define sexual availability outside of homosocial struggles; here availability and nonavailability refer to the cultural differential between lady and poet and not to whether another man has gotten to her before Wyatt. By superimposing the vocabulary of wildness and tameness onto the problem of gaining access to women who may belong to other men, Wyatt opens paths to social relationships that push against the limits of homosocial competition.

Wyatt exploits the ambivalence between tameness and wildness to open forms of relationship that are not contained by homosocial competition in "They Flee from Me." This poem is structured by a dramatic change in Wyatt's life in which women who had once been available have ceased to be so, a change that he tries to represent as their becoming wild:

> They flee from me that sometime did me seek
> With naked foot stalking in my chamber.
> I have seen them gentle, tame, and meek
> That now are wild and do not remember
> That sometime they put themself in danger
> To take bread at my hand; and now they range
> Busily seeking with a continual change.
>
> (1–7)

Here women have become wild and therefore reject Wyatt; they do not remember "that sometime" they put themselves in danger to feed at his hand. Yet the wild/tame vocabulary is not completely stable, for when women were gentle, tame, and meek they nonetheless stalked into Wyatt's chamber like wild animals. Equally to the point, insofar as the sort of wildness that makes women unavailable to Wyatt is marked by "busily seeking with a continual change," it seems like a variation on the "newfangleness" and calculating refinement that marks women as creatures of the court, a world that seems to Wyatt both tame and utterly wild, both human and utterly inhuman, both civilized and barbaric. In the concluding stanza of the poem Wyatt returns to hyper-refined, courtly ways of interacting:

It was no dream: I lay broad waking.
But all is turned thorough my gentleness
Into a strange fashion of forsaking.
And I have leave to go of her goodness
And she also to use newfangleness.
But since that I so kindly am served
I would fain know what she hath deserved.
(15–21)

Wyatt here glances at the beloved's polite, genteel ways of rejecting her suitors; telling him that he has "leave to go" is evidently the way she says "no" to Wyatt. Her rejection and her use of polite language are, for Wyatt, two sides of the same coin. Here "newfangleness," the "strange fashion" that has infected the social world, is presented as a bewildering code that defines a form of life from which Wyatt is alienated but which the beloved evidently calls home. The beloved's ambiguous wild/tame quality tokens membership in the circles of the courtly elite. Interestingly, this is a quality that Wyatt himself acquires when he plays at newfangled refinement in the concluding lines of the poem. In those lines Wyatt uses the codes of good manners to express an aggression that exceeds (and is meant to exceed) the norms of good breeding that the lady polices. Between the frustrated and uncertain wild/tame ambivalence in the first and the third stanzas, Wyatt tries to compensate himself for the bad new world in which rules of good manners conceal fundamental duplicity by remembering a time when everything was different:

> Thanked be fortune it hath been otherwise
> Twenty times better, but once in special,
> In thin array after a pleasant guise,
> When her loose gown from her shoulders did fall
> And she me caught in her arms long and small,
> Therewithal sweetly did me kiss
> And softly said, "Dear heart, how like you this?"
>
> (8–14)

This sexual memory is allegedly compensatory, and may also represent something like an impulse to humiliate the class of women that the wild/tame beloved represents, since Wyatt reminds them that he has had them. Yet what ought to be the unambivalent remembrance of better things past is undercut by a profoundly unsettling sense of control by the lady. With her mysterious question, the lady undercuts Wyatt's masculinity; Stephen Foley even argues that the sexual memory is underpinned by an Ovidian impotence farce.[40] The lady's undercutting of masculine self-possession seems to derive from her strangeness; it is almost as if she belongs to an exotic tribe whose anthropological difference keeps Wyatt off balance.[41] But why would Wyatt want to remember (and write a poem about) a somewhat disturbing memory that hints at a bewildering encounter between a weak and potentially flaccid Wyatt and a powerful because deeply strange woman? Only if Wyatt posits pleasure in a relationship characterized by an unbalanced, asymmetrical encounter between characters who act according to very different social standards.

Like many Wyatt poems, "They Flee from Me" is addressed both, or sequentially, to a beloved and to some unnamed, potentially sympathetic reader or readers who are presumed to identify with Wyatt's masculine plight. A strange and disabling relationship with a woman might make relationships with these male readers seem comforting or compensatory. In fact, however, the emasculating memory that Wyatt offers these readers undermines the possibility of fleeing from a bad heterosexual relationship into the arms of some loving and understanding man; offering a humiliating story to his readers instead repeats between poet and readers the emasculating relationship depicted inside the poem. Much the same thing happens in the ballad "Lament My Loss," in which Wyatt invites masculine readers to lament for him who suffers from "the grief and long abuse / Of lover's law and eke her puissant might" (13–14). This poem defines the relationship with his beloved as sexual by announcing the pain that she causes him to a public of interested readers. The important point is that the relationship that Wyatt tries to open with other men through this lament is not so much compensatory as it is an opportunity to relive pain in a public context: "Yet well ye know it will renew my smart / Thus to rehearse the pains that I have passed" (17–18). The poem ends with a somewhat flat moral admonition (Wyatt offers himself as an example of what not to do), but the poison of eroticized pain that the poem injects into male-male relationships seems to persist.

Again and again in Wyatt's poems a homosocial relationship that promises relief from the deprivations of a cruel, beloved woman is transformed into—at best—a one-sided opportunity to relive that pain or—at worst—a mechanism for spreading that pain to other readers. Wyatt either positions himself as a sacrificial lamb or views a community of male readers as an echo chamber where pain is amplified without any payoff. The relationship between men that is based on a shared or multiplied pain that emanates from the massive asymmetry between the male lover and the female beloved is one important way that male-male bonds can be sexualized. Women are ambivalently wild/tame and men suffer, but this suffering becomes the basis for relationships between men that are as one-sided and as dysfunctional as relationships between male lovers and female beloveds.

One exception to this rule is provided by "The Pillar Perished," in which Wyatt uses a man directly to launch himself into the seas of eroticized pain that also define sexual connections with his tame/wild beloved. In this sonnet Wyatt seems to address a single male reader and patron who has ceased to listen to Wyatt's complaints because he

has died. In dying, however, the patron attains a degree of unattainability and even otherworldliness that is clearly reminiscent of Wyatt's
tame/wild beloved.

> The pillar perished is whereto I leant,
> The strongest stay of mine unquiet mind;
> The like of it no man again can find—
> From east to west still seeking though he went—
> To mine unhap, for hap away hath rent
> Of all my joy the very bark and rind,
> And I, alas, by chance am thus assigned
> Dearly to mourn till death do it relent.
> But since that thus it is by destiny,
> What can I more but have a woeful heart,
> My pen in plaint, my voice in woeful cry,
> My mind in woe, my body full of smart,
> And I myself myself always to hate
> Till dreadful death do cease my doleful state?

The Petrarchan precursor to this sonnet, "Rotta è l'Alta Colonna è
'l Verde Lauro," is addressed both to Petrarch's patron Giovanni Colonna
(whose name puns with the Italian word for "pillar") and to Laura, and
Petrarch's poem maintains a complex double vision throughout.[42] Of
course, Wyatt's poem loses the Colonna/column wordplay, but it nevertheless seems much more exclusively addressed to a male patron
than Petrarch's poem—though it does not pun with any actual patron's
name, Wyatt's "pillar" is notable for its phallic properties. The notion
that Wyatt's beloved and understanding reader has only just died suggests that the erotic pain of Wyatt's other poems should be understood
as a sort of tactical posturing at odds with the comfort and satisfaction
Wyatt himself has felt all along, he now claims, in this "strongest stay
of mine unquiet mind."[43] But here, too, any reassuring or compensatory male bonding is deflected insofar as, in absence, Wyatt's pillar
himself becomes the source of the eroticized pain that had heretofore
been caused by the beloved lady. Wyatt is assigned "dearly to mourn

till death do it relent" and the sestet delivers a blazon of suffering: "What can I more but have a woeful heart, / My pen in plaint, my voice in woeful cry, / My mind in woe, my body full of smart." The poetry that he will write now, in other words, is in no obvious way different from the poetry he has written in the past: the patron's inaccessibility and unassailability, like the beloved's, provokes a turn against the self that is also the opening (for Wyatt) to sexuality. Wyatt thus finishes the sonnet by asking what can I do but "I myself myself always to hate / Till dreadful death do cease my doleful state." In death, the patron has precisely the effect on Wyatt that the cruel beloved had, and if he remembers a happy period of homosocial bliss (when the bark had not yet been rent from the tree of "all my joy"), Wyatt nevertheless only writes a poem about his patron once he is dead and has become an occasion for pain.[44]

In "The Pillar Perished," Wyatt uses a vocabulary of powerful emotions—notably, overwhelming grief—to chart the powerful ties that connect him to his erstwhile patron in ways that exceed all available social vocabularies, including the powerful geometries of homosocial desire and competition. Throughout Wyatt's poems powerful emotions provide a grammar of the ties that spring up when functional social ties between people have withered away. Such emotions do not point to a psychologically deep self; rather, they document and, indeed, define a powerful form of sexual bonding. One poem that depicts an interpersonal relationship that has been stripped of all functional social indices save an emotional grammar is "What Rage Is This?" Here the beloved and the speaker appear not as socially legible persons but only as hypotheses to account for the felt reality of intense, emotional pain:

What rage is this? What furor of what kind?
What pow'r, what plague doth weary thus my mind?
Within my bones to rankle is assigned
        What poison pleasant sweet?

                                        (1–4)

The fact that Wyatt does not know what significance to attribute to these affects ("What rage is this?") suggests that he has no privileged relation to them in the way modern readers tend to assume that they have a privileged relation to their own emotions. These emotions do not tell Wyatt anything about himself or about his personal interests, nor do they seem to require action to restore something like emotional balance or interpersonal functionality. What they do tell him is that he is in the grip of a painful tie with a beloved who appears only as a delivery vehicle for pain. Yet it is precisely this painful interpersonal dynamic that the poet and the poem seek to prolong, indefinitely:

> Oppress thou dost, and hast of him no cure,
> Nor yet my plaint no pity can procure.
> Fierce tiger fell, hard rock without recure,
>   Cruel rebel to love!
>   (13–16)

Here an impasse in the terms of a functional relationship between Wyatt and his beloved (Wyatt earlier reminds the lady that "Thy friend thou dost oppress" [12]) is represented as a sort of metaphysical problem, the problem of domesticating a tiger or softening a rock. Such problems are obviously irresolvable, and the value of this framework is to enable us to imagine an abiding limit experience that embodies simultaneous attraction to the beloved and profound, even violent repulsion from her. The interpersonal dynamic charted in this poem is perfectly calibrated to produce a pain whose felt reality and generative power is the only real topic of "What Rage Is This?"

> Lo, see mine eyes swell with continual tears.
> The body still away sleepless it wears.
> My food nothing my fainting strength repairs
>   Nor doth my limbs sustain.
>   (5–8)

These physical symptoms seem to represent the outer limits of Wyatt's social persona. They are a publicly legible index to a set of ties that go beyond normal channels of socializing, a set of ties that spring up when the functional social dimensions of a relationship between Wyatt and his beloved have withered away. What is left is a beloved, who manufactures pain, and Wyatt, who absorbs it.

In this poem and throughout his work, Wyatt takes as his task, as a poet, to explore the in-between spaces where social relationships between men and women and between men and other men break down and remain broken. Wyatt's is a poetry of social corrosion; in a gesture that borders on the suicidal, it tears the speaker out of the social world within which he (or sometimes she) is normally embedded. But if poems like "What Rage Is This?" represent a zero point in which Wyatt indulges in the fantasy of suicidal renunciation, they also document a breakthrough to an alternative social world whose existence is felt in intense and painful emotions inscribed on the body. Wyatt's poetry celebrates suicidal despair, murderous hatred, fear, and contempt of self and other as the luxuriant signs of a new form of pleasure that combines a profound turn away from others with a brazen disregard for the limits of the self. These poems heighten early modern turmoil between competing social visions in order to unmoor themselves from the social world and to give themselves wholly to the exploding emotions that capture the social structure of passion before intimacy.

☙

CHAPTER 2

Intimacy and the Eroticism of Social Distance: Sidney's Astrophil and Stella and Spenser's Amoretti

I have suggested that from Wyatt's first translations of Petrarchan sonnets into English the genre is a privileged bearer of the massive early modern contradiction between, on the one hand, a modern vision of a shared and interconnected social universe that projects the ideal of a shared humanity and, on the other hand, a premodern vision of the social world in which social distinction, personal identity, and group membership are defined a priori, as it were, by blood alone, and in which hereditary status is the basic engine of social relationships. I have also suggested that part of the power of Petrarchan poetry comes from its ability to fuse this contradiction into an unsettled and unsettling experience of emotionally mediated sexuality that glues bodies together when a functionally social connection between socially legible persons has been short-circuited.[1]

By comparing Spenser's sequence of sonnets, the *Amoretti,* with Sir Philip Sidney's *Astrophil and Stella,* I will show how representing an asocial erotic experience is an essential part of Spenser's peculiar self-conception as a "self-crowned laureate," a professional, career author who takes all of his poetry, including his sonnet sequence, with the utmost seriousness.[2] As Richard Helgerson notes, this self-conception was quite unusual in the Elizabethan literary system where courtly writers more commonly presented themselves as gentlemanly amateurs who wrote only for amusement and recreation. Sidney is perhaps the best example of this courtly mode of writing, and my central argument is that Sidney's and Spenser's different modes of authorial self-presentation are linked to the very different accounts of sexuality they develop in their sonnet sequences. In particular, I will argue that beneath Sidney's claim that his poetry is trifling, gentlemanly play lies a fantasy of profound intimacy with his beloved that is secured through shared aristocratic class. To return to the terms I used in chapter 1, Sidney anticipates the modern category of intimacy that Luhmann sketches, but for Sidney, intimacy can join only members of a noble elite; for Sidney, culture and sexuality join people whose shared blood makes them almost interchangeable. For Spenser, by contrast, poetry and sexuality are the only links between himself and a beloved who is almost biologically different from him and with whom any functionally social relationship (including an intimate relationship) is therefore impossible. The work of poetry as Spenser defines it in the *Amoretti,* like the work of the asocial sexuality he represents in the sequence, lies not in connecting members of a courtly elite who are very close to one another in social space, but in connecting people who are so far from one another in social space that they can barely recognize each other as social persons.

SIDNEY

Sidney's *Astrophil and Stella* was probably written in 1582 to celebrate an affair Sidney had with Penelope Rich. For the speaker of the sonnets (Astrophil, who is transparently a version of Sidney), writing about his love for Stella is often only the occasion for elaborate self-compliments and predictions about his own destiny as a Protestant soldier or statesman. One example of a sonnet that seems designed to remind readers of Sidney's and his family's importance is sonnet 30, which turns on the conceit that Astrophil is so distracted by love that he is hard-pressed to respond to all the urgent political issues that are put to him for consideration. These issues include "how Ulster likes of that same golden bit / Wherewith my father once made it half tame," a reference to his father's service as the regent of Ireland. Picking up on such moments, many critics of the sequence argue that for Sidney "love" is merely an excuse for advancing extraerotic personal ambitions. Borrowing a line from Shakespeare's sonnets to describe Sidney's poetry, Arthur Marotti argues that "love is not love" and that love language in Sidney's sonnets merely encodes political desires and ambitions.[3]

I suggest, however, that the *social* agenda of Sidney's sonnets is, in fact, utterly bound up with a certain, very seriously intended account of *erotic* practice. For beyond simple name-dropping, the fundamental project of the sequence is to allow Sidney to lay claim to a blood-borne nobility, and here love is a central part of the equation. In sonnet 62, for example, when Stella tells Astrophil that he only "true love in her should find," Sidney says:

I joyed, but straight thus watred was my wine,
That love she did, but loved a Love not blind,
Which would not let me, whom she loved, decline
From nobler course, fit for my birth and mind[4]

Here Sidney claims that the lady withholds certain favors because he is too noble (she will not allow him to "decline / From nobler course, fit for my birth and mind"). The beloved who educates her lover in refined love is a standard trope of Neoplatonic and Petrarchan conventions. It is noteworthy, however, that Stella derives her standards for love from Sidney's allegedly high birth. In other words, the kind of eroticism that Stella sanctions is *itself* important evidence of Sidney's nobility; in the mode of love she will countenance, Stella holds Sidney to the high standard he was born to.

As it happens, Sidney's genealogical credentials and his title to the "nobler course" Stella insists on were not so strong, something he was obviously self-conscious about throughout his life. Though his mother was a Dudley, the sister of the Earl of Leicester, Sidney's father was a socially rising bureaucrat who had gotten his start by being schooled together with the future Edward VI and had advanced largely by maintaining his reputation as a learned and cultured asset to people with power. Sidney successfully affiliated himself with his mother's family, but he remained sensitive to a certain paternal weakness in his genealogical credentials. Finessing this problem he wrote:

> I am a Dudley in blood, that Duke's [Northumberland's] daughter's son, and do acknowledge, though in all truth I may justly affirm that I am by my father's side of ancient and always well esteemed gentry and well matched gentry, yet I do acknowledge, I say, that my chiefest honour is to be a Dudley, and truly am glad to have cause to set forth the nobility of that blood whereof I am descended.[5]

The defensiveness about his father is palpable in, for example, the way "ancient and always well esteemed gentry" morphs into the rather more telling "well matched gentry." Well matched or not, Sidney was nevertheless born without a title and was only knighted in 1583 to satisfy a point of protocol in a diplomatic ceremony. It is especially ironic that despite his efforts to ally himself with his mother's relatives, Sidney was forced to adopt his father's strategy of accumulating culture to offset the absence of blood, a strategy his father recommended to him in a letter he posted from Ireland: "remember, my son, the noble blood you are descended of, by your mother's side; and think that only by virtuous life and good action you shall be an ornament to that illustrious family; and otherwise, through vice and sloth, you may be counted *labes generis* [a spot on your family], one of the greatest curses that can happen to man."[6] Strictly speaking, needing to add good behavior to good blood means that one's blood is not quite good enough to insulate one from the danger of becoming a spot on the family tree. Sidney's background doomed him to wage an eternal war of monumental (if also sometimes genuinely unconscious) social pretension, and his chosen weapon in this war was also his father's: culture.

The problematic conjunction of good blood and sophisticated culture at which Sidney and his father found themselves points to the central contradiction of early modern English society in which a social imaginary that emphasizes hereditary class is being slowly and unevenly displaced by one that emphasizes successful competition on the cultural terrain. While a culturally mediated status system ultimately supersedes the hereditary system, in Sidney's day the cultural economy was just powerful enough to cause a lot of turbulence but not (yet) to displace heredity. Throughout his career Sidney aims to resolve this contradictory fissure to his advantage by trying to leverage successful acculturation into a claim to the good blood that he was not so sure he possessed. In doing so Sidney picks up the cues of the humanist education program—whose product he was—that claimed to teach the wellborn how to act wellborn. Within the discourse of humanist pedagogy and civility, to be "gentle" often meant, first and foremost, to be gentle-born. Erasmus's iconic conduct manual, *Civility in Boys,* for example, is addressed to a young prince, and in his preface Erasmus suggests that lessons in civility are at once especially appropriate and superfluous for so high-ranking a young man:

> You, of course, are not in any great need of these rules, having been, in the first place, brought up from infancy at court, and then having obtained in Johannes Crucius an outstanding teacher of the very young. Nor is everything that we shall set forth apposite to you who are of princely blood and destined to rule.[7]

Erasmus notes the importance of growing up in a courtly milieu and getting a good education, but he ends by invoking blood as a fundamental social horizon that limits (supposedly) the range in which culture can operate. Erasmus's dedication embodies a dense, transitional situation in which the power of culture to define social status is acknowledged but harnessed, as it were, to express a hereditary form of class. The effort to attach behavioral expectations to genealogical class is one of the most important effects of the civilizing process, and it is just the claim we see Sidney putting into the mouth of his beloved when she demands that in his erotic behavior Astrophil act in a way fit for his "birth and mind." In essence, Sidney here positions Stella as a humanist tutor to princes while eliding the low social position occupied by actual tutors.[8]

At the Elizabethan court, poetry plays an essential role in the project of using culture to express aristocratic birth and status. If the humanist discourse of civility suggests that class should be expressed by behavior, then early modern sonneteers frequently saw Petrarchan conventions as a way to demonstrate the refined language—essentially good behavior in language—that would mark one as a member of the courtly elite. Indeed, refinement in language was associated with sonnets right from their introduction into English literary history.[9] Puttenham writes of Surrey and Wyatt, the first translators of Petrarchan sonnets into English and premier members of the "new company of courtly makers" that "sprong up" during Henry VIII's reign, that

> having travailed into Italie, and there tasted the sweete and stately measures and stile of the Italian Poesie as novices newly crept out of the schooles of Dante Arioste and Petrarch, they greatly pollished our rude & homely maner of vulgar Poesie, from that it had bene before, and for that cause may justly be sayd the first reformers of our English meetre and stile.[10]

Puttenham writes during the Elizabethan age, but even the earliest commentators on Petrarchan adaptations in English expressed a palpable sense of relief that an English still marked by the barbarism of German might be capable of the linguistic elegance of continental Romance languages.

As the cultural sociology of Pierre Bourdieu reminds us, however, linguistic refinement is a social category that requires a socially significant differential to remain operative, and in Sidney's day the social differential of Petrarchan rhetoric is increasingly hard to secure. At the Elizabethan court, Petrarchan conventions had become so widespread that they had been debased as a social currency, which means that the poetry that Sidney ought to be able to use to express his (supposedly elevated) class is itself classed as low, clichéd, or even vulgar.[11] One mark of Sidney's ambition, and one explanation for his elevation after death into an icon of Elizabethan gentility, is that he not only recognized but foregrounded the inability of Petrarchan writing to anchor a claim to being wellborn. Disappointed that he cannot simply use standard Petrarchan rhetoric, Sidney begins the sequence by complaining that despite "oft turning others' leaves, to see if thence would flow / Some fresh and fruitful showers upon my sunne-burn'd braine," he nevertheless lacks what he calls "invention" (1). From the standpoint of humanist schooling, invention would be understood as the construction of a new argument from the commonplaces culled from reading others' texts, from "turning others' leaves." Sidney's desire for "invention" is not a wish for originality but instead points to a devaluation in Petrarchan rhetoric.

Sonnet 15 evinces a sophisticated sociological perspective that leads Sidney to conclude that what makes the Petrarchan rhetoric of "others' leaves" inadequate is its *social* debasement, for everyone at court speaks Petrarchan as if by rote. Addressing some of the authors whose "leaves" he has often turned, Sidney says:

> You that do Dictionarie's methode bring
> Into your rimes, running in ratling rowes:
> You that poore *Petrarchs* long deceased woes,
> With new-borne sighes and denisend wit do sing;
> You take wrong waies, those far-fet helpes be such,
> As do bewray a want of inward tuch

The poems that one reads for invention have become virtual reference books, and copying such rhetoric will make Sidney a dictionary poet himself. Sidney makes his point with a sort of poetic joke, as the alliteration of line 2 invokes the excessively precise rhyming that comes from using the dictionary method. Though Sidney goes on to accuse his poetic contemporaries of literary theft ("at length stolne goods do come to light"), this charge is inseparable from a complaint about the overavailability of Petrarchan conventions. Petrarch's imitators in English have betrayed the legacy of Petrarch ("poore Petrarch") and in so doing have made it impossible for Sidney to adopt the Italian master as a literary model in the way Puttenham says Surrey and Wyatt, Petrarch's first translators, could.

In complaining about the debasement of Petrarchan rhetoric, Sidney is pointing to a very real problem in a key institution of early modern cultural transmission, the manuscript circle. Arthur Marotti and Wendy Wall have both made important studies of this institution in which copies of poems are passed from hand to hand rather than relying on centralized publication and distribution.[12] Relying as they did on

33

social networks, these manuscript circles did seem to promise a certain alignment of class with access to poetry (just the alignment Sidney wishes for). If the circuits of manuscript circulation could indeed restrict access to poetry to actual elites, then readers could make new poems by imitating the rhetoric they read without debasing the currency. Readers and writers both would be using a sort of restricted—essentially, a private—language that could not be copied by outsiders masquerading as insiders.[13] Readers who were potential writers would be marked as the social equals of writers who would be marked as the social equals of readers; poems would mediate not between persons who were socially distant from one another but between friends. In practice, however, the restrictiveness of manuscript circuits was, by Sidney's day, quite weak. Such circuits had become permeated by upwardly mobile poets seeking to pass themselves off as well connected; it is this institutional crisis that appears inside Sidney's sonnets in the form of complaints about the social debasement of Petrarchan rhetoric.

It is precisely here that the *erotic* experience *Astrophil and Stella* depicts becomes central to the sequence's *social* agenda. For even as sonnet 15 registers the problem of debased Petrarchan rhetoric, it proposes to shift away from insufficiently restricted cultural circuits to restricted *sexual* circuits. After all, Sidney ends the poem by advising himself and other poets that if "you seeke to nurse at fullest breasts of Fame, / Stella behold, and then begin to endite." The sequence goes to some trouble to remark the fact that "Stella" is Sidney's code name for the very real Penelope Devereux, sister of the Earl of Essex and wife of the prominent (and rich) Lord Rich; the rich/Rich pun is everywhere present, most strongly in sonnet 37, which ends with the decisive "Rich she is." Under such circumstances, a poetic based on physical access to "Stella" has real consequences, apparently excluding poets less well connected (sexually) than Sidney is. If the clichéd Petrarchan language of love is not restricted enough to express refinement, physical love with restricted persons may be. Indeed, throughout the sequence, Sidney sets up a sort of zero-sum economy in which physical love of Stella gradually displaces writing Petrarchan poetry about that love, as in sonnet 81's witty request for a kiss:

O kisse, which doest those ruddie gemmes impart,
Or gemmes, of frutes of new-found *Paradise,*
Breathing all blisse, and sweetening to the heart,
Teaching dumbe lips a nobler exercise;
O kisse, which soules, even soules together ties
By linkes of *Love,* and only Nature's art:
How faine would I paint thee to all men's eyes,
Or of thy gifts at least shade out some part.
But she forbids, with blushing words, she sayes
She builds her fame on higher seated praise:
But my heart burnes; I cannot silent be.
Then since (deare life) you faine would have me peace,
And I, mad with delight, want wit to cease,
Stop you my mouth with still still kissing me.

Stella is cross because Sidney's poetry makes a public scandal of their love, and she seeks to build her fame on higher-seated praise; but if Stella wishes to drag Astrophil back to the true nobility that makes him worthy of her, she need only stop his mouth from speaking poems by "teaching" his "dumbe lips a nobler exercise." Nobility is nobility of birth; kissing would confirm Sidney's membership in the aristocratic elite in a way writing conventional Petrarchan poems cannot. The kind of physical, erotic access to elite ladies like Stella that is advertised by the kiss of sonnet 81 promises to distinguish Sidney from the Petrarchan "Cupids" who, in sonnet 11, are more interested in exteriors than in substance, a mode of superficial erotic practice that is likened to children playing with books rather than opening them up:

For like a child that some faire booke doth find,
With guilded leaves or colour'd Velume playes,
Or at the most on some fine picture stayes,
But never heeds the fruit of writer's mind

Cupid's erotic practice parallels the universe of writers who just raid each other's books for superficial tropes and pretty pictures, and the sonnet ends by calling Cupid a "foole" because he seeks "not to get into her hart," the interior that passes show; it is an interior exclusive enough to mark those like Sidney who allegedly have access to it as distinct from the dictionary poets who must content themselves with surfaces. If the "inward tuch" that dictionary poets lack is distinctive in a way that writing Petrarchan poems is not, it is so because not all have (or can even reasonably claim to have) sexual access to the Stellas of the world.[14]

From this standpoint, Sidney's problem in *Astrophil and Stella* is how to point to physical access to elite ladies like Stella without resorting to the debased rhetoric of Petrarchan love. Sidney sometimes experiments with new rhetorics and new poetic forms that might point to the reality of elite love as Petrarchan conventions cannot. Toward the end of the sequence, for example, longer poems or songs come to interrupt or even to displace the sonnets; it is as if Sidney has come upon the limits of what can be said within the discursive universe of Petrarchan sonnets and must move beyond it. Song 5, for example, departs from Petrarchan conventions both formally and thematically: Astrophil threatens to blackmail Stella if she does not comply with his desires. The song ends with a fairly shocking catalog of the rumors that Sidney might spread about her:

> You then, ungratefull thief; you murdring Tyran you,
> You Rebell run away, to Lord and Lady untrue;
> You witch, you Divill, (alas) you still of me beloved;
> You see what I can say; mend yet your froward mind,
> And such skill in my muse you reconcil'd shall find,
> That all these cruell words your praises shall be proved.

In a world where witches could still be burned, Sidney's threats are more than metaphorical. By hinting at real skeletons in Stella's closet, as well as his own willingness to *compel* the lady to requite his love, Sidney departs dramatically from the normative Petrarchan story of a chaste and inaccessible beloved refusing the advances of a hapless lover. Another hint of a dark "realism" beneath these artfully contrived poems appears in song 2, in which Astrophil steals a kiss from the sleeping Stella. This song ends with Stella awaking and Astrophil fleeing:

Oh sweet kiss—but ah she is waking,
Lowring beautie chastens me:
Now will I away hence flee:
Foole, more foole, for no more taking.

Sidney here anticipates Richardsonian writing to the moment; it may have seemed like a spectacular special effect. More to the point, the violation hinted at here—about which Stella is angry in subsequent sonnets—and the concluding wish that he had taken greater liberties, anticipate the dark erotic subtext of song 5. As it happens, these dark songs pick up (and retrospectively organize) clues about Stella's character that run through much of the sequence and have the effect of giving the sequence a felt reality that is sometimes absent from more conventionally Petrarchan sequences. There is a sense that there is another, far less conventional courtship rippling beneath the surface of these sonnets, a courtship that anticipates the pointedly anti-Petrarchan rhetoric of Shakespeare's sonnets about the Dark Lady.

It is important, however, not to overstate Sidney's inventiveness in pushing the envelope of Petrarchan conventions. As Heather Dubrow notes, anti-Petrarchan conventions are very much a part of the history of Petrarchan conventions.[15] In fact, I want to argue that Sidney ultimately solves his problem of using poetry to announce physical access to elite ladies by laying claim to an experience of intimacy that *cannot* be represented; that is to say, Sidney finally develops a *discourse* of non-discursive intimacy. When Sidney does represent erotic consummation in sonnet 69, for example, he points to an experience that combines an intimacy explicitly based on class homogeneity with the claim that this experience cannot be shown:

O joy, too high for my low stile to show:
O blisse, fit for a nobler state then me:

Envie, put out thine eyes, least thou do see
What Oceans of delight in me do flow.
My friend, that oft saw through all maskes my wo,
Come, come, and let me powre my selfe on thee;
Gone is the winter of my miserie,
My spring appeares, ô see what here doth grow.
For *Stella* hath with words where faith doth shine,
Of her high heart giv'n me the monarchie:
I, I, ô I may say, that she is mine.
And though she give but thus conditionly
This realme of blisse, while vertuous course I take,
No kings be crown'd but they some covenants make.

The most surprising figure here is the friend who seems to intrude on this private moment. This "friend" has appeared elsewhere as an advocate (with Stella) of Sidney's giving up the behavior (including the poetry) that threatens to pull him down from his true status. But the imaginary class prophylactic provided by an erotics of intimacy between the great allows Sidney to imagine pouring himself onto his friend at the very same moment that he secures the right to pour himself onto his beloved; at this level of access, all are "friends" and all are interchangeable.[16] Moreover, the felt erotic connection with Stella and the friend reduces Sidney—normally quite voluble—to stuttering speechlessness or, more precisely, a careful rhetorical imitation of stuttering speechlessness: "I, I, ô I may say, that she is mine." The intimacy that joins Stella and Astrophil and friend cannot be communicated to those not swept up by its embrace, outsiders who can only look on in mute envy: "Envie, put out thine eyes, least thou do see / What Oceans of delight in me do flow."

But the nondiscursive intimacy that Sidney's stuttering points to does have some positive emotional content that is fleshed out in the sonnet that follows the ménage à trois consummation of Sidney and beloved and friend. In sonnet 70 Sidney hints that a poetics of joy would be able to capture the erotic intimacy of elite social circles. "Sonets be not bound prentise to annoy," he says, ruling out in one breathtaking phrase the entire Petrarchan tradition. If busy poets perform erotic pain and disappointment, then the nobles who enjoy access to the bodies of the great will be free to write sonnets of joyous consummation. Sidney ends sonnet 70 with the apparently deflationary claim that "wise silence is best musicke unto blisse;" he might be conceding the impossibility of writing about sexual joy, but he might just as well be referring to the "sound" of a poetics of joy to those who remain outside the charmed circle.[17] Anticipating the eighteenth-century discourse of emotional intimacy, in which emotions are the sin qua non of intimacy precisely because they seem hidden and private, Sidney finally claims that he cannot represent his joy but only point to a reality that goes beyond the words that, unlike bodies, are available to all, indiscriminately.

Sidney's project in *Astrophil and Stella* is, in a sense, to prop up the social value of words by trying to imagine words that are tied to a sort of biological gold standard, the physical bodies of elite ladies and friends to whom some have access and others do not. A mode of cultural production adequate to high love would thus have to be as unavailable, as silent, as the elite love that passes show is. It would have to be—in Wittgenstein's parlance—a private language.[18] Astrophil's love for Stella and his friend is socially distinctive only as long as it is not represented in a public language; it must remain a "joy, too high for my low stile to show." Stella can give her body to Sidney and his friend alike, but she has no choice but to condemn any nonprivate poetry that represents the experience to outsiders and thus gets in the way of an intimacy that might otherwise be perfect. This intimacy that cannot be understood by those who do not share the experience is not a metaphysical problem—for example, of gaining access to the mind of the other— so much as it is a social problem; it invokes a social border. In the context of Sidney's poetic project, the discourse of nondiscursive intimacy his sonnets develop amounts to a powerful mobilization of a biopolitics in which culture is propped onto the radically restricted currency of the body, a body that automatically evokes the blood that Sidney in fact lacked and that no amount of culture could compensate him for.

SPENSER

In the *Amoretti* Spenser breaks simultaneously with Sidney's account of an intimate sexuality protected by a class prophylactic *and* Sidney's stance that public poetry is a trifling distraction that should ultimately be abandoned in favor of the noble love that it cannot quite represent. Spenser never saw poetry as a trifling distraction, and he certainly never imagined that his own poetry should be discarded. Spenser had a real career, as an administrative secretary and a civil servant in the brutal English regime in Ireland, but in contrast to self-avowed courtly amateurs like Sidney, Spenser always asserted that literature was his true profession; this stance is especially evident in the *The Faerie Queene,* where he rarely misses an opportunity to remind his readers that the epic costs him "endlesse worke" and should be rewarded accordingly.[19]

In the midst of working on *The Faerie Queene,* Spenser courted and married Elizabeth Boyle, and this essentially private affair gave rise to the *Amoretti,* which Spenser published together with an epithalamion in 1595. In the *Amoretti,* Spenser sometimes casts the sonnets, as well as his courtship of Boyle, as a sort of vacation from his real work as the poet of *The Faerie Queene*—in sonnet 80, for example, he complains about the long race that he has run through "Faery land" while compiling "those six books," and asks "leave to rest me being halfe fordonne, / and gather to my selfe new breath awhile." It is as if courtship and the quasi-biographical sonnets that courtship spawns were a restful break for a busy poet worn down by serious cultural labor. More characteristically, however, Spenser claims that the sonnets are themselves difficult work and that they threaten to displace the writing of the *The Faerie Queene.* Moreover, whenever Spenser reflects on why these sonnets seem to take up so much of the time and professional energy that more properly ought to go into the queen's epic, he always points to an erotic experience of a very special kind. Addressing his friend Lodowick Bryskett in sonnet 33, for example, Spenser complains that the "tedious toyle" of writing the epic is impossible as long as his mind is "tost with troublous fit, / of a proud love, that doth my spirite spoyle." It is because love is in some as yet undefined way "proud" and tosses Spenser's mind with a "troublous fit" that the sonnets that represent love swell with the labored effort and the high stakes that would seem more appropriate for the epic.[20] Far from breaking with the professional stance that characterizes *The Faerie Queene,* the *Amoretti* repeat Spenser's literary professionalism, and they theorize this professionalism by means of the radically nonintimate sexuality that Spenser imagines in the sonnets.

The "proud love" that escalates Spenser's labor in the *Amoretti* is rooted in an experience of radical status heterogeneity very different from the fantasy of homogeneous, aristocratic intimacy on which Sidney's stance of gentlemanly amateurishness is founded. Unlike Stella, Spenser's beloved reminds Spenser not of the noble birth that he really shares with her, but rather of the low birth that he must purge in order to be worthy of her:

The soverayne beauty which I doo admyre,
witnesse the world how worthy to be prayzed:
the light wherof hath kindled heavenly fyre,
in my fraile spirit by her from basenesse raysed.

(3)

Class-inflected "baseness" in relation to an elevated beloved remains the guiding trope for understanding Spenser's relationship with Boyle throughout the sequence. It is difficult to know what the historical Boyle's class position was, though she was certainly not the high nobility that Spenser sometimes represents her as being.[21] For Spenser, the private erotic experience of the *Amoretti* seems impossible to imagine except through precisely the kind of class differential that would interfere with Sidney's model of erotic intimacy. Sonnet 3 makes clear that the erotic experience of the *Amoretti* requires both that the beloved be impossibly elevated *and also* that she hold out a faint, shimmering hope that Spenser might overcome the social divide, that his "fraile spirit [might be] by her from baseness raysed." Invoking the vexed terms of the discourse of civility, Spenser claims that his beloved might teach him the good behavior that would make him worthy of her, only to insist, again and again, that Boyle's good behavior is permanently out of reach for the lowborn Spenser. In other words, whenever the *Amoretti* announce the possibility of Spenser's becoming refined, they assert that Boyle possesses her refinement and sophistication by a birth that always excludes Spenser, who will therefore never complete the journey of his ceasing to be "base," the "poor boy" of the Merchant Taylor's school.[22] Spenser here attributes to Boyle precisely the strange conjunction of acculturation and blood that Sidney consciously aims to achieve. But whereas for Sidney the conjunction of blood and culture is the opening to an experience of sexual intimacy with other highly acculturated bodies, for Spenser Boyle's paradoxical position as a hereditary cultural sophisticate defines a massive interpersonal impasse between them.

Sonnet 8 rehearses the social impasse between these lovers in a paradigmatic form; there the impervious lady's ability to quell "base affections wound" and to inspire instead "chast desires on heavenly beauty bound" has the effect of literally raising Spenser's birth: "well is he borne that may behold you ever." But being wellborn lasts only as long as his desire is blocked by a lady whose (class-specific) pride is synonymous with an imperviousness to any desire of her own. Spenser does not become refined so much as he comes to adopt his beloved's disgust of his own lowborn body. And it is precisely as an endlessly renewable source of disgust for his lowborn body that Spenser values his beloved. In sonnet 5, for example, Spenser dismisses a voice that complains that Spenser's beloved is too proud to requite Spenser's love; for Spenser, the lady's pride, her sense of permanent superiority over Spenser, is the source of her attractiveness. It is the lady's "self-pleasing pride" that Spenser "do[es] most in her admire" even though (or perhaps because) this pride entails her rejection of him: "For in those lofty lookes is close implide / scorn of base things, and sdeign of foule dishonor." Spenser's desire for the self-pleasing Boyle must therefore be understood as a low desire that desires its own elimination; for Spenser, consummation would entail identification with the self-pleasing lady who rejects Spenser as lowborn, and getting what he wants would be experienced as a self-abjection.[23] A benign terminus of self-abjection has already been announced in sonnet 3: "That being now with her

huge brightnesse dazed, / base thing I can no more endure to view."
The disgust Spenser comes to feel at his own baseness in sonnet 3 is
what sonnets 5 and 8 go on to represent as a species of consummation,
a satisfaction of a desire complex enough to desire its own supersession.

Loving someone because they cannot or will not return love
amounts to a love that seeks rejection. If this asymmetrical dynamic is
weirdly appealing to Spenser, then it is also appealing to Boyle, for
in sonnet 10 her joy at seeing a massacre of Petrarchan lovers is not a
mark of hostility to the power of love but rather a sign of "licentious
bliss," something like erotic satisfaction.[24] The claim that the noble
body has somehow learned to take an infinite pleasure in rejecting
others has already been glimpsed in the "self-pleasing pride" of which
Boyle is accused in sonnet 5, and it is further described in sonnet 59:

> Such selfe assurance need not feare the spight,
> of grudging foes, ne favour seek of friends:
> but in the stay of her owne stedfast might,
> nether to one her selfe nor other bends.
> Most happy she that most assured doth rest,
> but he most happy who such one loves best.

The lady's self-assurance makes her impervious to others; she need not
"favour seek of friends," much less requite Spenser's love. Spenser sus-
pects that for Boyle there is an infinite pleasure lurking in this radical social indifference, and this indifference provokes a corresponding
pleasure in Spenser: "Most happy she that most assured doth rest, / but
he most happy who such one loves best." Spenser locates the lady's—
and his own—pleasure in the space of deferred or short-circuited
refinement whose condition is the lowborn body that disgusts both
him and his lady. The lady abjects the other (Spenser) whereas Spenser
abjects the self, and it is precisely in shared contempt of Spenser that
these radically different lovers become indispensable to each other as
they form something like a sadomasochistic compact.

The *Amoretti* glimpse in shared abjection a kind of minimum of sociability, a bare connection between lover and beloved verging on radical

disconnection; for Spenser, it is a space notably invested with erotic significance:

> The love which me so cruelly tormenteth,
> So pleasing is in my extreamest paine:
> that all the more my sorrow it augmenteth,
> the more I love and doe embrace my bane.
> Ne doe I wish (for wishing were but vaine)
> to be acquit fro my continuall smart:
> but joy her thrall for ever to remayne,
> and yield for pledge my poore captyved hart;
> The which that it from her may never start,
> let her, yf please her, bynd with adamant chayne:
> and from all wandring loves which mote pervart
> his safe assurance strongly it restrayne.
> Onely let her abstaine from cruelty,
> and doe me not before my time to dy.
>
> (42)

This poem is full of Petrarchan clichés that take on new meaning in the context of the *Amoretti*. The masochistic desire to suffer at the hands of the beloved, to "embrace my bane" in the name of prolonging "extreamest paine," is a desire that joins self-abjection and the abjection of the other, the desire of the speaker and the desire of the lady. Pain is evidently the only kind of experience that Elizabeth and Spenser can share for it preserves, indefinitely, their social incompatibility.

Departing notably from Sidney's (announced) reticence about representing the joy of elite intimacy, Spenser foregrounds a dynamic pain that seems to provide a public lexicon of an erotic connection. Pain— together with the pride and fear and self-loathing that deliver pain— defines a form of interaction between lover and beloved that bypasses any properly social tie. Pain is, of course, a standard component of conventional Petrarchan poems. In *The Faerie Queene*'s House of Busirane episode in book 3, cantos 11 to 12, which stages a kind of parody of a Petrarchan courtship, Busirane reads Petrarchan conventions as a torture manual: hearts will be torn out of living breasts, bodies will be chained to pillars of brass, flesh will be mortified with the oscillations of fire and ice. Busirane's victim is Amoret, the name of the sonnet sequence that seems to participate in the same economy of minimally social eroticism. What distinguishes the pain of the *Amoretti* (and perhaps also of the Busirane episode) from that of other Petrarchan poetry is the self-consciousness with which even pain (or first and foremost pain) is valorized as a species of erotic experience, a form of consummation. In sonnet 24, continual rejection leads Spenser to see his beloved as a sadistic Pandora come to visit physical punishment on him; he ends his poem, however, not by wishing to change the lady's mind, but by negotiating the terms of a punishment that may not end: "But since ye are my scourge I will intreat / that for my faults ye me will gently beat." But what in sonnet 24 nevertheless remains the temporary consequence of temporary rejection is revealed in sonnets 30, 31, and 32 to be the systematic result of an erotic economy that is fine-tuned toward the production of pain and social disconnection as the only kind of consummation these sonnets can countenance. In sonnet 30 the speaker's "hot desyre" does not melt the lady's "yse" but causes it to grow "harder," a perversion that sonnet 32 translates into the situation of a "paynefull smith" whose repeated beating with "heavy sledge" only makes the iron he is working on more resistant.[25] This perverse economy finds its origins in the class incompatibility that Spenser insists on, but by the time Spenser starts feeling the pain of rejection it has come to look like a satisfaction of sorts. In the House of Busirane episode and in the *Amoretti,* pain is valorized as a mode of erotic experience because it takes place in the nearly nonexistent space of an almost zero-degree social connection between the participants, the space of blocked identification.

The difficulty these sonnets face lies in the narrowness of the space they seek to occupy between the socially significant degradation of Boyle and the socially significant elevation of Spenser. It is only as minimally connected and barely responsive that Boyle's and Spenser's erotic experiences become possible, and it is precisely in the name of maintaining this precarious space of erotic affect that the sonnets seek to suspend their dysfunctional relationship indefinitely. Whereas Sidney imagines eroticism between people so similar in social status as to be interchangeable, Spenser defines eroticism as a force that brings together people who remain unable to engage with one another on any functionally social terms. The complex erotic bond of the *Amoretti* can be imagined by Spenser as occurring only when personal refinement is set against an insuperable class difference.

In order to imagine the erotic zero point generated by a process of blocked refinement, Spenser sometimes treats Boyle as a version of Queen Elizabeth, an equation he notes in sonnet 74 whose conceit turns on the name shared by the queen and by Boyle (and by Spenser's mother): "Most happy letters fram'd by skillful trade, / with which that happy name was first desynd." Treating Boyle as a version of the queen is what implants massive class disparity, which can never be overcome, into the heart of Spenser's relationship with her. But if endless refinement in relation to someone who is a version of the queen is the space of erotic experience, it is also the space of Spenser's professional engagement with literature. Spenser was born into a middle-class family, and his education was paid for by scholarships for "poor boys." To some extent, Spenser's literary professionalism represents the recognition that literature is the only road out of a low social status and his only link with the circles of power, and yet no matter how far he got he always imagined that the courtly and aristocratic readership he addressed was so distant in social space as to remain incomprehensible to him. Where Sidney's pretension to courtliness allowed him to imagine—in principle—a profound social intimacy with his readers, Spenser always insists on something close to species difference between himself and the court so that his own poetry can be invested with the endless, impossible task of overcoming that species difference. The *Amoretti* transfer the stance of being a rough, lowborn outsider that characterizes Spenser's professional relationship with the court into a personal relationship with his beloved, Elizabeth Boyle. By doing so, the sequence reveals a distinctive erotic charge in the experience of massive class disparity that is at the heart of Spenser's deviant literary professionalism.

The fact that the *Amoretti* offer an allegory of serious, careerist writing is highlighted in the sonnets in which the *Amoretti* threaten to displace *The Faerie Queene*. In sonnet 80 Spenser must remind himself to moderate his praise of Boyle since he must keep something in reserve for when he returns to praising the queen in *her* poem:

> Till then give leave to me in pleasant mew,
> to sport my muse and sing my loves sweet praise:
> the contemplation of whose heavenly hew,
> my spirit to an higher pitch will rayse.
> But let her prayses yet be low and meane,
> fit for the handmayd of the Faery Queene.

The fantasy that the *Amoretti* are mere recreation in "pleasant mew" is quickly sidelined by Spenser's fear that he is damaging his true poetic calling by allowing the beloved of the *Amoretti* to detain him from work on *The Faerie Queene*. Spenser reminds himself to moderate his praise by recalling his beloved's modest social standing—she is a mere "hand-mayd" to the "Faery Queene." But massive social disparity between poet and beloved is hardly separable from the kind of erotic experience Spenser imagines in the *Amoretti;* it is the structure of Spenser's love for Boyle itself that propels her and the poetry she inspires into their inevitable conflict with the queen and the queen's epic.[26] And if Elizabeth Boyle can (or must) be treated like a version of the queen, then the queen, too, must be *like* a version of Boyle; this reversible equation suggests that the experience of writing for the queen must be like the eroticism Spenser experiences in the *Amoretti*. By making a point of noticing that the *Amoretti* creep into the place that ought to be occupied by the epic, Spenser suggests that these sonnets, with their essentially nonsocial eroticism, both *embody* and *theorize* the cultural seriousness and self-conscious professionalism that marks his epic.

If, as Helgerson argues, Spenser invented the notion of a laureate writer by "abandoning all social identity except that conferred by his elected vocation," then the *Amoretti* reveal that this desperate celebration of literary work emerges only against the backdrop of an erotic cathexis of insuperable class difference.[27] The *Amoretti* suggest that the kind of cultural authority Spenser asserts for his self-consciously serious poetry is inseparable from the painfully erotic experience of loving someone who is socially so distant as to provoke endless self-abjection. As theorized by these sonnets, the compensatory social status Spenser's writing offers him is inseparable from an erotically valorized experience of shame that his low birth generates before the eyes of his beloved/ queen. By exploring the eroticism of massive social incompatibility, the *Amoretti* explore the affective side of Spenser's deviant careerism, theorizing his investment in poetry as work in language that is also work on the self, the repeated abjection of the part of the self that always limits perfect identification with the highborn beloved/reader to whom Spenser's cultural endeavors are addressed.[28] The dirty secret that poetry is a belabored effort to renegotiate the terms of a class system that excludes lowborn authors, the dirty secret that had to remain hidden in Sidney's poetics of restricted intimacy, is foregrounded here, where it becomes the basis of an eroticism of endless, unsuccessful self-refinement.

CHAPTER 3

Civility and the Emotional Topography
of The Faerie Queene

I have been arguing that the discourse of civility bears two incompatible social imaginaries: on the one hand a vision of potentially universal
humanity, and on the other hand a vision of heredity as the essential
engine of personal identity and social relationships. I have also described
how early modern poets can fuse this contradiction to define sexualized limit experiences in which bodies connect with other bodies in
the absence of functionally social ties between socially legible persons.
Describing this asocial sexuality is an important part of many early
modern literary texts; Edmund Spenser's *The Faerie Queene,* however,
is unique in its single-minded focus on excavating and archiving the
experience of an asocial sexuality that is triggered by the conflicting
social visions carried by the discourse of civility.

Spenser places the discourse of civility at the very heart of his project in *The Faerie Queene;* in the epic's prefatory letter to Sir Walter
Raleigh, Spenser famously claims that "the general end therefore of all
the booke is to fashion a gentleman or noble person in vertuous and
gentle discipline."[1] But if *The Faerie Queene* is a conduct manual, then
it is a very strange one for, as a genre, conduct manuals are marked
by an overwhelming degree of explicitness. Erasmus's *Civility in Boys,*
for example, gives rules for personal behavior that can strike modern
readers as embarrassing because they speak of things that ought to go
more or less without saying.[2] Any reader of *The Faerie Queene,* by contrast, knows that if rules for conduct are being offered at all, they are
almost impossible to understand. The models of conduct that appear in

Spenser's verses have an uncanny, self-revising, sometimes Kafkaesque quality, as though they were emanating from some mysterious and distant realm whose dictates remain baffling to Spenser even as he tries to explain them to his readers. And in a sense, the rules of conduct that the epic supposedly teaches do emanate from a distant and baffling realm, for Spenser always insists that his models of good behavior are the queen and the most elite courtiers, and at the same time that this class of persons is so distant from him in social space that he can barely understand them.[3]

By insisting that good behavior is the property of a courtly elite whose manners remain mysterious or even incomprehensible to those, like Spenser himself, who are not already part of their glittering world, Spenser is essentially moving backward in the history of civility. As Norbert Elias argues in *The Civilizing Process,* during the earlier Middle Ages rules for good conduct emerged as a way of distinguishing a courtly elite; they taught a "courtliness" that did not apply, even in principle, to other segments of the social world. During the sixteenth century, however, under the revolutionary pressure of humanist pedagogy, conduct manuals began to address a wider audience and to teach not a socially restricted "courtliness" but a potentially universal "civility."[4] And while sixteenth-century conduct manuals continued to frame good behavior as a way of looking high-class and as a technique of upward mobility, they also offered a radical new rationale for good manners: that they are a way of acknowledging and respecting a hypothetically universal human identity that is supposedly shared by everyone in the social world.

Spenser revives the notion of a socially restricted "courtliness" in order to block or short-circuit the emerging notion of universal civility designed to respect a universal humanity that his epic also registers.[5] On the one hand, insofar as he addresses his epic conduct manual to some wider, potentially national audience interested in being fashioned into "gentlem[e]n or noble person[s] in vertuous and gentle discipline," Spenser is very much drawing on the Renaissance extension and expansion of the project of civility to apply, in principle, to the whole social world as a set of universal norms for humane interaction. On the other hand, when Spenser frames the good conduct modeled by courtly elites as baffling or even inappropriate to those, like the poet himself, who are not members of this courtly elite, he frames manners as a socially distinctive "courtliness" that short-circuits any potentially universal "civility." The clash between these two very different social visions gives rise to a special form of sexual intersubjectivity that is defined when a potentially "civilized" relationship is blocked or undermined by the resurgence of the fundamental, almost genetic differences implied by the notion of courtliness. As is the case with the other texts I have examined, in *The Faerie Queene* this privileged sexual intersubjectivity is legible primarily in terms of powerfully depersonalized emotions that open and close bodies to one another when functionally social ties between socially legible persons have been short-circuited. In short, Spenser's epic uses the vexed discourse of civility to draw attention to the frictions and gaps that cut through early modern society and that energize a privileged experience of asocial sexuality that is the real subject of *The Faerie Queene*.

The beneficent social crisis that Spenser triggers by means of the internally contradictory discourse of civility is most pronounced in book 3, which is designed to illustrate chastity, the virtue definitively embodied by Queen Elizabeth. In the proem, Spenser suggests that teaching chastity amounts to copying the queen, a project that seems impossible or even incoherent from a standpoint outside the confines of court.

It falls me here to write of Chastity,
That fairest vertue, farre above the rest:
For which what needs me fetch from *Faery*
Forreine ensamples, it to have exprest?
Sith it is shrined in my Soveraines brest.
    (bk. 3, pr. 1)

When it comes to chastity, Spenser cannot invent fictional role models ("forreine ensamples" fetched from Faerieland). Rather, he must represent the queen herself and the exemplary behavior that is enshrined in her breast. Yet representing the queen is nearly impossible; Spenser writes that even the greatest graphical artists (Zeuxis and Praxitelles, evidently) would "faile, and greatly faint" at such an enterprise, tainting the queen's "perfections" with error. And though the representational power of poets "passeth [the] Painter farre / In picturing the parts of beautie daint," not even poets would "so hard a workmanship adventure darre / For fear through want of words her excellence to marre" (2). Spenser here deploys what Ernst Robert Curtius calls the topos of inexpressibility; the poet encounters something that is too great, too beautiful for him to bring it into language.[6] For Spenser, the queen constitutes an outer limit, and his claim to be unable to represent her is connected to the claim that she is somewhere beyond his social horizon, so distant that he cannot quite see her; Spenser cannot "presume so high to stretch mine humble quill" for he is a mere "apprentice of the skill, / That whylome in divinest wits did raine."[7] He sets out to teach chastity to a broader reading public but finds that this may be impossible because it would amount to imitating the queen directly, something that seems impossible or even incoherent because of her social distance.

To mediate between himself and the impossibly elevated queen, Spenser calls on a third character, his sometime patron and neighbor in Ireland, Sir Walter Raleigh. By doing so Spenser seems to invoke the homosocial ties between men that are among the building blocks of the early modern sex-gender system. But in the proem, Spenser draws on this homosocial geometry only to show how the social divide that yawns between himself and the queen defines an erotic charge that moves in ways that exceed homosocial propriety. Spenser contrasts his own situation as a mere apprentice who cannot quite picture the queen to that of Raleigh, who enjoys (at least when in favor) the kind of access to the queen that Spenser lacks. This access enables Raleigh's unfinished poem "The Ocean to Cynthia" to capture the queen in a way Spenser's *The Faerie Queene* cannot. If Spenser's poetry displeases the queen (because it "presumes" too high and may "marre" her excellence), then Raleigh's poetry will surely fit the bill.

But if in living colours, and right hew,
Your selfe you covet to see pictured,

Who can it doe more lively, or more trew,
Then that sweete verse, with *Nectar* sprinckeled,
In which a gracious servant pictured
His *Cynthia,* his heavens fairest light?

Part of the reason that Raleigh's poem seems superior to Spenser's is
that he enjoys a more elevated social status and, being her "servant,"
more access to the queen. Spenser asks Raleigh for help in mending
whatever Spenser, being a mere apprentice, mars ("But let that same
delitious Poet lend / A little leave unto a rusticke Muse" [5]); it is as
though Raleigh owned the business of representing the queen and the
good behavior she models. Spenser here conjures up a homosocial picture of the two Irish neighbors working together to please their difficult queen, or perhaps of Spenser as the reader-pupil learning the craft
of representing the queen from Raleigh as writer-master; both pictures
invoke the gendered homosocial grammar that is so central a part of the
early modern sex-gender system. But the fact that Raleigh can represent what Spenser can only mar also suggests a profound axis of exclusion between the two men, one a mere apprentice, the other quite at
home in the glittering precincts of absolute power, an axis of exclusion
that seems to repeat the initial separation between Spenser and queen.
And precisely because it throws a wrench into conventional homosocial interactions, the social asymmetry between Spenser and Raleigh
provokes an intense, and intensely sexualized, pleasure in Spenser, for
what begins as the suggestion that the queen will like Raleigh's poetry
quickly turns into an opportunity to testify to Raleigh's capacity to
please Spenser. When Spenser contemplates Raleigh's poem, "The Ocean
to Cynthia," he is himself "with his melting sweetnesse ravished, / And
with the wonder of her beames bright, / My senses lulled are in slom-
ber of delight" (4). At the same time, Spenser's sexualized pleasure at
Raleigh's poem—a poem born of social access—aligns Spenser and the
queen insofar as Spenser's pleasure is also imagined to be the queen's.
In place of a proper homosocial dynamic in which the two men are
aligned by the gravity of their difficult queen, the socially marginalized

Spenser ends up being aligned with his queen in shared melting pleasure at the hands of Raleigh. But this asymmetrical dynamic is built on another, equally asymmetrical dynamic in which it is Raleigh and the queen who are aligned because they are both the sources of Spenser's bliss: Raleigh because he represents the queen in ways Spenser cannot; the queen simply because she is the queen. In short, the example of Raleigh's poem (whose perfect representation of the queen is born of social access to her) allows Spenser to conceptualize a pleasure (at once literary and bodily) that is built on converting massive, unbridgeable social distance into pleasure, a pleasure that joins him, by turns, to the queen and to Raleigh. Spenser starts the proem by claiming that in order to write a conduct manual of chastity he would need to represent the queen, which seems impossible, but then Spenser sidesteps this problem by reinterpreting the social distance that had previously seemed like an impasse in his relationships with the queen as the origin of an intensely sexualized experience of ravished, melting pleasure that becomes the real subject of the proem.

The proem also illustrates that the eroticism of social distance, once sparked, produces effects that are hard to contain. While much of the proem suggests how the eroticism of massive social distance splits Spenser and Raleigh and undermines a functional homosocial tie by distributing these men in various arrangements around the erotic social distance defined by the queen and her incomprehensible chastity, in the final lines of the proem the men are rotated back into a position of relative equality, but an equality that is far from conventionally homosocial. Calling the queen by the name Raleigh has given her, Spenser ends the proem by inviting his queen to see herself in more than one mirror:

Ne let his fairest *Cynthia* refuse,
In mirrours more then one her selfe to see,
But either *Gloriana* let her chuse,
Or in *Belphebe* fashioned to bee:
In th'one her rule, in th'other her rare chastitee.

The multiplied mirrors Spenser names are the ones his own epic presents, for both Gloriana and Belphebe are characters in *The Faerie Queene*. In the prefatory letter to Raleigh, Spenser outlines his plan to split the virtues he wants to illustrate in the queen into public and private, producing one set of allegorical figures for each: Gloriana for the public side, Belphebe for the private. Yet there can be no doubt that Raleigh, too, holds up a mirror to the queen, and by calling Elizabeth by Raleigh's name for her, "Cynthia," and thus invoking an image of Cynthia staring at herself, Spenser suggests the profound narcissism that he assumes to be the name of the queen's pleasure: she cannot own enough mirrors or enough flattering literary representations. And here the queen's voracious narcissism projects a social space in which Spenser and Raleigh are again equated, both courtiers holding mirrors to the queen and hoping for her regard. But Spenser was no courtier, and to position Raleigh alongside himself, and thus Raleigh's ambitions alongside his own, is to suggest that they occupy a place in relation to the queen where relevant *social* differences between men are erased. Such a place can only be the place of the disregard or disgrace or even shame that is represented by the Ireland that both Spenser and Raleigh were obliged to call home.[8] Sending hopeful mirror flashes back across the sea, Raleigh and Spenser both appear in the light of disgrace and banishment, another instance of Spenser's drive to replace the flattening mechanisms of conventional homosocial bonding and conventional heterosexual passion with a very different geometry of sexuality.

Between the lines of a proem that announces the goal of teaching chastity, we can therefore read a very different project, to excavate and archive the possibilities for relationships that arise in spaces where the mechanisms and norms of conventional social bonding have been rendered inoperative by a fundamental early modern contradiction in the terms of social life. The proem's concluding vision of a homosociability of shame and the interpersonal constellations that appear arrayed around the massive social divide defined by the queen outline a basic framework for the experience of sexuality that becomes the real subject matter of the poem as a whole. The vocabulary that Spenser uses to codify and catalog this experience of sexuality is that of intense, asymmetrical emotions such as the bliss and the fear and the shame that are registered throughout the proem. These emotions are part of an emotional topography that defines connections between bodies that arise when functionally social connections, including homosocial connections, have been foreclosed; they are the deepest terrain and the real focus of *The Faerie Queene*.

To begin to sketch the submerged emotional topography that springs up around the social fissures defined by the discourse of civility, I turn now to the relationship between Belphebe and Timias. To some extent, this relationship repeats the massive social divide that operates in the proem. In the proem Spenser identifies Belphebe as one of his stand-ins for the queen, while Timias is often seen as a parallel to Sir Walter Raleigh.[9] The exchanges between Timias and Belphebe in book 3 illustrate both the way sexuality arises from the contradiction between universal and exclusionary forms of good behavior and the way that the felt reality of this sexuality can be captured by descriptions of powerfully asymmetrical somatic affects.

At the beginning of book 3, Timias, squire to the future King Arthur, becomes separated from his master when he chases after Florimel's attacker rather than after the lady herself as Arthur does. Timias eventually defeats the attacker but only at the cost of sustaining a nearly fatal injury, and he is in a fairly gruesome state of physical disrepair when Belphebe finds him while she is passing through the forest during a hunt with her damsels. Belphebe revives Timias through the deft (and historically ironic) application of tobacco leaves, but as soon as he awakes Timias mistakes her for an angel:

By this he had sweete life recur'd againe,
And groning inly deepe, at last his eyes,
His watry eyes, drizling like deawy raine,
He up gan lift toward the azure skies,
From whence descend all hopelesse remedies:
Therwith he sigh'd, and turning him aside,
The goodly Mayd full of divinities,
And gifts of heavenly grace he by him spide
(3.5.34)

Looking upward Timias sees what he imagines to be a heavenly creature, and it is only on such terms that he can imagine a relationship with Belphebe. Addressing her he asks, "Angell, or Goddesse do I call thee right? / What service may I do unto thee meete" (35).[10] The uncertainty about Belphebe's status (angel or goddess) is a sign of her distance from Timias, who casts himself as a mere human, but it is precisely because of this distance that the possibility of service enters the picture. Timias's "service" here has a religious resonance, marking it as different in kind from the service between men that joined Timias and Arthur. Indeed, gender difference is part of what intensifies status disparity between Belphebe and Timias since it seems to activate a whole Petrarchan tradition that Timias registers by ratcheting his adoration of Belphebe up into a religious register.

But crucial to the working of the Belphebe-Timias relationship, as Spenser represents it, is that Belphebe insistently blocks any relationship based on religious adoration or, indeed, any sense of insuperable status disparity. Blushing, Belphebe assures Timias that she is no angel and wants no "service" and that she will be content if Timias lives. Even more problematically for Timias, Belphebe attributes her desire to help Timias to a responsibility that all "mortals" share:

We mortal wights whose lives and fortunes bee
To commun accidents still open layd,
Are bound with commun bond of frailtee,
To succour wretched wights, whom we captived see.

(3.5.36)

Modern readers are likely to celebrate Belphebe's philosophy of the "commun bond of frailtee" for its humane enlightenment and to endorse the ethic of mutual care and concern that follows from it. This is not how Timias takes it, however, and perhaps not how Spenser thought anybody would take it. After all, in a poem in which she stands in for the sovereign queen *and* (at least in Timias's eyes) a deeply alien femininity, Belphebe's assertion of shared humanity may well be the most perverse thing she could do under the circumstances.

From Timias's perspective, *because* Belphebe's ideology of a "commun bond" undermines his desire to see her as impossibly elevated, it makes a relationship between them completely impossible. Because it blocks the religious service he proposes, Timias sees Belphebe's philosophy of shared humanity as a way of excluding him more fundamentally than any assertion of divine status would. And to some extent, the epic's narrator shares Timias's view, for he attributes the medical intervention that is the practical outcome of Belphebe's humanitarian philosophy to Belphebe's own supposedly elevated social standing; the narrator claims that she knows how to treat Timias because "she of hearbes had great intendiment, / Taught of the Nymphe, which from her infancy / Her nourced had in trew Nobility" (32). From the narrator's perspective, Belphebe's ideology of the "commun bond" is therefore strangely linked with, or even an expression of, a "trew Nobility" that reintroduces a fundamental social difference between her and Timias that the notion of shared humanity would seemingly undo.

Belphebe's "trew Nobility" raises the question of how she can be civilized if she has lived her entire life in the "salvage forests," a question that points directly to the incompatible accounts of social status and personal identity that are borne by the discourse of civility and swirl throughout *The Faerie Queene*. In canto 6 Spenser notes that some "faire Ladies" may well wonder about this issue:

> Well may I weene, faire Ladies, all this while
> Ye wonder, how this noble Damozell
> So great perfections did in her compile,
> Sith that in salvage forests she did dwell,
> So farre from court or royall Citadell,
> The great schoolmistresse of all curtesy:
> Seemeth that such wild woods should far expell
> All civil usage and gentility,
> And gentle sprite deforme with rude rusticity.
> (3.6.1–9)

The answer Spenser offers to this question makes Belphebe occupy the very contradiction that the discourse of civility opens, for in Belphebe

the refinement and civility that ought to be acquired only through acculturation, through exposure to the ways of court, "the great school-
mistresse of all curtesy," have been communicated to her instead by
blood or by genes.[11] The story the narrator provides to explain how
Belphebe came to possess such good manners begins with her mother's
impregnation by a sunbeam. Belphebe represents Queen Elizabeth, and
the difficulty of portraying the queen's birth as an instance of standard
human reproduction stems in part from her technically illegitimate status since Henry VIII had executed her mother and legally expropriated
her.[12] There are other instances where Spenser invents a nonhuman
mode of reproduction for the queen, notably in the April eclogue of the
Shepheardes Calendar in which the queen is born when a gust of wind
crosses Pan's (Henry VIII's) pipe (penis). In the Timias and Belphebe
story, however, the nonhuman impregnation of Belphebe's mother via
sunbeam attests to Spenser's willingness to see the courtly elite, especially the queen, as so radically different as to be endowed with a different biology and different mechanisms of reproduction. The question of
how Belphebe could come to be so civilized despite having been raised
in the forest thus elicits the suggestion that she possesses her civility in
virtue of the biology that distinguishes her from the generic inhabitants
of the savage forest. This biology therefore also distinguishes Belphebe
from Timias, who seems quite emphatically a creature of those "wild
woods [that] should farre expel / All civil usage and gentility."[13] After
all, Timias has just engaged in the aggressive violence that would get
any courtier exiled from the peace-loving court. Moreover, given that
Belphebe's genetic civility turns into a commitment to something like
shared humanity, Timias comes to seem excluded from her not only
because he has less sophisticated manners (as *he* insists) but also because
he seems closer to an animal than a human—after all, Belphebe is on
a hunt, following a trail of blood and expecting to find the carcass of
an animal she has killed, when she discovers the body of the squire.

  Here, at the point of maximum contradiction between incompatible terms for social relationships, is where the relationship between
Belphebe and Timias is at its most intense—and its most sexual. One
sign of the active presence of sexuality at the heart of what appears only

as the *absence* of sociability is the blush that overcomes Belphebe when she first encounters the body that may be an animal and only gradually comes to seem human. When Belphebe beholds the gruesome image of Timias, "all suddeinly abasht she chaunged hew, / And with sterne horrour backward gan to start: / But when she better him beheld, she grew / Full of soft passion and unwonted smart: / The point of pity perced through her tender hart" (30). It is tempting to believe that the blush ("all suddeinly abasht she chaunged hew") is caused by the gruesome wounds that Spenser has elaborately described in the preceding stanzas. Yet Belphebe regains her composure only by looking more closely at the mangled body that lies before her. The text never tells us what, exactly, Belphebe sees; we know only that a stern horror is replaced by a heart given over to the pleasures of pity ("the point of pity perced through her tender hart"). In Spenser's allegorical universe, Belphebe's blush suggests not (or not only) revulsion but something like temptation, and in a book in which she is an emblem of the textually organizing virtue of chastity, this moment of temptation can only be read in a sexual register. So, is it not horror of Timias's body that causes her to start up but rather love of it? What excites a figure as otherworldly, as nominally chaste as Belphebe, a figure who, moreover, stands in for the queen herself? What is the name of the desire of a character who loves no man? Belphebe is hunting, she is tracing a blood trail, she is expecting to see a corpse, and within the terms of the militant hunting ideology that Belphebe has taken over from the chaste Diana, she *wants* to see corpses, she *wants* to produce corpses. Her blush, therefore, seems to occur precisely at the moment she gets what she most wants (and what she is most allowed to have): the dead body of an animal she has shot.

One way of understanding why Belphebe feels shame, and why this shame registers the presence of sexuality, is to look at Silvan Tomkins's account of the emotion. As Eve Kosofsky Sedgwick and Adam Frank note in the introduction to their selection of Tomkins's work, the value of Tomkins's account of shame lies precisely in his emphasis on a sudden "strangeness" between individuals that has little to do with the codes of prohibition that are associated with the civilizing process as it is normally understood to operate.[14] Here is Tomkins describing shame:

> Like disgust, [shame] operates only after interest or enjoyment has been activated, and inhibits one or the other or both. . . . Such a barrier might be because one is suddenly looked at by one who is strange, or because one wishes to look at or commune with another person but suddenly cannot because he is strange, or one expected him to be familiar but he suddenly appears unfamiliar, or one started to smile but found one was smiling at a stranger.[15]

In Tomkins's model, shame is taken out of the juridical context of the forbidden and placed instead within a complex interpersonal space of incompletely reduced interest or excitement about another. And while Tomkins's model still projects an end point of mutual recognition between people who are *not* strangers, his description suggests a powerful way in which shame can define a relationship that cannot be defined in any social vocabulary. This model suggests that what is happening to Belphebe is a sort of incomplete reduction of interest in which what had seemed an animal (the animal she was trying to kill) suddenly comes to seem like something other than an animal. But her interest is reduced not all the way, as it were, but only to a sort of middle point where it becomes almost impossible to know what to do with Timias. It is precisely in this kind of foreclosed relationship, the flip side of Timias's hopeless struggle to fit Belphebe into the category of angel or goddess divine, that Spenser identifies sexuality. Belphebe's shame, like Timias's despairing uncertainty about how to approach Belphebe, indicates not repression but boundless indulgence in a pleasure defined by an interpersonal divide that cannot be healed. Insofar as shame occupies a space of foreclosed sociability, this emotion may be *foundational* for sexuality as Spenser understands sexuality, a fact that should not block attention to the plethora of other emotions that Spenser recruits in his epic to describe the kind of asocial or nonsocial sexuality that blooms between Belphebe and Timias. The *value* of emotions (including shame, but also including, in Belphebe's case, horror and pity) is that they can be treated as somatic, corporeal events that define modes of relationship, modes of interpersonal connection that are not functionally social at all and that therefore cannot be described in any of the terms early modern society uses to think about itself. In his use of shame, and in his use of other emotions, Spenser treats emotions not as signs of rich individual personalities, but as defining bodily states that open and close the body to other emotionally inflamed bodies when a functionally social connection between socially legible persons is impossible.

If Belphebe's blush suggests that her nonrelationship with Timias is sexual, then Timias's graphically illustrated emotional suffering is its precise counterpart, the very terrain on which the terms of their thoroughly nonsocial connection is worked out. Timias suffers from an emotional pain that has no single name but is defined, first and foremost, by its power to leech away the social registers of his identity that had previously connected him to other characters in his social world:

> Still as his wound did gather, and grow hole,
> So still his hart woxe sore, and health decayd:
> Madnesse to save a part, and lose the whole.
> Still whenas he beheld the heavenly Mayd,
> Whiles dayly plaisters to his wound she layd,
> So still his Malady the more increast,
> The whiles her matchlesse beautie him dismayd.
> Ah God, what other could he do at least,
> But love so faire a Lady, that his life releast?
>
> (3.5.43)

Since he is in the grip of a commitment to absolute status difference, Timias experiences Belphebe's humane, medical treatment as a form of torture. The application of the herbs whose knowledge testifies to Belphebe's "trew Nobility" thus has the effect of making Timias sick even as it heals him, of replacing his physical injury with a sickness of a more radical kind. On the terms of this sickness, the interaction between them may go on forever, and it is in order to capture the felt reality of this curious form of interpersonal bonding that the poem shifts to the purely bodily level. Whatever the name of the emotion that grips Timias here, it gradually strips him of other forms of identity until it defines the whole of his being, a being that is intimately and permanently attached to Belphebe.

At the heart of this shift to bodies and affects is a set of incompatible terms for social bonds (service, humanity, civility) that has been converted into an unstable, overdetermined complex.[16] Sexuality feeds on this social dysfunction and even codifies it. In the grip of the complex emotional pain that defines him as the subject of sexuality, Timias compulsively repeats the terms of the social contradiction that gives rise to it, a contradiction between the *inevitability* of hierarchical difference mediated by service and the *impossibility* of such service because of shared humanity. In stanza 47 Timias compares service to Belphebe with service to a Christianized God:

But foolish boy, what bootes they service bace
To her, to whom the heavens do serve and sew?
Thou a meane Squire, of meeke and lowly place,
She heavenly borne, and of celestiall hew.
How then? of all love taketh equall vew:
And doth not highest God vouchsafe to take
The love and service of the basest crew?
If she will not, dye meekly for her sake;
Dye rather, dye, then ever so faire love forsake.

(3.5.47)

Timias sets up an analogy to the Christian God (who evidently accepts all men's love, no matter their social position) only to end by suggesting that the analogy may not hold.[17] If the massive class divide that Timias insists on makes a legible social relationship impossible (he ends each of the three stanzas we are considering here with a version of the refrain "Dye rather, dye, then ever so faire love forsake"), it nevertheless gives Timias something that he evidently wants, for it articulates what makes the relationship look specifically sexual, and after rehearsing the social impasse, Timias yields himself completely to the "victour proud":

Thus warreid he long time against his will,
Till that through weaknesse he was forst at last,
To yielde himself unto the mighty ill:
Which as a victour proud, gan ransack fast
His inward parts, and all his entrayles wast,
That neither bloud in face, nor life in hart
It left, but both did quite drye up, and blast;
As percing levin, which the inner part
Of every thing consumes, and calcineth by art.
(48)

Timias's painful emotional state resolves the social impasse that his social reasoning leads to—in a way, it is relief; he finally gives in to its emotional reality—and it also provides a way of describing the reality of a relationship that cannot be understood or represented in any other way.[18] And if this is true for Timias, it is also true for the author of the Timias and Belphebe story, for by forcing the social contradiction between them to resolve itself into a blazon of emotive experience, Spenser frees an entire range of literary sources for deployment; the final image of Timias being pierced by lightning (paralleled by Belphebe's being pierced by pity), for example, is a reworking of the story of Zeus raping Semele as a lightning bolt.[19]

Once this shift *out of* social space and *into* emotional space, where bodies and affects are the terrain of relationship, has taken hold, it expands in scope to encompass interactions with other characters that Belphebe and Timias encounter. In the continuation of their story in book 4, Belphebe sees Timias comforting Amoret and flies into a fit of jealous rage that seems to parallel her earlier fit of shamed horror at first encountering Timias's (alluringly) mangled body:

Which when she [i.e., Belphebe] saw, with sodaine glauncing eye,
Her noble heart with sight thereof was fild
With deepe disdaine, and great indignity,
That in her wrath she thought them both have thrild
(4.7.36)

Disdain, a sign of her "noble heart," opens a space of debasement and disgrace that renders Timias's impossibly low social status literal; afterward, he lives like an "outcast thrall," a position with a recognizable social logic: "Well said the wiseman, now prov'd true by this, / Which to this gentle Squire did happen late, / That the displeasure of the mighty is / Then death it selfe more dread and desperate" (4.8.1).[20] Something worse than the martyr's death that Timias had decided on at the end of the first installment of his adventures with Belphebe has in fact befallen him, namely, the displeasure of the great that leads to ostracism and the complete eradication of all the marks of his social identity. Timias breaks his weapons, forswears speech, and tears his garments:

And eke his garment, to be thereto meet,
He willfully did cut and shape anew;
And his faire lockes, that wont with ointment sweet
To be embaulm'd, and sweat out dainty dew,
He let to grow and griesly to concrew,
Uncomb'd, uncurl'd, and carelessly unshed;
That in short time his face they overgrew,
And over all his shoulders did dispred,
That who he whilome was, uneath was to be read.
(4.7.40)

But far from giving up on "love," Timias enters more deeply into an emotional space that supplants the functional social world. Moreover, Timias's final reduction to *pure* emotion, to an emotional state that is now the sum total of his social identity, colonizes previously functional relationships, like the loving service that once joined him to his lord, Arthur. When "his owne deare Lord Prince *Arthure* came that way," he fails utterly to recognize Timias, though he does suspect him of having once been a "gentle swaine" (42, 45). Life as an "outcast thrall," life utterly outside of the normal mechanisms of the social world, a life in which one is "with griefe and anguishe overcum" (43, 44), is read by Arthur as prima facie evidence that Timias has entered a world of love. In *The Faerie Queene* the ruined human being simply *is* the erotically impassioned human being, and when Arthur sees the name of Belphebe carved in a tree, he correctly surmises that it names the object of the love that produces Timias's ruined state:

> And eke by that he saw on every tree,
> How he the name of one engraven had,
> Which likly was his liefest love to be,
> For whom he now so sorely was bestad;
> Which was by him B E L P H E B E rightly rad.
> Yet who was that *Belphebe,* he ne wist;
> Yet saw he often how he wexed glad,
> When he it heard, and how the ground he kist,
> Wherein it written was, and how himselfe he blist.
>
> (4.7.46)

The body that has been deprived of its social marks, that has been cast out of all available forms of functionally social relationship, is simultaneously the body inflamed by passion; Arthur can recognize the bodily reality even as he fails to recognize his own beloved squire—the social person—about whose loss he is said to be heartbroken.[21]

Once Arthur touches the sexuality defined at the level of emotions rather than social identities, it infects him, too, by providing the terms for a new kind of relationship with his ex-squire. The relationship between these two men comes to seem sexual in just the way Timias's relationship with Belphebe does insofar as Arthur knows just how to relate to him (now only a body, an impassioned one) on the terrain of affects alone: he pronounces Belphebe's name, which makes Timias "wexe glad," a procedure whose therapeutic value is largely eclipsed by its ability to increase Timias's pain. Though he ostensibly aims to reduce Timias's pain, Arthur in fact has the effect of eliciting or heightening the affective responses that indicate the reality of a sexual connection. The sexuality that emerges out of the social impasse between Timias and Belphebe comes to infect a formerly functional, indeed a formerly foundational, male-male relationship between aristocrats, the most highly valorized *social* relationship in Spenser's real historical world as well as in the imagined world of Faerieland.

If the relationships between Timias and Belphebe in books 3 and 4 and between Spenser and Raleigh in the proem to book 3 hint at the complex paths between a gendered relationship to the queen and male-male sexuality, the Castle Joyeous episode with which book 3 opens investigates sexuality between two women characters: Malecasta, the queen of Castle Joyeous, and Britomart, a lady dressed as a knight and the announced hero of book 3.[22] Like the sexuality that joined Timias and Belphebe, the poem diagnoses a kind of sexual force that binds Malecasta and Britomart, a force born of massive and systemic confusion between terms for properly social relationships that is expressed as incompatible notions of civility or courtesy.

At the beginning of book 3, Britomart and Redcrosse enter the lavish Castle Joyeous and the world they encounter inside is an alien one, full of things that neither they nor the narrator are well equipped to understand:

> But for to tell the sumptuous aray
> Of that great chamber, should be labour lost:
> For living wit, I weene, cannot display
> The royall riches and exceeding cost,
> Of every pillour and of every post:
> Which all of purest bullion framed were,
> And with great pearles and pretious stones embost,
> That the bright glister of their beames cleare
> Did sparckle forth great light, and glorious did appeare.

> These straunger knights through passing, forth were led
> Into an inner rowme, whose royaltee
> And rich purveyance might uneath be red;
> Mote Princes place beseeme so deckt to bee.
> Which stately manner when as they did see,
> The image of superfluous riotize,
> Exceeding much the state of meane degree,

> They greatly wondred, whence so sumptuous guize
> Might be maintayned, and each gan diversely devize.
>
> (3.1.32–33)

In Castle Joyeous the "straunger" knights encounter something fundamentally alien, and their sense of the strangeness of the castle is echoed by Spenser himself. In language that repeats the claims of inexpressibility made in the proem to book 3, Spenser writes that Castle Joyeous may be difficult or even impossible to represent: "For living wit, I weene, cannot display / The royall riches and exceeding cost." Here the difficulty of depicting the castle is tied to its lavishness, what the speaker goes on to describe as a "royaltee" that "might uneath be red."

The castle is, of course, an emblem of the courts of absolute monarchy that are characterized by the lavish riches that seem strange to "old-style" feudal aristocrats represented by Britomart and Redcrosse. Helgerson sees the retrofeudalism of *The Faerie Queene* (expressed in both the feudal knights and in the pseudo-Germanic language Spenser uses) as part of an invidious ideological project of reimagining the English nation as composed of recalcitrant, autonomous aristocrats modeled on the Earl of Essex whom Spenser served as a young man.[23] I suggest that rather than advocating an actual return to a fundamentally feudal social form, Spenser is deploying the aristocratic perspective in order to alienate the historically new absolutist court. Moreover, this alienation can be accomplished as readily from the middle-class perspective that Spenser (the narrator) adopts when he complains that the castle's trappings are "superfluous riotize" that exceed "meane degree." The middle-class moralizing impulse of the resentful lyrical speaker (Spenser wonders how much it must all have cost) enters into an alliance with old-style aristocratic revulsion at the new absolutist court; what they have in common is a sense of profound exclusion from what Castle Joyeous represents.

Part of what seems sinful to Spenser and strange to his feudal knights is the highly refined behavior that takes place in the Castle Joyeous. The knights who have previously fought with Britomart reappear in new clothes and in a new guise:

For they all seemed curteous and gent,
And all sixe brethren, borne of one parent,
Which had them trayned in all civilitee,
And goodly taught to tilt and turnament

(3.1.44)

The "civilitee" of the inhabitants of Castle Joyeous seems to provide the
terms on which Britomart and Redcrosse can be brought into the castle; "civilitee," in other words, seems to provide the terms for a humane
relationship that will displace the spectacular violence of the battle
between Britomart and the knights at the beginning of the episode.
But viewed from a perspective that is at once feudal and middle-class,
the courtesy that ought to embrace Britomart and Redcrosse disgusts
them. Civility is converted from a potentially universal set of norms for
interpersonal behavior into the property of a class of people who are
associated with the absolutist court and who are as essentially different
from Britomart and Redcrosse as the queen is different from Spenser.
    The ambivalent welcoming and blocking of civility is most con-
centrated in the scandalously sexualized courting that Britomart and
Redcrosse encounter at court and which C. S. Lewis ties to the highly
elaborated behavioral codes of courtly love:[24]

And all was full of Damzels, and of Squires,
Dauncing and reveling both day and night,
And swimming deepe in sensuall desires,
And *Cupid* still emongst them kindled lustfull fires.

And all the while sweet Musicke did divide
Her looser notes with *Lydian* harmony;
And all the while sweet birdes thereto applide
Their daintie layes and dulcet melody,
Ay caroling of love and jollity,
That wonder was to heare their trim consort.
. . . .

[But] they sdeigned such lascivious disport,
And loath'd the loose demeanure of that wanton sort.
(3.2.39–40)

The flirting that is identified as highly refined and civilized is "sdeigned" because it seems sinful, and its seeming sinfulness is inseparable from its being transformed into a mark of social distance. The denunciation of a promiscuous and excessive sexuality is here the mark of the social exclusion of the knights from the behavioral codes of court.

The text seems to identify the hyperrefined sexuality of the Castle Joyeous as repugnant or even socially dangerous. But insofar as this denunciation is itself a mark of the social divide yawning between Redcrosse and Britomart and the inhabitants of the Castle Joyeous, it points toward a very different way of defining sexuality that steers clear of sexual panic. This alternative sexuality is located not in a space of social danger or disruption but in the contradiction between incompatible terms for social relationships that we have also seen in the proem and in the relationship between Timias and Belphebe and that reappears in the vexed but intense tie between Britomart and Malecasta.

Britomart and Malecasta, in fact, experiment with an eroticism that is defined by the friction between the "civilitee" that produces scandalous courtship and Britomart's own code of good behavior, at once middle-class and feudal-aristocratic. When Malecasta expresses an aggressively civilized desire for Britomart, Britomart cannot simply refuse her because that would be "discourteise":

For thy she would not in discourteise wise,
Scorne the faire offer of good will profest;
For great rebuke it is, love to despise,
Or rudely sdeine a gentle harts request;
But with faire countenance, as beseemed best,
Her entertayned; nath'lesse she inly deemd
Her love too light, to wooe a wandring guest:

Which she misconstruing, thereby esteemd
That from like inward fire that outward smoke had steemd.

(3.1.55)

In reluctantly accepting Malecasta's offer of love, Britomart is partly
drawing on the traditional medieval code of courtly love, but partly,
too, on a much more modern notion of a shared human condition,
since Spenser tells us, in the preceding stanza, that it is Britomart's
capacity to empathize or even to identify with Malecasta that leads her
to "credit" Malecasta's professions of love:

Full easie was for her to have beliefe,
Who by self-feeling of her feeble sexe,
And by long triall of the inward griefe,
Wherewith imperious love her hart did vexe,
Could judge what paines do loving harts perplexe.

(3.1.54)

It is a shared human condition that Britomart seems to acknowledge
here. But the point is that Britomart's humane "courtesy" (since "she
would not in *discourteise* wise, / Scorne the faire offer of good will profest") leads her to misrecognize Malecasta's love as something like courtly
dedication of a lord to his lady, just as Malecasta's much more restricted
"civilitee" leads *her* to misrecognize Britomart's courtesy as requital of
flirtatious love on her own terms. Two different brands of courtesy, one
that excludes both old-style aristocrats and middle-class moralizers and
the other that excludes hyperrefined representatives of the absolute
monarchy, are fundamentally indistinguishable to these characters. And
this confusion, this misrecognition, opens the door to sexuality, for in the
grip of her "mistaken" belief that Britomart shares her love, Malecasta
makes her way toward the chamber in which Britomart is sleeping and
lies down next to her. Despite her belief that Britomart shares her own
desire, however, Malecasta fearfully ascertains whether "any member
mooved" (3.1.60). Lying, fearfully, next to the unconscious body of
Britomart and trying not to wake her is, evidently, what Malecasta sees

as consummation of a shared erotic passion; satisfied, she emits an "inward sigh." This sigh suggests that the erotic relationship she seeks here is defined by a kind of inability or refusal to relate at all.

When Britomart awakes to find Malecasta lying next to her she responds with an aggressive burst of violence. Her violence seems to bespeak a refusal of sexuality:

> She lightly lept out of her filed bed,
> And to her weapon ran, in minde to gride
> The loathed leachour.
>
> (3.1.62)

These lines, and the violence that ensues, suggest a profound revulsion at a sexuality whose presence Britomart had not suspected; needless to say, given the encouragement Britomart offered Malecasta in the name of courtesy, the hypothesis that Britomart had no idea what Malecasta's intentions were seems improbable. Indeed, the burst of violence seems finally to be an *emblem* of a sexual relationship that is based on social disconnection. The fact that Britomart sustains an injury whose description is highly sexualized seems to confirm that the violence and aggression with which the episode ends are at least as much a continuation of a sexual relationship as they are an expression of an impulse to eliminate or repress sexuality. Britomart's wound is literally caused not by Malecasta but by the knight Gardante:

> But one of those six knights, *Gardante* hight,
> Drew out a deadly bow and arrow keene,
> Which forth he sent with felonous despight,
> And fell intent against the virgin sheene:
> The mortall steele stayd not, till it was seene
> To gore her side, yet was the wound not deepe,
> But lightly rased her soft silken skin,
> That drops of purple bloud thereout did weepe,
> Which did her lilly smock with staines of vermeil steepe.
>
> (3.1.65)

Though it is not Malecasta who fires the wounding arrow, within the terms of the allegory in which Gardante stands for the gaze that Britomart allowed, it is the relationship with Malecasta that has caused Britomart this sexualized wound. Again, it is a nonrelationship, a relationship characterized by the failure to establish a functional social tie, that is identified as the essence of sexuality. In the "drops of purple bloud [that] thereout did weepe, / Which did her lilly smock with staines of vermeil steepe," the presence of a seemingly absent nonrelationship is registered by the body in a way that bypasses the conscious intentions of that body's owner.

In the Castle Joyeous episode, and throughout *The Faerie Queene,* Spenser uses the vexed discourse of civility to achieve a perspective that allows him to treat the absolutist court not as the celebrated center of a functional collective life but as the source of social contradictions that generate a powerful experience of emotionally mediated sexuality. Again and again in the epic Spenser treats the figure of the queen and her absolutist court not as objects of social veneration or respect but as a way of importing a sexual charge into socially unstable relationships at its margins, directly between Spenser and the queen in the proem and again between Spenser and Raleigh, Timias and Belphebe, Timias and Arthur, and Britomart and Malecasta. But this "use" of the absolutist court inside the epic finally poses the question of how the epic and its author are supposed to relate to the court and the queen to whom the epic is addressed.

As I noted in chapter 2, Spenser is an emblematic figure in a massive sixteenth-century transformation of the terms of literary ambition and authority. Helgerson argues that Spenser, together with other sixteenth-century writers, turned away from the court and the notion of being an "amateur gentleman writer" and invented a new conception of the autonomous, professional writer and new criteria for a successful literary career.[25] But the role of autonomous writer only makes sense within an institutionalized literary field that authorizes purely literary ambition. Absent such an institution, Spenser's literary ambition can appear only as a kind of creative negation of the role of courtly poet. I suggest that the chief expression of Spenser's historically anomalous ambition is a discourse of sexuality that displaces serious literature from the court by actively displacing the court within serious literature.[26] Thus, while Spenser claims that his epic is designed to serve the queen, as he must, he quietly devotes almost all of his literary energies to exposing the social discontinuities and contradictions that swirl around the court and that pepper the fabric of his epic with a socially dysfunctional sexuality that is, in some sense, its real focus.[27] In short, if Spenser sought to make it in the historical world he had been born into by serving the queen and being recognized as a courtly writer, he nevertheless also sought to displace the chief mechanisms of that historical world in a gesture that could be redeemed only in literary history.[28]

An equation of a historically anomalous, even dysfunctional, literary ambition *and* an impulse to explore sociosexual alternatives that lie beneath or alongside the historical social world he had been born into is, in fact, evident throughout Spenser's biography. It appears, for example, in Spenser's early friendship with his pompous, ambitious, and ultimately self-defeating Cambridge colleague, Gabriel Harvey.[29] As Jonathan Goldberg has argued in his discussion of the exchange of letters these men published, Spenser and Harvey plotted their own future careers in the realm of literature by representing their friendship as a secret and potentially troubling networking of young men.[30] Spenser's early relationship with Harvey suggests that if Spenser found himself ineluctably *in* the social world, he was nevertheless drawn, profoundly drawn, to the borders, the limits, the test cases of Elizabethan sociability, and that he associated literature with this urge from the start. Overdetermined and radically unstable, friendship with Harvey is just one instance of a whole range of marginal positions to which Spenser returned again and again, in life and in an epic poem that aims to document a form of sexuality that drives people together precisely in those moments when conventional social norms have been short-circuited. Alongside the ambitious writer eager to secure the queen's accolades and her money, we must, perhaps, learn to see another Spenser, one who found in the "endless work" of writing a way of keeping the normative operations of the social world at bay.[31] At the time of Spenser's death in 1599, *The Faerie Queene* was left unfinished at some thirty-six thousand lines; he had planned a work twice the length and had suggested that when he finished *The Faerie Queene* he would write a second, complementary epic of equal length. John Guillory sees the desire to rest as the greatest moral danger Spenser's characters ever face, but rest may also be the greatest danger their poetic progenitor faced, for in rest lay the inevitable return of the conventional social world and conventional social ties that had been laboriously pushed beyond the writing desk.[32] It is Spenser's radical wish to move beyond the normative terms of his historical social world that turns *The Faerie Queene* into an archive of a hidden emotional topography that ripples beneath—and alongside—early modern society.

CHAPTER 4

At the Limits of the Social World: Fear and Pride in Shakespeare's Troilus and Cressida

I have been describing a discourse of sexuality that is forged out of an early modern contradiction between incompatible ways of defining class or status and incompatible ways of envisioning the social world as a whole. This underlying social contradiction is generated by the slow, uneven, and often traumatic emergence of a modern social formation in early modern England, and it is theorized by the important early modern discourse of civility. I have argued that the discourse of civility projects the ideal of a universal humanity that must be respected by all and lays the foundation for a kind of social distinction that results from competition with others for the showy courtesy that marks one capable of "humane" relationships. I have also argued that this modern social vision is consistently unable to displace an older, essentially premodern or feudal vision of the social world in which social distinction, personal identity, and group membership are defined a priori, as it were, by blood alone.

In Shakespeare's plays, as in the other literary texts I have examined, this underlying social contradiction is fused to define a special class of sexual intersubjectivity. Caught between the logic of a potentially universal humanity and the logic of heredity, Shakespeare's characters are driven together by the shimmering possibility of a shared humanity only to be repulsed by the resurgence of a blood-borne sense of incompatibility that seems to violate the hypothesis of shared humanity. This historically specific form of interpersonal breakdown shatters characters out of the social world and into a kind of parallel world of sexuality, and like Sidney and Spenser, Shakespeare catalogs the specific interpersonal experiences available in this parallel realm through a vocabulary of intense, depersonalized, painfully pleasurable emotions including fear, pride, anger, and shame. These emotions define a nexus of sexual connections between bodies that arise when functionally social connections between socially legible persons have been foreclosed.

Although this form of sexuality is an important part of many of Shakespeare's plays, critics have had a hard time recognizing it because they have often framed representations of sexuality as either endorsing the patriarchal norms of early modern society or transgressing them.[1] Naturally, the plays do register early modern sex-gender norms, and they do represent forms of sexuality that are sanctioned by these norms as well as forms of sexuality that challenge them.[2] But Shakespeare's plays *also* use the central social contradictions of his society to generate a form of sexual intersubjectivity that flourishes alongside or beneath early modern sex-gender norms, neither attacking nor affirming them. In that sense, Shakespeare's plays offer a kind of X-ray vision that cuts through the nominal heteronormativity of early modern culture to reveal a special class of sexual relationships that flourish quietly beneath the surface of Renaissance society as we have grown accustomed to seeing it.[3]

I will focus on *Troilus and Cressida* because this play's jaundiced or skewed relationship to Elizabethan culture positions it perfectly to catch the traces of the emotionally mediated sexuality that ripples beneath conventional social life. Formally, *Troilus and Cressida* is structured by a quasi-carnivalesque impulse to debase the Homeric figures that are among the most highly valued cultural icons in Elizabethan society, and several commentators, notably Eric S. Mallin, have examined the strange and disorienting ways the play resonates in the context of the Earl of Essex's efforts to style himself a modern Achilles.[4] If the disorienting effect of the play results, in part, from Shakespeare's customary mixing of high and low cultural materials (here, the Homeric epic with a bedroom farce), there is nevertheless reason to think that *Troilus and Cressida* seemed especially unsettled—and unsettling—to Shakespeare's contemporaries. One sign of this is the 1609 quarto that famously contains a publisher's preface that insists, falsely it seems, that the play had never been publicly performed and was meant only for culturally sophisticated readers.[5] If this preface is a ham-fisted effort to market the play to self-identified cultural sophisticates, it nevertheless *also* has the effect of highlighting a persistent uncertainty about who the intended audience of the play really is and about what they are supposed to do with it.[6]

It is precisely the culturally unsettled and unsettling status of the play's formal structure that positions it to catch the traces of a fundamentally asocial sexuality that flourishes just beneath the surface of early modern society and that is indifferent to that society's needs and anxieties. One of the most basic assumptions of Renaissance society toward which *Troilus and Cressida* turns a notably jaundiced eye is the homosocial traffic in women—in which women are used to cement ties between men by being given in marriage or used to produce heirs—that is one of the pillars of the early modern sex-gender system. The story of the Trojan War seems to affirm the preeminence of homosocial ties in the most canonical form; the Greeks, after all, are fighting to restore the marriage bond on which the homosocial order is founded. Moreover, the movement of Cressida, at the very midpoint of the play, from the Trojan camp to the Greek camp suggests an impulse to restore the imbalance in the relationship between the two groups of men caused by the abduction of Helen by giving the Greeks a Trojan woman who is said at every turn to be nearly interchangeable with Helen.[7]

But most of Shakespeare's warriors seem weary of the homosocial bonds that are secured through the bodies of women, a weariness that is expressed in the misogyny that afflicts the Greek warriors who look on Helen as a garden variety "whore," as well as the Trojan princes who—somewhat shockingly—think that Helen should be given up. Troilus, for example, begins the play by announcing that Helen is "too starved a subject for my sword" (1.1.89), and Hector argues that Helen should be handed back to the Greeks because she is "a thing not ours" (2.2.22). Helen is "not ours" both because she is Greek and because she is a woman.[8] Referring to the warriors who are also Trojan princes,

Hector asks, "If we have lost so many tenths of ours / To guard a thing not ours nor worth to us / (Had it our name) the value of one ten, / What merit's in that reason which denies / The yielding of her up?" (2.2.21–25). The Greeks share Hector's point of view. During the prisoner exchange Diomedes goes out of his way to tell Paris that the Greeks love their warriors more than they love Helen. She is, says Diomedes, "bitter to her country: hear me, Paris— / For every false drop in her bawdy veins / A Grecian's life hath sunk; for every scruple / Of her contaminated carrion weight / A Trojan hath been slain" (4.1.70–74). In the love for his own men Diomedes finds the only possible common ground with his enemy; he appeals to Paris on the grounds that the Trojans love Trojan men as much and in the same way as the Greeks love Greek men—and in both cases, it is a love that dictates turning against women. Shakespeare's version of the Trojan War is thus troubled from the outset by the fact that men on both sides seem disinclined to fight for or about women, or to use women as a currency for negotiating relationships between men.[9]

But if the structure of the original Homeric story makes this weariness with homosocial ties seem like a major social crisis that must be overcome so that war can be resurrected on a heroic footing, the energy of Shakespeare's retelling of the story is nevertheless almost completely devoted to preventing such a return to sociosexual "normalcy" and to exploring the alternative sexual order that springs up in the hiatus. For Troilus, the titular hero of the play, fatigue with homosocial ties is valuable because it opens the door to a form of relationship with his beloved Cressida that feels sexual *because* it is not part of the web of homosocial ties in which men use women to cement social bonds between men or to compete with other men. For Troilus, love for Cressida separates him in a somewhat humiliating fashion from the duty he owes to his kinsmen as a Trojan warrior and prince, and his first action in the play is, in fact, to disarm: "I'll unarm again," Troilus says, asking, "Why should I war without the walls of Troy, / That find such cruel battle here within?" (1.1.1–3).[10] A war within his own breast displaces him from the seemingly homosocial war without, but if this separation is humiliating then it is also valuable, for it sets

Troilus's love for Cressida apart from the bland heterosexual homosociability that seems to structure the war and Greek/Trojan society as a
whole. Indeed, under the pressure of his love for Cressida, Troilus manages to look in on the homosocial order from the outside, as it were,
for when he complains that "Helen must needs be fair, / When with
your blood you daily paint her thus" (1.1.86–87), he comes close to
disclosing the open secret that "love" for Helen is merely a vehicle for
desire and competition between men and for masculine self-assertion.

Unlike love for the blood-painted Helen, Troilus's love for Cressida
is almost *defined* by its leading him away from the homosocial regard
of other men on which his social status depends; far from reaffirming
his social self, Troilus's sexuality seems fundamentally and essentially
self-defeating or even self-shattering.[11] When long-desired consummation with Cressida is finally within sight, Troilus imagines not secure
intimacy but something dangerous, something as dangerous as a battle
that he is losing.[12] Imagining sex with his beloved, Troilus fears "that
I shall lose distinction in my joys, / As doth a battle, when they charge
on heaps / The enemy flying" (3.2.25–27). But what seems like a simple case of what Adorno might call the bourgeois fear of sex in which
the brutishness of sexual pleasure threatens the dignity of the individual (what Troilus calls his "distinction") is in fact the opposite, the fear
that an exalted style of love will threaten Troilus's brutish self. Troilus
claims that Cressida is unimaginably more sophisticated than he and
that she represents a kind of personal status or identity that is permanently out of reach for him.[13] Resorting to the digestion metaphors
that saturate this play, Troilus claims that the moment that his "wat'ry
palates taste indeed / Love's thrice-repured nectar" will spell death:
"Death, I fear me, / Swooning destruction, or some joy too fine, / Too
subtle-potent, tuned too sharp in sweetness / For the capacity of my
ruder powers. / I fear it much" (3.2.19–24). Troilus's palate is "wat'ry"
but his "ruder powers" will fail to digest the subtle, "thrice-repured"
and altogether too sweet nectar of Cressida.

When Troilus imbues Cressida with the allure of "thrice-repured
nectar," he seems to draw on the world conjured up by the discourse
of civility in which status, and especially the status of a new courtly

elite, depends on successfully achieving the elegant and sophisticated manners that mark one as capable of entering into a humane relationship with others. But while Cressida's achievements seem facts of acculturation that ought to be learnable, Troilus insists that she possesses a kind of symbolic supercachet that is hers by birth and blood and that makes her *biologically* different from him; in essence, Troilus injects an aristocratic social imaginary (in which status and identity are hereditary) into the potentially universal logic of acquired and acculturated civility, and he does so to block any sense of a reassuring, functionally social courtship between the two. It is noteworthy, after all, that Troilus is a prince and Cressida an aristocrat, if also the daughter of a traitor, and that their shared membership in the Trojan elite would seem to make them perfect candidates for a courtly affair, which is exactly the way Cressida's uncle, Pandarus, looks at it, something I shall discuss shortly. Troilus deflects such a conventionally courtly tie by insisting on a radical, almost corporeal incompatibility between himself and his beloved. In a sense, Troilus has erotically cathected social and interpersonal breakdown; he insists on a massive incompatibility between himself and Cressida because, from his perspective, it is the total impossibility of a functionally social tie on *any* terms with an alien Cressida that generates the excitement of sexuality. Cressida's love is like food from another world, food that Troilus wants even though, or because, he fears he will choke on it.

In *Troilus and Cressida,* the space of sexuality that is generated out of a rather abstract sociological contradiction between culturally mediated social status and biological essence is filled in and given texture by powerful corporeal emotions that define connections between bodies when functionally social connections have been short-circuited. For Troilus, the relationship becomes legible primarily in terms of the intense fear he feels when looking on the social aporia constituted by Cressida (as he sees her) and that seems to glue him to her as nothing else can. Offering a blazon of fear, Troilus says that when he gazes on Cressida, "Even such a passion doth embrace my bosom / My heart beats thicker than a feverous pulse, / And all my powers do their bestowing lose / Like vassalage at unawares encount'ring / The eye of majesty" (3.2.34–38). Fear is the essence of the erotic tie as Troilus experiences it, and to give himself that loving feeling he props Cressida onto the position of the absolute monarch ("the eye of majesty") and imagines himself as a cowering "vassal." Making Cressida into a version of the queen equips Troilus's fear with an entire sociology, for at the end of the Middle Ages and the beginning of the early modern period the absolutist courts were vanguards of courtly refinement, sites for the elaboration of ever more highly articulated forms of behavior that gradually increased the cultural separation of the world of the court from the popular milieu. Though the Jacobean theory of divine right hints at the state autonomy that the future held, throughout the early modern era the state was still closely associated with a social elite, and the authority of the state depended on the cultural cachet of this social elite and the shock and awe they could generate in spectators.

The awesome separateness of a glittering, otherworldly court has value for Troilus because it enables him to define his relationship with Cressida: this relationship is impossible in just the same way that a relationship with members of the Elizabethan court would be impossible for a country bumpkin; the only possible terrain for a tie that is caught in this contradiction is in the awed anxiety and fear that Troilus suffers (and enjoys) when he contemplates Cressida. When Troilus says his "heart beats thicker than a feverous pulse," he labels a relationship that cannot be named in any other way because it is *defined* by the absence of social recognition. By using a graphically depicted fear to sketch the glue that joins Troilus to Cressida, Shakespeare approaches the question of sexuality from the standpoint of neither sexual identities nor a homosociality that uses sex to affirm social ties between men; rather, he approaches sexuality from the standpoint of what Foucault terms an *ars erotica*. Shakespeare's project in the play is to reveal how the contradictions of social life invest specific relationships with the powerful affects that designate early modern sexuality and set it apart from functional social life.

It is often the case in Shakespeare's plays that an erotic charge is generated by massive interpersonal incompatibility arising from the very structure of the imagined society of the play; this is true, for example, in *Othello,* in *Romeo and Juliet,* as well as in *All's Well That Ends Well,* in which the relationship of the self-consciously lowborn Helena and the noble Bertram is sexualized precisely to the degree that it seems socially impossible or even absent: Helena manages to get Bertram to impregnate her without his conscious participation. The kind of interpersonal impasse or breakdown that triggers sexuality in these plays, like the impasse that triggers sexuality between Troilus and Cressida, is not simply class incompatibility (between highborn and lowborn, say, or even between rival blood clans) but a more radical and more unstable contradiction between altogether different ways of defining status or identity and of envisioning the social world as a whole. The specific social contradiction that triggers sexuality in *Troilus and Cressida* is between, on the one hand, a vision of a culturally mediated society structured by the hypothesis of a shared humanity and, on the other hand, the insistence that blood and heredity define basic, nonnegotiable differences between persons. The most vital relationships that appear in Shakespeare's plays act like chemical catalysts that force together these totally incompatible visions of status or identity until they fuse into a sexuality that departs from either vision to define a special class of sexual intersubjectivity, a sexuality that stands apart from social life.

   This emotionally mediated sexual bonding does not attack the homosocial ties that underpin early modern society; it simply ignores them. In the case of *Troilus and Cressida,* the fact that Troilus's eroticism of fear ignores normative homosocial ties rather than attacking them is emphasized by the supposedly comic Pandarus subplot. Pandarus is Cressida's uncle and acts as a go-between for Cressida and Troilus; as an orthodox homosocialist, Pandarus thinks of the women he is related to as chips to be traded to other men, and he views setting up a liaison between the lovers as a means of securing a liaison with Troilus for himself. "Had I a sister," muses Pandarus, "[who was] a grace, or a daughter [who was] a goddess, he [i.e., Troilus] should take his choice. O admirable man!" (1.2.227–28). And when word comes that Cressida must be handed over to the Greeks, Pandarus's sole concern is for his prospective nephew-in-law: "Would thou hadst ne'er been born!" he says to his niece, "I knew thou wouldst be his death" (4.2.86–87).

But the distance of the Pandarus-Troilus relationship from a functional homosociability in which relations between men are secured through women is announced from the beginning when Troilus complains—with a hint of humiliation—that he must woo Pandarus as much (or in the same way) as he woos Cressida: "And he's as tetchy to be woo'd to woo / As she is stubborn-chaste against all suit" (1.1.92–93). And indeed, Pandarus ends the play with an epilogue in which he seems not like someone who traffics in women but like the object of traffic himself, afflicted with the venereal "diseases" (5.11.56) that Shakespeare's sources give Cressida as ritualized punishment for her being a "whore."[14] Kenneth Palmer, editor of the second series Arden edition, is disturbed by this and remarks in a footnote that "there is no natural reason why a panderer should become infected by his trade; but Pandarus is a kind of surrogate for Cressida."[15] If Pandarus can become a surrogate for Cressida (as Palmer rightly notes), then the model of homosociability that Pandarus supposedly embodies proceeds at some tangent to the functional homosociability in which women are used to forge socially useful connections between men. Since Pandarus does not seem to offer Troilus any social advantages anyway, the fact that Troilus must woo Pandarus is simply another opportunity to emphasize how distant Troilus's motivations in loving Cressida are from the red-blooded competition with real-world stakes that functional homosociability is supposed to represent. By declining to use Cressida to engage in real-world competition and negotiation with other men for status or power, Troilus converts a mode of heterosexual courtship that has real-world consequences into the source of a fear (and shame) that singles him out as the subject of sexuality.

The Pandarus subplot hints that the asocial love Troilus cultivates toward his beloved can spill over to infect relationships between men—between Troilus and the Pandarus he must woo and, once Cressida is handed over to the Greeks halfway through the play, between Troilus and his Greek enemies. On its face, the transfer of Cressida to the Greeks threatens to force Troilus back into the homosocial competition with men (this time with the Greeks) that he had been at pains to avoid within the walls of Troy. What actually seems to happen is that the asocial sexuality that Troilus first experiences in relation to Cressida is shifted into the heart of his relationship with his social enemies.

As soon as he gets the news that Cressida will be handed over to the Greeks, Troilus worries that she will desire the Greek youths because they possess the symbolic refinement that Cressida has and Troilus claims to lack. "The Grecian youths are full of quality," Troilus muses,

Their loving well compos'd, with gift of nature flowing,
And swelling o'er with arts and exercise.
How novelty may move, and parts with person,
Alas, a kind of godly jealousy—
Which I beseech you call a virtuous sin—
Makes me afeard.

(4.4.75-81)

In Troilus's eyes, Cressida belongs with the Greeks because she is as civilized as they are. René Girard sees this as a symptom of homosocial (his word is "mimetic") desire, and he glosses the passage as follows: "Everything Troilus says confirms the mimetic nature of his relationship to the Greeks. He certainly wants to acquire the talents and achievements that he admires in them. Which young man in love would not?" Girard writes that the only way out of fear and jealousy for Troilus would be "a Greek education," which would make Troilus Greek, an education that Girard thinks impossible only because it would take more time than Troilus has at this moment of crisis.[16] But Troilus fears that the asocial sexuality defined by the *refusal* to use Cressida to enter into a functionally (if competitive) homosocial relationship will be closed off as Cressida establishes functional ties with the Greeks (to whom she is "naturally" similar anyway) and forces Troilus to compete with them—in orthodox homosocial form—for her hand. Rather than fighting with the Greeks for Cressida, Troilus therefore somewhat theatrically insists that the Greeks are as sophisticated as Cressida and that he himself is unequal to both. Troilus's refusal to compete with the Greeks by engaging in what Girard calls a Greek education is a (somewhat desperate) effort to preserve the gulf that divides him from Cressida by introducing that same gulf into his relationship with the Greeks who have adopted her. In Girard's view, loving Cressida is merely a cover for the homosocial envy and competitiveness Troilus feels toward the Greeks; Girard indicts Troilus for not loving Cressida enough.[17] But far from demonstrating too little love and too much social calculation, Troilus here suffers from a sort of explosion of a sexuality that infects even his relationship with his supposed social rivals.[18]

Troilus manages to keep homosocial relations at bay for a time after Cressida is transferred to the Greek camp, but Cressida's vulnerability in the Greek camp leads her to embrace homosocial ties. Indeed, the asymmetry of gender makes Cressida's experience of sexuality more ambivalent than Troilus's throughout the play; in a ruthlessly patriarchal world, it is difficult for Cressida to indulge in a sexuality that leeches away the real-world stakes of a relationship between a man and a woman. Like Troilus, Cressida sees sexuality as dangerous to her social standing and dignity, but absent the privilege of being a man, Cressida cannot accept the risk of indulging in such passion.[19] Just before she is handed to the Greeks, Cressida gives a powerful image of a sexuality she fears when she asks Troilus to "bid me hold my tongue, / For in this rapture I shall surely speak / The thing I shall repent" (3.2.125–27). Specifically, she fears that

If I confess too much you will play the tyrant.
I love you now, but till now not so much
But I might master it. In faith, I lie;
My thoughts were like unbridled children, grown
Too headstrong for their mother. See, we fools!
Why have I blabbed?

(3.2.115–20)

Cressida's desire for Troilus is as unsettling as "unbridled children," and Cressida sees sexual refusal or unattainability as the only safe position for a woman to be in, famously claiming that "Women are angels, wooing; / Things won are done" (1.2.277–78). And when Cressida wishes to become a man ("I wished myself a man, / Or that we women had men's privilege / Of speaking first" (3.2.123–25), it is only partly because men are authorized to woo; Cressida also hints that men can take risks that women cannot, that men may indulge in a desire that is almost defined by its tendency to undermine social credibility, dignity, and authority. It is because of the difficulties her gender causes her that Cressida must struggle with and, I think, finally conquer a powerful sexual impulse to which Troilus simply surrenders.

This ambivalent experience of sexuality is part of the explanation for the speed and ease with which Cressida embraces the role of coquette once she has been removed to the Greek camp. When the Greek leaders paw at her minutes after she has left her lover, Cressida coolly plays with their desires. Although her coquettishness does not get her far (it elicits an aggressively misogynist reply from Ulysses), Cressida may well be making the most of the extraordinarily weak hand she has been dealt. This realistic resignation sets Cressida up for the charge of faithlessness, yet there is a sense in which it allows her own desire for Troilus to remain more or less intact, still defined as something deeply dangerous to the social self that threatens at every turn to undermine her tenuously held position in the Greek camp. This may account for Cressida's profound struggle with herself in the scene in which she gives in to Diomedes' request for a favor—a sleeve to display on his helmet during battle as a token of her sexual submission and a taunt to Troilus. It is surprising not that Cressida finally gives in to Diomedes, but that she comes close to holding out in what would surely be a suicidal gesture. When Cressida tells Diomedes that the pledge he has just taken from her belonged to one "that loved me better than you will" (5.2.96), it sounds as if she were resigning herself to the claims of reality, for if Troilus loved her better than Diomedes, Diomedes can certainly protect her better in the Greek camp. Here, Cressida essentially chooses a homosocial relationship over an erotic one, but in so doing she preserves that erotic relationship as a dangerous, potentially suicidal urge within herself.

Although Cressida preserves an erotic connection to Troilus as an unrealized potential deep within herself, her tactical alliance with Diomedes condemns Troilus to the homosocial competition from which he had previously felt pleasurably excluded. After witnessing Cressida's apparent betrayal while he spies on her and Diomedes, Troilus heads off vowing revenge on his rival, and insofar as the Cressida-Troilus-Diomedes story replays the Helen-Menelaus-Paris story in reverse (a parallel emphasized by Thersites while he spies on Ulysses and Troilus while they spy on Cressida and Diomedes),[20] Troilus's desire for revenge promises to finally inject some energy into the war as a whole. In the very next scene Troilus argues with his brother Hector, who is prone to flamboyantly chivalric gestures of mercy on the battlefield:

> For th' love of all the gods,
> Let's leave the hermit Pity with our mothers,
> And when we have our armours buckled on,
> The venomed vengeance ride upon our swords,
> Spur them to ruthful work, rein them from ruth.
>
> (5.3.44–48)

Troilus began the play in the grip of thoroughgoing disaffection from combat, but he now becomes a spokesperson for total war, urging Hector to turn his back on both an outdated code of honor and the entreaties of his wife, sister, and father, who beg him to sit out the day's combat. In the battle that takes up most of act 5, Troilus's actions stand as an emblem of the Trojan War as it *ought* to look; Ulysses, for example, says admiringly that Troilus has "done today / Mad and fantastic execution, / Engaging and redeeming of himself / With such a careless force and forceless care / As if that lust, in very spite of cunning, / Bade him win all" (5.5.37–42). Ulysses even worries that his own famous "cunning" will be no match for Troilus's "careless force." Yet by describing Troilus's force as "careless," Ulysses hints that deep within an apparently revitalized commitment to the public responsibilities of war lies a turn against the self that indicates the persistence of a sexual comportment in Troilus's newfound martial interest. Troilus, too, hints that there is something *abnormally* careless in his bravery when he cries out, "Fate, hear me what I say! I reck not though thou end my life today" (5.6.26–27), and at the end of the play, after the catastrophe of Hector's

89

death, Troilus presents himself not as the second Hector and the best hope of his people but as the harbinger of final destruction:

> Sit, gods, upon your thrones and smite at Troy!
> I say at once: let your brief plagues be mercy,
> And linger not our sure destructions on!
>
> (5.11.7–9)

This is almost the last word in the play, and it suggests how heroism in defense of motherland can come to seem like a death wish. Thus, even as Cressida's anguished turn to Diomedes returns Troilus to homosocial life and a war for women in which he had previously lost interest, it also, perhaps secretly, shifts the sexualized, socially tangential comportment he had adopted toward her onto the battlefield.

One way of approaching the question of whether the war as it finally appears in act 5 of Shakespeare's play is still structured by conventional homosocial desire is through the figure of Achilles, who holds up the Greek war effort by keeping to his tent and refusing to fight. Achilles triggers an asocial or socially tangential sexuality between himself and other men in the Greek camp that parallels the fearful sexuality Troilus experiences in relation to Cressida. Like the sexual relationship between Troilus and Cressida, the sexuality Achilles generates around himself is rooted in the incompatible social imaginaries spawned by an emerging modernity. Paying attention to the ways Achilles exploits social contradictions to generate a sexuality between himself and the other men in the Greek camp will confirm what is merely suggested by Troilus's erotic carelessness in the final battle: the Trojan War as it is finally constituted by the encounter of Achilles, Hector, and Troilus on the battlefield of act 5 is neither the continuation of conventional social life nor its inversion, but the resurrection of society on the ambiguous foundation of sexuality.

That Achilles does not fit into the normal procedures of his social world is the obvious problem faced by the Greek leadership. The terms of social ordering against which Achilles rebels are invoked by Ulysses in the act 1, scene 3 speech in which he famously defends the hierarchy that Achilles undermines by disobeying direct orders to return to battle:

> The heavens themselves, the planets, and this centre
> Observe degree, priority, and place,
> Insisture, course, proportion, season, form
> Office, and custom, all in line of order
>
> (1.3.85–88)

Throughout this speech, Ulysses relies on the eating metaphors that permeate the play to express his vision of the disciplined army, using digestion as the privileged metaphor for integrating Achilles into social life. "When that the general is not like the hive / To whom the foragers shall all repair," Ulysses asks, "What honey is expected?" (1.3.81–83).[21] Ulysses understands Achilles' recalcitrance as bad primarily because it interferes with the orderly production and consumption of food in which the bees both bring food to the general and are eaten by him. A derangement of appetite is what ensues:

> Then everything includes itself in power,
> Power into will, will into appetite,
> And appetite, an universal wolf,
> So doubly seconded with will and power,
> Must make perforce an universal prey,
> And last eat up himself
>
> (1.3.119–24)

This last phrase, of course, "and last eat up himself," is Shakespeare's slogan for the disease that afflicts the Young Man of the sonnets, namely, pride. Agamemnon says simply, "he that is proud eats up himself" (2.3.152), and Ulysses describes "the proud lord" as "bast[ing] his arrogance with his own seam [i.e., fat, grease]" (2.3.181–82). Self-consuming pride leads Achilles to withhold his body from the collective, just as the proud Young Man does by declining to reproduce, and from Ulysses' standpoint, Achilles' indigestible pride threatens to stick in the throat:

"Great Agamemnon," Ulysses concludes his act 1 forensic exercise, "This chaos, when degree is suffocate, / Follows the choking" (1.3.124–26). The general is in danger of choking on the indigestible Achilles, a point later made by the general himself when, speaking of Achilles' virtues, he says that "yet all his virtues, / Not virtuously on his own part beheld, / Do in our eyes begin to lose their gloss, / Yea, like fair fruit in an unwholesome dish, / Are like to rot untasted" (2.3.115–19). Achilles is or is becoming rotten, rotten food that might ruin the appetite or stick in the throat. For Ulysses, pride refuses to enter into social bonds and seems impervious to the demands of social life, a situation figured in the Greek camp as producing nausea. In the play Ajax offers to return Achilles to the general food supply by making him into bread: "I will knead him, I'll make him supple" (2.3.222). It is apparently the hope of breaking Achilles' pride and thereby making him edible that leads Ajax to wish that Achilles "were a Trojan" (2.3.230), and the entire Greek leadership shares Ajax's view that there is something treacherous about Achilles that makes him more dangerous than the Trojans.

Like Troilus's fear, Achilles' pride is the effect of a contradiction between social imaginaries. If Achilles breaks with Ulysses's vision of a great chain of command in which everyone knows his place and in which social status derives only from one's position in the hierarchy, then he nevertheless also denies that his social status or identity depends on culturally mediated competition with and recognition from others— what the play terms "fame." In act 3 Ulysses asserts that "no man is the lord of anything, / Though in and of him there be much consisting, / Till he communicate his parts to others; / Nor doth he of himself know them for aught, / Till he behold them form'd in the applause" of others (3.3.116–20). It is precisely this function of praising him, of applauding him, that Achilles denies the other members of his social world; Ulysses's argument notwithstanding, Achilles does indeed believe himself to be "lord" even when he does not "communicate his parts to others." What makes Achilles so radically unsocial is that he seems to believe that he has some status deep within himself that makes it possible for him to *secede* from social life. By laying claim to a kind of permanent, extrasocial fame, Achilles props a sociological distinction,

premised on successful competition within a competitive social totality, premised, that is, on eliciting praise from others with whom he
shares a world, on an outdated aristocratic imaginary in which status
derives from blood alone. Achilles is like an old-style aristocrat in the
modern world, and his pride defines a massive social impasse that seems
to make any social relationship with him impossible. The same is true
in the sonnets where the Young Man's pride results from his belief that
he does not depend on anyone's praise for his social status. Moreover,
in the sonnets, the injection of culturally mediated status into the veins,
as it were, makes it hard to tell whether the Young Man is an aristocrat
or, as William Empson puts it, a career-minded arriviste.[22] This confusion of status also afflicts Achilles and for exactly the same reason. In
both cases, pride identifies a peculiar moment of social dysfunction that
draws on the most fundamental social contradictions of Shakespeare's
society and makes it impossible for characters to relate to Achilles in a
legibly *social* way. Ajax summarizes the prevailing view in the Greek
camp by asking simply, "Can he not be sociable?" (2.3.207). The question of sociability, the question of the terms on which Achilles can be
integrated into the normal procedures of social life and thus the question of the terms on which a relationship with pride is possible, is the
central question faced by the Greek camp, and since, as Ulysses puts it
at the end of his set speech, "Troy in our weakness stands, not in her
strength" (1.3.137), it is in some sense the central question faced by the
play as a whole.

While Ulysses sees Achilles' pride as antisocial, as an attack on the
social order over which King Agamemnon presides, the play suggests
that pride is not so much antisocial as it is *asocial* or *differently social*.
Ulysses thinks of Achilles' pride as a massive social crisis that must
be overcome, but Achilles' pride does not really seem to block strong
interpersonal relationships between Achilles and others as much as it
redefines them by placing them on a sexual footing. Ajax himself trans-
fers the disgust Achilles' pride makes him feel into the sexual register:
"I do hate the proud man as I do hate the engendering of toads"
(2.3.156), an image also used by Othello to describe the disgust he feels
at the thought of Desdemona's sexual infidelity.[23] This is just what

happens in the sonnets where the pride of the Young Man invests the relationship between him and Shakespeare with a sexual allure that is paradoxically captured in Shakespeare's obsessive feeling that he, as a lyric speaker, is superfluous, pointless, without function. Ulysses knows the feeling, for to encounter Achilles is also to encounter an aporia, to feel useless, to feel more or less supplementary—to feel like the subject of a sexual relationship as Shakespeare understands it.

In this context, Ulysses's obsessive efforts to frame Achilles as antisocial or socially deviant, as a danger to society that must be crushed through violence or guile, actually amounts to a refusal to fully acknowledge the perverse claim of sexuality that Achilles insists on. It is a defense that other characters engage in as well, notably Thersites who tries to contain Achillean sexuality by deploying the scapegoating notion of sodomy. Everyone in the Greek camp knows that Achilles is sleeping with Patroclus, and Thersites calls Patroclus "Achilles' male varlet" and his "masculine whore" (5.1.14, 16). As Gregory Bredbeck observes, by deploying sodomy Thersites frames the Achilles-Patroclus relationship as a sign of the degeneration of the entire body politic; but by attaching overwhelming (overwhelmingly negative) social consequences to the relationship, Thersites essentially covers up sexuality.[24] The same kind of disavowal of sexuality is accomplished by Nestor, though in precisely the opposite direction, when he contentedly "uses" Patroclus's death to get Achilles back onto the battlefield by telling the soldiers to "Go bear Patroclus' body to Achilles."[25] In both cases, a sexuality that is built on the absence of a functional social ground is denied in favor of a relationship with overwhelming social consequences, whether those consequences are bad or good.[26]

The real challenge posed by Achilles' pride is that it defines a kind of interpersonal bonding that is essentially *outside* or *indifferent* to social concerns, and the only vocabulary that captures this form of intersubjectivity is the one Ulysses obsessively returns to—the accusation of pride. To say, as Ulysses does, that Achilles is proud is to name a relationship that can be labeled in no other way. This pride seems to draw people together in interpersonal formations that have no social consequences whatsoever, neither bad nor good. Worse still, pride is catching.[27] Near the beginning of the play, Ulysses provides an image of the spiraling reproduction of socially marginal, prideful couples in the "factions," the Greek warriors who, in "envious fever / Of pale and bloodless emulation" (1.3.133–34), imitate Achilles' pride by keeping to their tents as he does. Like a virus, pride enacts a cascading conversion of the social into the sexual by encouraging others to become proud and thereby to open specifically sexual relations with still other members of the social world. As Shakespeare represents it, pride projects a matrix of sexual relationships between men that threatens to replace the functional social ties on which the war effort is founded. In a sense, Achilles' pride opens and keeps open—indeed, it widens the purview of—the asocial or nonsocial sexuality that first appears in the Troilus-Cressida relationship and that is first named by Troilus's fear.

We get one powerful image of the socially indifferent sexuality that threatens to replace the functional social ties on which the war effort is founded in Ulysses' scandalized description of what goes on in Achilles' tent. In act 1, scene 3, Ulysses describes how Patroclus entertains Achilles in his tent with slanderous, theatrical lampoons of the Greek leaders. In keeping with his other attacks on Achillean sexuality, Ulysses believes these theatrical lampoons undermine the authority and credibility of the Greek leadership in reality. But as he makes this complaint, Ulysses more or less inadvertently suggests how Patroclus and Achilles in fact use theatricality—and the idea of the Elizabethan theater—to harness and redirect real social pressures and contradictions to energize a sexuality that simply proceeds at a tangent to official social life:

> The great Achilles, whom opinion crowns
> The sinew and the forehand of our host
> Having his ear full of his airy fame,
> Grows dainty of his worth, and in his tent
> Lies mocking our designs: with him Patroclus
> Upon a lazy bed the livelong day
> Breaks scurril jests,
> And with ridiculous and awkward action,
> Which, slanderer, he imitation calls,

He pageants us. Sometimes, great Agamemnon,
Thy topless deputation he puts on,
. . . like a strutting player, whose conceit
Lies in his hamstring and doth think it rich
To hear the wooden dialogue and sound
'Twixt his stretch'd footing and the scaffoldage.
(1.3.142–56)

Like a strutting theater player, Patroclus reduces affairs of state to a
comic pageant while Achilles acts like a member of a rowdy Elizabethan
theater: "Achilles, on his pressed bed lolling, / From his deep chest
laughs out a loud applause: / Cries 'Excellent! 'Tis Agamemnon right!/
Now play me Nestor . . .'" (1.3.162–65). Ulysses goes on to complain
that through Patroclus's parodies the "achievements, plots, orders, pre-
ventions" of the Greek high command are reduced to "stuff for these
two to make paradoxes" (1.3.181, 184). Ulysses gives his view of the
normative way subjects *ought* to relate to the state:

There is a mystery—with whom relation
Durst never meddle—in the soul of state,
Which hath an operation more divine
Than breath or pen can give expressure to.
(3.3.203–6)

Ulysses suggests that the state's social legitimacy depends on the awe
that social distance or detachment produces; for him, the state's "mystery" is coeval with a refusal of any "relation" to the social world; what
he finds objectionable in Patroclus's theater is that it makes the state
visible and even familiar.[28] But Patroclus's theater aims not to decon-
struct state power in reality but only to produce erotic pleasure. By
aping the Greek generals, Patroclus allows Achilles to indulge his pride
by violating the state in a self-consciously theatrical way whose only
real effect is to affirm the emotional reality of a sexual tie between
these men. In Patroclus's hands, the theater is a machine for converting real social contradictions and discontinuities into a form of sexual

intersubjectivity that differentiates itself from the conventional registers of early modern social life. This use of the theater depends, in turn,
on the *difference* between theatrical representations and reality, a difference that Ulysses fails to recognize when he complains that the theater undermines respect for the state *in reality*. Ulysses complains that
Patroclus is a bad actor, that his imitations of the Greek leaders are as
little like their models as "Vulcan and his wife" (1.3.168), but this difference, and the fact of representation (or the fact of the difference
between culture and the real) that it foregrounds, is obviously part of
the pleasure Achilles takes in consuming Patroclus's parodies.[29] Patroclus's comic theater does indeed foreclose the distance that Ulysses says
ought to divide the court from the people it governs as it brings the
awesome power of the state into the bedroom, not in reality but only
as cultural representation, and not in the name of political critique but
only in the name of a pleasure that is radically unhinged from the anxieties and concerns of early modern society.

When Shakespeare makes Patroclus's playacting into a powerful
emblem of asocial sexuality, he relies, in part, on the special status of
the early modern theater as an institution that stands apart from the
rest of social life.[30] Critics and theater historians have described the
special status of the early modern theater as an early version of cultural
autonomy. Drawing on the important work of Stephen Mullaney, Louis
Montrose writes:

> [T]he actual process of theatrical performance, marked off in both time
> and space from the normal flow and loci of social activity, offered to its
> audience—and, of course, to its performers—an imaginative experience
> that partially and temporarily removed them from their normal places,
> their ascribed subject positions. In this sense, for the Queen's common
> subjects, to go to the public playhouse to see a play was to undergo a
> marginal experience; it was to visit the interstices of the Elizabethan
> social and cognitive order.[31]

But the example of Patroclus's bedroom theater suggests that the ability of the theater to set itself apart from the "normal flow and loci of

social activity" could only be the contingent, recurring achievement of a theater systematically geared toward converting the social divides and the contradictions of social life into a socially unreactive pleasure.[32] Like the Puritan antitheatrical critics of Shakespeare's day, Ulysses complains that Patroclus's performance is *antisocial,* that it is an attack on a certain imagined national community. However, insofar as it hijacks real social pressures only to produce pleasure, Patroclus's theater seems merely *nonsocial* or *asocial,* endowed with a degree of apartness from society that is premised on a perverse indifference to the real-world concerns that Ulysses articulates and a perverse refusal to either serve or attack any functional communities however imagined.[33] It is this nonsocial or asocial quality that makes theater both the engine and the emblem of the asocial sexuality that drives Achilles and Patroclus together without providing the terms for a conventional social connection between them. Patroclus uses the theater to define a place apart from the conventional registers of social life, a sort of social bubble within which a special class of sexual intersubjectivity can flourish, but a bubble that stays open only as long as the self-consciously theatrical estrangement from the claims of the social world accomplished by Patroclus's lampoons remains in effect.[34]

Attacking the comic theater in Achilles' tent is only one instance of Ulysses' running effort to break Achilles' pride and thereby break the claim of the asocial sexuality he insists on. But the radical question of sociability that is constituted both by Achilles' pride and by his self-consciously theatricalized relation to Patroclus is finally solved not by Ulysses' cunning but by love: "I have a woman's longing," Achilles finally announces, "An appetite that I am sick withal, / To see great Hector in his weeds of peace, / To talk with him, and to behold his visage / Even to my full view" (3.3.239–43). The appetite for another that pride retards is opened precisely on the enemy; but if the desire for Hector in his weeds of peace seems to open a space of humanity and restraint in the midst of the ravages of war, the encounter itself makes war seem not like a violation of the terms of social life but like the very essence of social life conceived in a new way. For Achilles, beholding the visage of Hector is evidently perfectly compatible with, even premised on, the desire to destroy that visage. When the heroes do meet they are like two bodybuilders admiring one another's dangerously built-up musculatures. "Now, Hector," says Achilles, "I have fed my eyes on thee; / I have with exact view perus'd thee, Hector, / And quoted joint by joint" (4.5.231–33). But this loving gaze is merely a prelude to (or the expression of) the desire to destroy those joints. Achilles continues:

> Tell me, you heavens, in which part of his body
> Shall I destroy him? Whether there, or there, or there
> That I may give the local wound a name,
> And make distinct the very breach whereout
> Hector's great spirit flew. Answer me, heavens!
>
> (4.5.242–46)

Achilles invites Hector to gaze back, "Behold thy fill," and takes offense when Hector says he has already seen enough. Achilles assumes that Hector enjoys looking at the muscles of a man who promises to use them to inflict pain. Being invited to enter into a relationship with Achilles on these terms makes Hector uneasy, an uneasiness that he can only label by invoking the pride that names the only way anyone can have a relationship with Achilles. "It would discredit the blest gods, proud man," Hector says, "To answer such a question" (4.5.247–48).[35] To call Achilles proud does not deny a relationship with him but affirms the presence of a very special bond indeed. The theatrical dynamic of staring at an enemy's body, admiring not only the body on which one will inflict wounds but also the muscles that may inflict wounds in return is in the nature of a relationship with pride, and on these thoroughly unsocial terms the relationship may go on forever. Hector articulates this latter possibility when he departs from Achilles with a warning:

> Henceforth guard thee well;
> For I'll not kill thee there, nor there, nor there;
> But, by the forge that stithied Mars his helm,
> I'll kill thee everywhere, yea, o'er and o'er.
>
> (4.5.253–56)

When Hector can kill Achilles "everywhere, yea, o'er and o'er," the desire to kill the proud Achilles becomes a condition for a relationship as much as its abrogation. The hole within the normal operations of the social world that is opened by the pride that admits of no appetite for others and that refuses to allow others to eat it is here converted into the ground of a relationship that is intensely real if also deeply strange. In place of a reassuringly masculine homosocial bonding, these heroes define a mode of relationship that proceeds from recognition of radical similarity (Hector and Achilles are mirror images of one another) to a theatrical form of social practice that is premised on making the relationship itself seem impossible, over and over again, by killing each other, over and over again. It is a form of relationship whose closest modern analogue may in fact be sadomasochism, but a historically specific form that is rooted in the most profound sociological contradictions of early modern society.

An awareness of the *historical* condition of a sexuality that we would term sadomasochistic is perhaps the most profound insight *Troilus and Cressida* delivers. The most explicit statement of this recognition comes in the prisoner exchange in which the Trojan Aeneas greets the Greek Diomedes "in human gentleness" but continues: "By Venus's hand I swear / No man alive can love in such a sort / The thing he means to kill, more excellently" (4.1.22, 24–26). For Aeneas, the assertion of shared humanity is only a prelude to its spectacular violation through a violence and aggression that he identifies as a kind of erotic practice: Aeneas loves the thing he means to kill. This ambivalent love is rooted in the social contradiction that also drives the love of Troilus and Cressida and Achilles and Patroclus, for if "human gentleness" gestures toward some shared humanity that joins even enemies, then "gentleness" nevertheless also points to a very different notion of blood-borne status that is rooted in blood and lineage and that shades into the repeated hints throughout the play that the Greeks and the Trojans are *racially* different. But if Aeneas's hatred is partially explained by some sense of blood-borne or tribal difference between himself and Diomedes, then this hatred becomes erotic only when it is *felt* as the repudiation of a powerfully binding humanity. Here a benign vision of a hypothetical humanity is valued as much for the powerfully inclusive, if competitive, form of social life it projects as for the failures it inevitably foregrounds, the moments of social weakness in which the forces of shared humanity break down.[36] Like other Shakespeare plays, *Troilus and Cressida* charts a path from such breakdowns of a shared humanity to an ungrounded and ungrounding sexuality that stands apart from social life and is defined only by the asymmetrical emotions that join bodies when functional social connections between socially legible persons have been foreclosed: Aeneas greets Diomedes in the name of a human gentleness he wants to violate, Troilus cringes before Cressida with loving fear, Achilles stares at Hector with a woman's longing to kill, and Achilles laughs at Patroclus with disdain for the social universe both inhabit. These relationships foreground erotic breakdowns within the universal humanity dreamed of by the civilizing process, and taken together, these relationships also gesture toward an alternative form of social life in which the most fundamentally social desire is also Hector's desire: the desire to kill, everywhere, over and over again.[37]

CHAPTER 5

Poetic Autonomy and the History of Sexuality in Shakespeare's Sonnets

I have described the emergence, at the very cusp of modernity, of a form of sexuality that arises out of the contradictions of sixteenth-century society and constitutes a special class of interpersonal bonding that, like the modern notion of intimacy, stands apart from the rest of social life even if, unlike modern intimacy, it is not rooted in a private, domestic sphere. A central character in this story has been the poetic tendency called Petrarchanism. From its first appearance in English, in the work of Wyatt and Surrey, Petrarchan poetry is the bearer of two contra-dictory visions of society: one emphasizing inherited, blood-borne identities, and the other celebrating some universally shared humanity. While the social contradiction between these two visions is not itself gender-specific, since it refers only to different ways of defining class or status, Petrarchan poetry vectors this social contradiction through gender in complicated ways. Thus far, I have read the conventional beloved lady of Petrarchan poetry as representing the emerging ideals of restraint and humane regard that are part of a modern social vision that is unable to dislodge an older, aristocratic social imaginary typi-fied by the aggressively desiring masculine speaker who fails to live up to the ideal of the beloved and therefore fails to attain her on her terms. In Petrarchan poetry, what is really the encounter of differently constituted social identities emanating from different social worlds is made to look like the encounter of two genders doomed to wage eternal gender war. To some extent, the tradition of Petrarchan poetry allows the historical contradiction between two incompatible social imaginaries to be absorbed by a gender-building program that is meant to supersede the social contradiction.

More important than Petrarchan poetry's efforts to resolve the real contradiction it points to is its ability to develop unexpected social alternatives out of the contradiction itself. In essence, Petrarchan poetry acts as a catalyst that forces the contradiction between these two social visions to resolve itself into an explosion of intense, depersonalized emotions that testify to the beginning of a sexual experience at a tangent to any available social norms. My slogan has been that sexuality emerges when a humane relationship is foreclosed or undercut by a resurgent emphasis on aristocratic identity and autonomy. An allied formula is that sexual ties emerge when one segment of society tries to secede, in the name of inherent, blood-borne status, from the complex, self-regulating social totality that is projected by the ideal of a humane relationship. Both situations are imported into English literary history by Petrarchan conventions.

Shakespeare's sonnets have always seemed a bit of an exception within the history of Petrarchan poetry, in part because they appear to depart from the gendered situation typical of Petrarchan sonnets. The first 126 of Shakespeare's sonnets are addressed to or are about a Young Man whom the speaker evidently loves, and when a Dark Lady appears after sonnet 127 she seems to have an affair not only with the speaker but also with the Young Man, who remains the center of gravity throughout the sequence. That Shakespeare's sonnets are suffused with evidence of erotic desire between men has been the focus—explicitly or implicitly—of commentary on the sonnets since the seventeenth century.[1] Indeed, the effort to disavow the homoerotic content of the sonnets has given rise to some of the most comically inept critical and editorial treatments of the sonnets. The most scandalous of such treatments is surely John Benson's edition of 1640, which went so far as to change the pronouns in at least some of the sonnets to straighten out the narrative.[2]

But the theory that Petrarchan poetry is canonically heterosexual and that Shakespeare's sonnets are therefore a scandalous exception is quite incorrect. For one thing, there are other instances of Petrarchan sonnets that explicitly address male-male (and even female-female) love; one example is the collection of sonnets published by Richard Barnfield.³ And beyond *Petrarchan* treatments of homoerotic desire lies an entire classical traditional of homoerotic verse that is still very much alive in the Renaissance. Equally to the point, even sonnet sequences that are nominally heterosexual are almost always *also* suffused with homoerotic desire. To cite just one example, which I discussed in chapter 2, in *Astrophil and Stella* Sidney makes a point of saying that, at the very moment he (or the speaker) is allowed some kind of sexual access to his beloved Stella, he also experiences sexual access to his (male) friend; the sexual ecstasy the speaker feels is directed interchangeably to a woman and to a man. In Sidney's case, the explanation for this phenomenon turned out to lie in a project of making courtly behavior seem to reside in the blood or the genes, but the presence of homoerotic desire is fairly widespread in sonnets. Petrarchan poems often seem to be in the business of using women to negotiate connections between men, whether they are rival suitors or friends or a poet and his patron. In short, Petrarchan poetry generally folds easily into Eve Kosofsky Sedgwick's notion of homosocial desire in which men use women to establish relationships with one another, and in this context, cross-gender desire could be perfectly compatible with same-sex desire.

I argue that Shakespeare's sonnets represent a departure from the Petrarchan tradition not because they represent male-male eroticism but because they seek to do so in a context *not* defined by the geometry of homosocial desire. In fact, while trying to find a vocabulary that captures the nature of his desire for the Young Man, Shakespeare runs through a whole world of homosocial ties between men (they are like male rivals for a beloved, but also like a master and a pupil, a lawyer and a client, a patron and a poet, a judge and a lawyer) only to find them all deficient or disappointing in some critical respect.⁴ What is more, the world of poetry also contains vocabularies for conventional (and conventionally desiring) ties between men, and as Bruce Smith points out, Shakespeare is as little satisfied by the traditional poetic resources available to him to represent desire between men as he is by the resources provided by a male-dominated society. "The problem with the sonnets," writes Smith, "is that 'he' [the Young Man] is not the usual male object of desire in poems ranging from late antiquity all the way down to *Venus and Adonis:* to wit, a beardless boy with a lovely white neck and a ripe ass. Instead, he is an active subject in his own right, someone who can have sex with his mistress as readily as the speaker can."[5] But what Smith identifies as a problem is in fact a carefully constructed solution to another, almost opposite, problem: Shakespeare *fears* that his relationship with the Young Man will be absorbed by a whole range of essentially homosocial vocabularies that can cover (and, in essence, cover *up*) a sexual relationship between men in early modern England. Shakespeare aims to represent the relationship in a different light, and he does so by portraying the Young Man as something other than a conventional homosocial partner.

Shakespeare goes to some lengths to break with both the homosocial grammar of his society and with a whole poetic tradition of homoerotic verse in order to open the door to a sexualization of relationships between men that is energized by the same underlying social contradiction that Petrarchan poetry typically frames in terms of an encounter across gender. In other words, in his sonnets Shakespeare implants the central social contradiction of sixteenth-century society in the heart of his relationship with the Young Man *rather than* his relationship with the Dark Lady.[6] It is in relation to the Young Man that Shakespeare experiences the kind of asocial sexuality that I have been discussing, and I will suggest that the felt reality of this sexual tie is captured in a discourse of depersonalized and depersonalizing melancholy. In a sharp departure from the gender conventions of Petrarchan poetry more generally, the Dark Lady triggers a very different kind of sexual experience, one that is based not on insuperable difference but on a deep sense of similarity and mutual dependency, a development that I, following Joel Fineman to some extent, see as being of some moment in the history of sexuality.[7] Smith has remarked on the intimacy of their relationship, even if it is a disturbing intimacy for Shakespeare. "For all their cynicism," Smith writes of the Dark Lady poems, "sonnets 127 to 154 communicate a mutuality, a sensual understanding between speaker and listener, that so often is painfully not the case in sonnets 20 through 126."[8] Margreta de Grazia argues that this mutuality is based on a shared social status—a status that she, suggestively, calls middle-class. I believe that the intimacy of Shakespeare and the Dark Lady arises from a fundamental reworking of the underlying gender assumptions of Petrarchan poetry in which the female beloved and the male lover represent very different social universes, one civil and one aristocratic; the relationship Shakespeare has with the Dark Lady represents the triumph—an ironic triumph, to be sure—of civility alone as a personal ideal.

It is true that the Dark Lady does not use the standard terminology of humanist civility—she does not seek to teach Shakespeare restrained and civilized manners as other Petrarchan beloveds do. Nevertheless, the Dark Lady operates within the folds of civility in two respects: she depends on a kind of personal identity that is explicitly not rooted in aristocratic blood but instead depends on being recognized and affirmed by others with whom she shares the social world, and she insists that Shakespeare respect a social identity he finds repugnant by offering her flattering poems. Most characteristic of the intimacy that joins Shakespeare and the Dark Lady is Shakespeare's peculiar acceptance of the Dark Lady despite her perceived failings. In sonnet 130 Shakespeare admits that his beloved is not the Petrarchan ideal, but he is drawn to her nonetheless:

My mistress' eyes are nothing like the sun;
Coral is far more red than her lips' red;
If snow be white, why then her breasts are dun;
If hairs be wires, black wires grow on her head;
I have seen roses damasked, red and white,
But no such roses see I in her cheeks;
And in some perfumes is there more delight
Than in the breath that from my mistress reeks.
I love to hear her speak, yet well I know
That music hath a far more pleasing sound;
I grant I never saw a goddess go;
My mistress when she walks treads on the ground.
    And yet, by heaven, I think my love as rare
    As any she belied with false compare. [9]

This poem is sometimes read as a romantic assertion that Shakespeare loves the Dark Lady despite her imperfections, but it is certainly worth noting, in this regard, that Shakespeare finally says only that she is as "rare" as anybody, and that before he does so he goes out of his way to remark on the Dark Lady's faults. The fact that the Dark Lady is not herself beautiful (all the world agrees that she is not in sonnet 148 where Shakespeare wonders, "If that be fair whereon my false eyes dote, / What means the world to say it is not so?") only makes her more obviously in need of the flattering attentions of her poet. The real point of this poem is that even as Shakespeare says that he will not deliver a traditional blazon, a flattering catalog of the beauties of the beloved, he also registers how hard it is not to. Indeed, in refusing to deliver a blazon, Shakespeare comes closer than elsewhere to actually evoking an image of the beloved, and we get more of a sense of what she actually looks like here than anywhere else. The bad faith that the poem performs (Shakespeare gives an image despite himself, writes a poem despite himself) is apparently driven by the lady herself, who embodies a world defined by duplicity and cosmetic falseness. If "in the old age black was not counted fair," then the Dark Lady points to a comparatively modern world where lack of (inherent) beauty is no obstacle to being called beautiful, and where being called beautiful in some sense makes it so. Whether ironically or not, Shakespeare fulfills the lady's desire to see herself praised so that her physical deficiencies might be supplemented.

Here, as elsewhere, Shakespeare's sonnets to the Dark Lady are characterized by the felt difficulty of *not* providing her with what are nevertheless said to be inflated or exaggerated compliments. Sonnet 147 ends with "For I have sworn thee fair, and thought thee bright, / Who art as black as hell, as dark as night." Sonnet 152 rewrites the concluding couplet of sonnet 147 to emphasize that he swears she is fair even as he knows she is not: "For I have sworn thee fair: more perjured eye, / To swear against the truth so foul a lie."[10] If Shakespeare is affirming the Dark Lady's social value despite himself, then in some ironic way she also affirms his social value; from Shakespeare's perspective, lying to the Dark Lady is part of lying to himself:

Thus vainly thinking that she thinks me young,
Although she knows my days are past the best,
Simply I credit her false-speaking tongue;
On both sides thus is simple truth suppressed.
(138)

Shakespeare agrees to pretend that his mistress is truthful in order to believe her when she claims to believe that he is young and naïve. More generally, by recognizing and affirming the Dark Lady despite her faults, Shakespeare is testifying to the triumph of culture over nature in himself, too, for he apparently feels an almost instinctive drive to hurl insults at his beloved and casts his ability to check these impulses as an act of perverse and Herculean self-control. Two ironically civilized selves meet each other in the Shakespeare–Dark Lady relationship, and they affirm in one another an identity that makes no reference to underlying facts of blood.

As should be obvious given the language I have used to characterize their relationship, in fundamental respects these characters fulfill the conditions of intimacy that Luhmann describes in *Love as Passion*. Neither Shakespeare nor the Dark Lady has a stable social identity outside of something like a personality, and their personalities depend on recognition and affirmation by other persons. Shakespeare and the Dark Lady essentially inhabit the same social universe, and what follows from this is a certain locker-room breeziness in Shakespeare's interactions with the Dark Lady that makes a relationship between a man and a woman approximate (in tone) a relationship more characteristic of men. These characters enter into a dance of recognition and affirmation that marks a real departure from conventional Petrarchan poetry, for the relationship between this Petrarchan speaker and his beloved is defined not by turbulence between civility and a residual aristocratic conception of social ties but by civility alone. In emphasizing a (perverse) mutuality between male lover and female beloved, Shakespeare essentially breaks down the gender-inflected cultural difference of the conventional Petrarchan beloved.

The desire that joins Shakespeare and the Dark Lady may point forward to the domestic intimacies of eighteenth-century fiction, but it does so with a difference. In eighteenth-century fiction, intimate private relationships that are consensual and felt as compensation for an alienating public existence are sanctioned by the public world; in a key respect such relationships become the very cornerstone of social life. In the earlier historical moment of the *Sonnets,* however, sexualized intimacy, especially intimacy across gender difference, seems profoundly disturbing and even dangerous, and this danger is essential to the way Shakespeare characterizes the relationship he has with the Dark Lady. As I argued in chapter 1, in the early modern period the experience of intimacy is often seen as the flip side of a disturbing withdrawal from social life denoted by sodomy. A number of commentators have noted that desire for the Dark Lady is in fact represented as fundamentally disruptive of orderly life, and Goldberg argues that if sodomy—the category of dangerous and feared desire—arises anywhere in the sequence, it is surely in relation not to the Young Man but to the Dark Lady who is "outside marriage and promiscuous and dangerous to the homosocial order."[11] The disruptive and dangerous nature of the desire Shakespeare feels for the Dark Lady is spelled out in the opening quatrain of sonnet 129:

> Th'expense of spirit in a waste of shame
> Is lust in action; and till action, lust
> Is perjured, murd'rous, bloody, full of blame,
> Savage, extreme, rude, cruel, not to trust

Valerie Traub argues that sodomy can be transferred to what we would term a heterosexual relationship because early modern heterosexuality was so completely focused on using the bodies of women to produce heirs and secure relationships between men that actual *erotic desire* for a woman seems disruptive.[12] Traub's discussion suggests that *heterosexual desire* (as opposed to the strategic aim of reproduction) is as antithetical as sodomy is to the privileged relationships between men on which the unabashedly patriarchal society of early modern England rests.

The ability of the Dark Lady to absorb, within the context of a nominally heterosexual relationship, many of the attributes of sodomy has begun to seem like a deeply important fact for any reconstruction of the early modern sex-gender system and of the place of Shakespeare's sonnets within it.[13] What is at stake here in making desire for the Dark Lady seem so profoundly antithetical to social life is, I believe, the struggle to define a relationship with the Young Man outside the homosocial geometry that threatens to cover up sexuality between men.[14] As I argued in chapter 1, sodomy is the dark twin of functional homosocial intimacy, and Shakespeare uses the Dark Lady to absorb functional homosocial intimacy *and* the dysfunctional intimacy of sodomy that is its obverse. If homosocial intimacy and sodomy both accrue to the bond between Shakespeare and the Dark Lady, then the tie between Shakespeare and the Young Man is left to be defined in some other way. In other words, by allowing the dark flowers of sodomy to well up in his own relation to the Dark Lady, Shakespeare seeks to shield the Young Man (and the relationship Shakespeare has with him) from the entire homosocial/sodomitical dynamic.

By having the Dark Lady have an affair with both Shakespeare and the Young Man, Shakespeare paradoxically confronts the danger of homosociability in its purest form. Indeed, for Sedgwick, the ménage à trois of Shakespeare, the Young Man, and the Dark Lady is the founding example of a homosocial triangle. Describing the way male-male love functions seamlessly within a homosocial dynamic defined, in part, by the Dark Lady, Sedgwick writes: "within the world sketched in these sonnets, there is not an equal opposition or choice posited between two such institutions as homosexuality (under whatever name) and heterosexuality. The *Sonnets* present a male-male love that, like the love of the Greeks, is set firmly within a structure of institutionalized social relations carried out via women; marriage, name, family, loyalty to progenitors and posterity, all depend on the youth's making a particular use of women that is not, in the abstract, seen as opposing, denying, or detracting from his bond to the speaker" (35). But for Shakespeare, as for the other authors I have examined in this study, there is something profoundly disappointing about the love that is firmly and functionally

rooted in the homosocial dynamics of early modern society. To whatever extent Shakespeare and the Young Man become homosocial part-
ners—whether because they compete *for* the Dark Lady or because
Shakespeare protects the Young Man *from* the Dark Lady—the relationship will be endowed with a functional sociability rather than the
nonfunctional asociability that opens up a sexual experience for Shakespeare. Here the threat of sodomy does its work; Shakespeare jams up
the homosocial framework by cutting "deals" with the Dark Lady in
which he agrees to a relationship with her (on her, essentially, sodomitical terms) if she will agree to abandon her claim on the Young Man:
"Prison my heart in thy steel bosom's ward;" he pleads with the Dark
Lady, "But then my friend's heart let my poor heart bail" (133). The
effect of these deals is to emit the Young Man from the homosocial
gravity that the gendered situation of standard Petrarchan poetry con-
stantly reasserts. By explicitly facing the homosocial triangle and by
allowing the Dark Lady to absorb the unsettling and disruptive charge
of sodomy that more typically shadows functional relationships between
men, Shakespeare seeks to guard the Young Man from the charge of
being a sodomite and at the same time to make it clear that the experience of the Young Man he himself desires must be defined outside
the whole continuum of homosociability. Pinning sodomy on the Dark
Lady is part of a strategy of protecting the Young Man from the homosocial funny mirror that joins sodomy and intimacy between men.

By trying to emit the Young Man from the homosocial intimacy
that joins Shakespeare and the Dark Lady, Shakespeare frames the Young
Man as a sort of unreactive particle within the world of homosociability. The relationship that ensues between these men is not based on
fundamental similarity or mutual need, as the relation with the Dark
Lady is; rather, it is based on a kind of irreducible social difference that
culminates in a sort of constitutive indifference. There are, of course,
some sonnets where Shakespeare does imagine a fairly intense intimacy between himself and the Young Man that is at least reminiscent
of the intimacy he experiences with the Dark Lady. Foremost in this
regard are sonnets where physical interpenetration of bodies seems to
model the relationship. In sonnet 24, for example, Shakespeare and the

Young Man see images of one another in the surfaces of each other's eyes, but the confusion of frame and image (the Young Man is contained by and contains Shakespeare) culminates not with a sense of intimacy but with a renewed sense of separation. Shakespeare claims that his talent (for "painting" the Young Man on the surface of his eyes) lies in his ability to reproduce "perspective," the painterly illusion of distance, and the concluding couplet emphasizes the persistence of difference between speaker and beloved: "Yet eyes this cunning want to grace their art: / They draw but what they see, know not the heart." Here the "heart" seems to be the part of the Young Man that remains irretrievable, but it is also the part of Shakespeare (the love, presumably) that the Young Man cannot see in all the pictures that Shakespeare gives him. The debate between heart and eyes becomes a trope for several poems in the sequence that points to the continuing split between Shakespeare and the Young Man that is echoed in an internal split inside Shakespeare himself. In sonnet 46, for example, Shakespeare's "eye and heart are at a mortal war / How to divide the conquest of thy sight," a debate that is only temporarily resolved through a skewed legal proceeding (the jurors are all financially dependent on the heart). The debate is resolved again in sonnet 48 where the eye and heart work out a visitation schedule that allows them to divide their time with the Young Man. The disconnected debate between Shakespeare's own eyes and heart repeats a disconnect between his whole body and the beloved.

The distance between Shakespeare and the Young Man (and between Shakespeare and Shakespeare), which persists even in the sonnets that come closest to framing the Shakespeare–Young Man bond as intimate, points to a bond of another kind, one that rises beyond the homosocial dynamic. Central to this other mode of interpersonal bonding is the Young Man's weird social positioning, which has been a vexed issue in commentary on the sonnets. Early editors tended to identify him as an aristocratic patron like the Earl of Pembroke, while Oscar Wilde imagined him as a poor actor; William Empson simply refers to the opposed views of the Young Man as aristocrat and vulgar careerist.[15] The fact that a certain ambiguity surrounds the Young Man's social status is an effect of the game Shakespeare is playing. I will argue that Shakespeare positions the Young Man as a representative of a blood-borne aristocratic status while also emphasizing that this social ideal is outdated in the social context defined by the Dark Lady and is therefore somewhat imaginary.[16] By giving him an imaginary social status, Shakespeare invests the Young Man with a sort of socially unreactive power that jams up all the forms of social relationships and all the poetic practices that might join Shakespeare to him. The result is to endow the Young Man with a curious quality between plasticity (Sedgwick calls him a dumb blonde) and irreducible alterity. Being somewhere between utterly unattainable and utterly plastic seems to endow the Young Man with the social ambivalence that seems to lie at the heart of the erotic relationship as Shakespeare conceives of it.

One reason to suppose that the Young Man is an aristocrat in a world without a place for aristocrats is Shakespeare's tendency to treat him as an embalmed mummy. In sonnet 68, for example, the Young Man is an archive of a social world now dead, and he therefore indicts the modern world of endless struggle for a veneer of acquired graces that can supplement, or even occlude, the facts of birth and biology:

Thus is his cheek the map of days outworn,
When beauty lived and died as flowers do now,
Before these bastard signs of fair were born,
Or durst inhabit on a living brow;
Before the golden tresses of the dead,
The right of sepulchers, were shorn away,
To live a second life on second head;
Ere beauty's dead fleece made another gay:
In him those holy antique hours are seen,
Without all ornament, itself and true,
Making no summer of another's green,
Robbing no old to dress his beauty new;
   And him as for a map doth Nature store
   To show false art what beauty was of yore.
      (68)

Shakespeare complains that symbolic attributes, the "signs of fair," have become systematically decoupled from the bedrock of a biological reality that is at the same time a social reality. This makes it hard to understand why the Young Man is still alive—in essence, the Young Man is so outdated that he ought to be dead, a point Shakespeare in fact makes in sonnet 67 where he complains that people are stealing fashion ideas from what, in the Young Man, is not fashion but biological essence:

Why should false painting imitate his cheek,
And steal dead seeing of his living hue?
Why should poor beauty indirectly seek
Roses of shadow, since his rose is true?
Why should he live, now nature bankrupt is,
Beggared of blood to blush through lively veins?
For she hath no exchequer now but his,
And proud of many, lives upon his gains.
    O, him she stores, to show what wealth she had
    In days long since, before these last so bad.

On the one hand, Nature keeps the Young Man around to steal from him (as the violets do in sonnet 99), but on the other hand, she keeps him around to provide a sort of platinum yardstick in relation to which the modern world can be found sorely wanting. The Young Man becomes a reservoir of the blood that the rest of nature lacks, a lack that leads the rest of the world to resort to proud compare as, of course, the Dark Lady does. But if the sonnet asks, "Why should false painting imitate his cheek," the answer it implicitly offers is: it should not. The Young Man is so profoundly outside of the transactions of modernity that he ought (Shakespeare seems to say) simply be left alone. It is as if the modern world cannot even recognize the critique that the Young Man offers by his mere and extraordinary existence. Shakespeare makes the Young Man into the representative of a social status that has no place in the modern world and then comes close to deciding that he should simply keep this secret to himself since no one else will understand anyway.

The Young Man's aristocratic identity allows him to secede from the modern world altogether, indicting the struggle for a veneer of civility, for personal identity defined culturally rather than biologically. There has, of course, never been a form of social life wholly free of symbolic or cultural competition, but I would say that the fantasy of such a social world is necessarily projected by modernity, and here the Young Man represents this fantasy in an intensified form. As such, the Young Man projects a social force field around himself in a way that is very different from the Dark Lady, and if it is painfully easy for Shakespeare to relate to the Dark Lady, in poetry as in life, it is pleasurably hard to relate to the Young Man, in both poetry and life. By forcing him to occupy a breaking point where the interconnected social world projected by the discourse of civility is undermined or suspended, the Young Man is invested with a radical alterity that is at the core of the discourse of emotionally mediated sexuality I investigate.

The aristocratic emphasis on an identity that is delivered by blood alone, and the connection between this fantasy and a mode of sociability that fundamentally excludes Shakespeare, are spelled out in the reproduction sonnets with which the sequence begins. Sedgwick reads the reproduction sonnets as so powerfully homosocial that they can encompass even overt male-male eroticism. From this standpoint, Shakespeare asks that for love of him, the Young Man reproduce ("Make thee another self for love of me, / That beauty still may live in thine or thee" [10]). But the specificity of sexuality for Shakespeare seems to lie in his odd positioning as a spokesman for aristocratic values that he does not share and from which he himself will not benefit.[17] As Sedgwick notes, in these early sonnets reproduction is represented as an all-male affair; women are only vessels. But the males who are involved in the drama of reproduction are clearly not Shakespeare but members of the Young Man's family, his father and his imagined sons. Shakespeare advises the Young Man that "You had a father; let your son say so" (13), presumably on the occasion that the son becomes the Young Man's heir and displaces the "worms" who inherit the Young Man's wealth in sonnet 6. In sonnet 10 it is "the roof" and in sonnet 16 the "lines of life" that the Young Man is called on to restore, an ancestral home and pedigree that have no obvious place for Shakespeare. The aristocratic social imaginary projects a form of sociability so profoundly mediated by blood that it simply excludes nonkinsmen.

The reproduction sonnets are sometimes represented as an attack on the Young Man's narcissism or his pride; Shakespeare accuses him of feeding his "light's flame with self-substantial fuel" (1), of having "traffic with [him]self alone" (4), of harboring "no love toward others" (9)—as if those were bad things. But there is a real sense in which Shakespeare represents reproducing as a more perfect narcissism that would exclude Shakespeare in a way that failure to reproduce does not, by returning the focus to a blood-borne social status that Shakespeare lacks. Emphasizing the biological immanence of the Young Man's identity, Shakespeare argues that the Young Man's sons would be genetic clones enabling the Young Man to see himself as young even when he has become old; as the couplet of sonnet 2 puts it: "This were to be new made when thou art old, / And see thy blood warm when thou feel'st it cold." The compensation of seeing warm blood is rendered questionable by the somewhat disturbing image of the Young Man's feeling cold blood flowing through his veins. The only kind of personal identity that would be gratified by this poetic image would be rooted not in the life of the self but in the life of the clan mediated by a bloodline.

Shakespeare is not advocating that the Young Man check his narcissistic impulses but that he redirect those impulses toward the pseudo-biology of the bloodline he shares with kin. In this sense, the sonnets actually provoke and reaffirm the Young Man's narcissism, purifying it of the dross of modernity and refocusing it on the outdated ideal of an aristocratic endogamy. In the process, Shakespeare makes the Young Man's narcissism count as a profoundly unsocial kernel that excludes vast reaches of the social world in the name of social values that are profoundly outdated. For in the *modern* world the aristocratic autonomy that Shakespeare invites the Young Man to assert amounts to deep-rooted sociopathy. Shakespeare writes that ideally the Young Man would reproduce himself hundreds of times:

That's for thyself to breed another thee,
Or ten times happier, be it ten for one:
Ten times thyself were happier than thou art,
If ten of thine ten times refigured thee

(6)

This sonnet goes on to reintroduce the claim of the "immortality" (of the self via the family) that the Young Man seems not to find compelling, but the image of one hundred Young Men in the lifetime of the original Young Man nevertheless suggests that the Young Man might refigure the world in his image, might found a social order in which the original narcissistic desire to traffic with himself alone would find literal gratification, by creating a world in which he could literally traffic only with versions of himself. And as sonnet 11 makes clear, Shakespeare *wants* the Young Man to reproduce himself so that he will traffic only with versions of himself and thereby actually *displace* the rest of the world:

If all were minded so, the times should cease,
And threescore year would make the world away:
Let those whom nature hath not made for store,
Harsh, featureless and rude, barrenly perish;
Look whom she best endowed, she gave the more,
Which bounteous gift thou shouldst in bounty cherish:
    She carved thee for her seal, and meant thereby
    Thou shouldst print more, not let that copy die.

By repopulating the world with versions of the Young Man himself, he abolishes the rest of the social world: "let those whom nature has not made for store,/ Harsh, featureless and rude, barrenly perish." The Young Man's family becomes a sort of premodern tribe that can secede from the shared social world projected by civility—and then displace that world altogether. It is membership in this tribe that gives the Young Man his alluring narcissism, which now seems the flip side of a homicidal impulse to do away with the rest of society.

The real payoff of this effort to intensify the Young Man's self-contained narcissism comes in the difficulty of writing poems to him that it triggers, a difficulty that really becomes the subject matter of the sonnets. Faced with the social black hole that the Young Man represents, Shakespeare declines to write him poems as conventionally conceived:

So is it not with me as with that Muse,
Stirred by a painted beauty to his verse,
Who heaven itself for ornament doth use,
And every fair with his fair doth rehearse,
Making a couplement of proud compare
With sun and moon, with earth and sea's rich gems;
With April's first-born flowers and all things rare
That heaven's air in this rondure hems;
O let me true in love but truly write,
And then believe me: my love is as fair
As any mother's child, though not so bright
As those gold candles fixed in heaven's air:
    Let them say more that like of hearsay well,
    I will not praise, that purpose not to sell.

(21)

Above all, Shakespeare avoids making the Young Man seem in any way to depend on the inflated and flattering comparisons and the social recognition that are the very essence of the poetic function in relation to the Dark Lady. The Young Man should not be painted because he is not already a "painted beauty" as the Dark Lady is—someone whose social identity relies utterly on symbolic attributes and social recognition. Only those beauties who depend on cosmetics (the sort of thing the Dark Lady does compulsively), in other words, only those beauties that have already been inflated, are appropriate targets for further inflation; treating the Young Man this way makes him seem at once counterfeit and womanly. In sonnet 83 Shakespeare observes, "I never saw that you did painting need, / And therefore to your fair no painting set," and in 103 Shakespeare asks, "Were it not sinful, then, striving to mend, /

To mar the subject that before was well?" And noting that other poets write flattering poems to the Young Man, Shakespeare advises him to reject them since "their gross painting might be better used / Where cheeks need blood; in thee it is abused" (82). Blood here defines an identity that is fundamentally resistant to flattering or exaggerating poetry.

In this context, Shakespeare aims to write a kind of poetry that does not add anything to the Young Man but *reminds* him of an identity that exists utterly within himself, and reminds him that he does not need other people to certify his social status, poets least of all. Shakespeare distinguishes his own poetry as so radically truthful and noninflationary that he turns down metaphor itself so as to make it clear that he is not doing anything for the Young Man that the Young Man could not do for himself. In the context of the Young Man's aristocratic status, Shakespeare simply asks, "Who is it that says most? Which can say more / Than this rich praise: that you alone are you" (84). Instead of poems that paint the virtues of the Young Man, Shakespeare will merely refer to a social status that does not depend on poetry.[18]

Fineman argues that Shakespeare's sonnets signal the death of an epideictic tradition of praise poetry that is organized around the desire to identify with the object of praise. I would emphasize, however, that for Shakespeare the difficulty of praising the Young Man arises not out of the paradoxes inherent to the literary discourse of praise poetry but out of a massive social impasse characterized by an aristocratic autonomy that militates ferociously against a social world increasingly defined by the interconnection of all. The Young Man is hard to praise in poetry because he represents a social breaking point; he is so profoundly self-contained that he needs no recognition from anyone, poetic or otherwise. Shakespeare's stance that the truer his poetry is, the less it does for the Young Man is inseparable from his experience of a relationship with the Young Man that crosses this social breaking point, a relationship almost defined by making Shakespeare feel useless and unneeded. In fact, throughout the sequence Shakespeare regularly imagines altogether abdicating as the Young Man's poet; in sonnet 77 Shakespeare gives the Young Man a notebook in the hope that the Young Man will write his own poems. More typically, however, Shakespeare invites the

Young Man to actively *reject* poetry, and he rarely misses an opportunity to insult his own poems. The concluding couplet of sonnet 72 casts the sonnets as trash, or worse, that ought to be rejected by the Young Man: Shakespeare says, "For I am shamed by that which I bring forth, / And so should you, to love things nothing worth." Much the same scenario is played out in sonnet 71:

O if (I say) you look upon this verse,
When I, perhaps, compounded am with clay,
Do not so much as my poor name rehearse,
But let your love even with my life decay;
   Lest the wise world should look into your moan,
   And mock you with me after I am gone.

The Young Man must stop loving the poems so that Shakespeare will not get any credit for them, and thus, by extension, not get any credit for the Young Man either. At stake is a certain brand of love that requires that the Young Man not feel indebted to Shakespeare or to the products of Shakespeare's pen.[19] When Shakespeare does imagine that the sonnets will remain of interest to the Young Man after Shakespeare has died (in sonnet 74, for example), he does so only by identifying the sonnets as the part of Shakespeare that was not really Shakespeare at all: "When thou reviewest this, thou dost review / The very part was consecrate to thee." Shakespeare seems to want to foreclose, here as elsewhere, a contractual relationship in which poet and patron enter into the dialectics of real-world ambition, and he wants to substitute a radical narcissism by the Young Man in which he consumes images of himself. Rather than wrapping him in a veneer of fine culture, Shakespeare's poems aim only to remind the Young Man that he has good blood flowing through his veins; such poems deserve no credit from the Young Man, and if Shakespeare does get credit then it is because his poems were not really his; they were merely copies of the Young Man.

This embarrassed attitude toward his own poems points to Shakespeare's erotic experience of the Young Man. The relentlessness with which Shakespeare casts himself, qua poet, as worthy of being rejected suggests that, in the context of the Young Man, Shakespeare has cathected rejection itself. The speaker of the sonnets is weirdly eager to get broken up with, and the sonnets are full of reasons the Young Man should think of Shakespeare as a bad catch (he's old, he's working-class, he's a bad poet). In sonnet 88 Shakespeare promises that when the time comes for the Young Man to reject Shakespeare, he will help the Young Man to write his Dear Will letter, being "With mine own weakness . . . best acquainted," "Upon thy side, against myself I'll fight." In sonnet 49 the reasons the Young Man will inevitably offer for failing to find Shakespeare attractive are endowed with a legally compelling force: "To leave poor me, thou hast the strength of laws, / Since why to love, I can allege no cause." But the Young Man's court case is compelling because of Shakespeare's own eagerness to lose that case; in sonnet 89, for example, Shakespeare agrees to fabricate evidence against himself, promising to limp should the Young Man claim to find Shakespeare lame: "Speak of my lameness, and I straight will halt, / Against thy reasons making no defense." Shakespeare declares quite emphatically: "Thou canst not, love, disgrace me half so ill, / . . . As I'll myself disgrace, knowing thy will."

For Jean Laplanche, a certain degree of masochism is foundational for sexuality. In *Life and Death in Psychoanalysis,* Laplanche argues that sexuality arises as a defense by an infant against the fear that its emerging and therefore still fragile ego will be overwhelmed.[20] The infant responds by investing the possibility of being overwhelmed with a pleasurable charge. In Leo Bersani's reformulation of Laplanche's claims, sexuality is geared toward a pleasurable self-shattering. The Laplanche-Bersani account is not, however, historicized; as I argued in chapter 1, it seems obvious that early modern authors do not often assume the sort of well-defined, well-defended self that is pleasurably shattered in Bersani's account of sexuality. In fact, New Historicists have been at pains to demonstrate that self-fashioning is still very much on the agenda during the early modern period. For this reason, in Shakespeare's sequence as in the other texts I have examined, masochism is not dialectically tied to an already fashioned self; rather, it arises within the context of a social relationship that occupies one of the social breaking points of the early modern social world. In other words, what appears as masochism is the flip side of a concrete form of interpersonal tie that is opened when the Young Man's aristocratic narcissism intrudes into a modern, inclusive world.

The simultaneity of feeling a self and feeling that self shattered is marked everywhere in the sequence; it occurs only in the context of a relationship with the Young Man. Only by identifying with the alluringly extrasocial Young Man does Shakespeare feel like the owner of a genuine, authentic self not exposed to the ravages of a competitive and disillusioning world. In sonnet 22, for example, Shakespeare feels young as long as the Young Man is young, as if the Young Man's pristine body were Shakespeare's own: "My glass shall not persuade me I am old / So long as youth and thou are of one date." In sonnet 25 Shakespeare says that having the Young Man makes him feel better than if he were the favorite of a prince, in part because real favorites must submit to endless fawning and flattering and compromise.[21] At the same time, however, the Young Man offers Shakespeare a better, more authentic self only to the extent that he remains infused with an aristocratic identity that requires, for its preservation, that Shakespeare be rejected. Shakespeare's experience of a stable self, in other words, is inseparable from his feeling repelled, almost physically repelled. Unlike Shakespeare's relationship with the Dark Lady, his relationship with the Young Man is not geared toward affirming the self or advancing its interests; it may, indeed, be premised on the recurring interpersonal failure that Shakespeare foregrounds and that gives this speaker his persistently mournful tone.

The mournful tone of many of the Young Man sonnets is not at all incidental to the discourse of sexuality they sketch. Melancholy is the name that the sonnets apply to Shakespeare's characteristic experience of pleasurable self-splitting, a self-splitting that is the result of a relationship with something that does not admit of any relationship.[22] In sonnet 45, for example, Shakespeare claims to be "oppressed with melancholy" because the two lightest of his four elements, "slight air and purging fire," have flown to the Young Man so that the rest of his body, now composed only of heavy earth and water, "sinks down to death." While Shakespeare here conflates the four Aristotelian elements (water, air, fire, earth) with the four humors (phlegm, blood, black bile, yellow bile), the point is clear enough: because affects are conceived of as arising from physical imbalances of the body, an affect is not part of a private psychology but a social fact, in principle available to others. Moreover, because melancholy is a social fact, it can name a relationship with the Young Man: it is, after all, because a piece of Shakespeare is imagined to be *with* the Young Man that he feels melancholy. In sonnet 45, the relationship that is named by melancholy is located only in psychological space as Shakespeare's "fire" and "air" become a yo-yo that flies back and forth between Shakespeare and the Young Man, but in sonnet 44 the relationship is located in physical space as Shakespeare imagines a geographical distance that separates Shakespeare from the Young Man but also from his own "thought" that is nimble enough to ignore the constraints of space and time. The point in both cases is that melancholy names not a psychological state but a relationship that is imagined as physical, and that the relationship named is based on a physical separation that is reproduced as a mental separation. As such, melancholy is the affective counterpart of the pride or narcissism that the Young Man feels and that, as we have seen, Shakespeare actively encourages in him. Melancholy and pride both name an interpersonal relationship that is caught in a contradiction between two sets of social terms.[23] These emotions define ties between bodies that arise when functionally social ties are foreclosed. Like the fear that names Troilus's experience of Cressida, in Shakespeare's *Troilus and Cressida,* or the pride that names Ulysses' experience of Achilles, like the anger and shame that name Spenser's experience of his beloved Elizabeth Boyle, Shakespeare's melancholy traces a real social relationship defined according to a social grammar that emerges, spontaneously, out of the contradictions that wrench apart sixteenth-century English society.

Following the path of melancholy traced by the Young Man sonnets suggests a new way of reading some of the sonnets about the Dark Lady as well. As we have seen, by and large the Dark Lady inhabits a modern world and demands that Shakespeare relate to her as a person stripped of external status markers who both seeks and gives social recognition. But a certain persistent melancholy suggests that the Dark Lady also rebels against this modern form of intimate sociability. By attending to the persistent subtext of sadness in the Dark Lady sonnets, we may begin to hear the Petrarchan lady, normally suffused with the responsibility of bearing the world historical project of civility, speak to reveal a sexual experience that has remained largely unavailable thus far in my discussion.[24] In sonnet 127, the compulsively false qualities of the Dark Lady (associated with modern, antisocial, criminally ambitious desire) are gradually commuted into a melancholy that opens the door to alternative forms of relationship:

In the old age black was not counted fair,
Or if it were, it bore not beauty's name;
But now is black beauty's successive heir,
And beauty slandered with a bastard shame:
For since each hand hath put on nature's power,
Fairing the foul with art's false borrowed face,
Sweet beauty hath no name, no holy bower,
But is profaned, if not lives in disgrace.
Therefore my mistress' eyes are raven black,
Her eyes so suited, and they mourners seem
At such who, not born fair, no beauty lack,
Sland'ring creation with a false esteem;
    Yet so they mourn, becoming of their woe,
    That every tongue says beauty should look so.[25]

The Dark Lady embodies a modern world defined by the unmooring of symbolic attributes from the alleged bedrock of the biological that is referred to by the outdated aristocratic imaginary. As such she represents the triumph of a "bastard shame" over the legitimate reproduction that ensures the continuity of bloodlines. The most puzzling word in sonnet 127, however, is the "therefore" that marks the transition from the initial octet to the concluding sestet: "*Therefore* my mistress' eyes are raven black." This logical marker apparently endows the concluding sestet of the sonnet with the force of a logical conclusion. Shakespeare seems often to be interested in positions that logic forces him into, even if he would prefer to avoid them; in the sonnets, logic is often a way of continuing the self-torture that he sees as constitutive of a sexual relationship with the Young Man, as when Shakespeare is logically forced to acknowledge his own inadequacy. But the logic that structures sonnet 127 seems to be false insofar as the black countenance of the mistress is not *caused by* but rather *exemplifies* the falsity of the age that Shakespeare complains about in the opening octet. The falsity of the age is marked by the use of the heavy makeup and mascara that the Dark Lady uses to make her eyes dark. In using makeup to cover suspected blemishes, the Dark Lady is an *example* of a dark age and not a victim of it as "therefore" seems to hint.

One possible resolution of the difficulty is to say that when Shakespeare describes an example of a state of affairs as a logical consequence of that state of affairs, he simply betrays the fact that the Dark Lady is a *pure* example, fabricated for the purpose of exemplifying whatever needs to be exemplified. On this view, the reasoning of the sonnet can be reconstructed as follows: Because I, Shakespeare, use the figure of the Dark Lady to exemplify all that is bad in the world, and because the world's badness is manifested primarily by the replacement of "fairness" with blackness, *therefore* my mistress's eyes are raven black. The Dark Lady is dark because all modern ladies are dark. She is the perfect example of something that could be found elsewhere, too.

But there is also a "strong logic" interpretation of the sonnet, for part of the reason the lady's eyes are black is that she is in a state of mourning. The first time the word "mourning" is used it is only as a metaphor, one that the sonnets imply may be false: "Her eyes so suited, and they mourners seem." It is as if Shakespeare were saying that she *seems* to be mourning, but this is just more of her compulsive falseness. By the concluding couplet, however, the possibility of "real" melancholy seems to have entered the field of interpretation to stay: "Yet so they mourn, becoming of their woe, / That every tongue says that beauty should look so." The Dark Lady has black eyes because she mourns—perhaps because a cloud hangs over her brow, so to speak, and perhaps also because her mascara runs with tears—and she mourns so well that she seems beautiful, making "every tongue" say that beauty should look just like the Dark Lady when she is sad. The apparent irony of the sonnet is as follows: Shakespeare begins by complaining that beauty has been replaced by a falseness that is tokened by blackness, but then Shakespeare discovers in blackness an alternative form of beauty that takes him in, even though he should know better. Moreover, the strong logic interpretation of the poem suggests that the name of Shakespeare's pain is also the name of the Dark Lady's pain insofar as she mourns for just the same reason he does: the world is full of falseness and "*therefore* my mistress' brows are raven black." She is beautiful only because she (like Shakespeare) hates the modern world, yet she is beautiful only *in* the modern world. As such the Dark Lady seems to mourn the very terms on which she becomes desirable, and thus she mourns the very terms on which a relationship with her becomes possible. In essence, the Dark Lady is sad about the kind of social tie that she herself insists on; it is just the kind of interpersonal catch-22 that might become the basis for a very different tie between the speaker and her. On the one hand, the Dark Lady herself insists on the "falseness" of flattery, but on the other hand, her sadness about this falseness seems to cut in a very different direction, opening the door to a different experience of herself and of others. Thus, in the cases of both the Young Man and the Dark Lady, mourning or melancholy diagnoses a weakness in the social fabric even in the midst of what is normally territory pretty securely held by the armies of modernity, and it is the kind of social weakness that, from Shakespeare's point of view, energizes sexuality.

Throughout this study I have suggested that cataloging the kind of emotionally mediated, asocial sexuality that Shakespeare feels in relation to the Young Man, and perhaps also in relation to the Dark Lady, comes to define literature as a semiautonomous discourse that inhabits its own region or pocket within social life. In fact, in the sonnets Shakespeare suggests that he can capture the alluringly nonsocial relationship he has with the Young Man *only* by writing poems that are utterly autonomous, in the sense that they have no ulterior, extraliterary motives.[26] This is striking because, as New Historicist critics have shown convincingly, early modern poetry as conventionally understood is still very much bound up with day-to-day struggles for social prestige and power. This is especially true at the court where self-consciously courtly poetry, like sonnet sequences, was used to announce ambitions, cement alliances, secure patronage, and pass social gossip; such poetry seems less like art and more like a continuation of politics by other means.[27] In the sonnets the rival poet or poets represent the social context in which poetry is big business. The rival poets who compete with Shakespeare for the Young Man's attention model poetry that is utterly bound up with the day-to-day struggle for real-world prestige and recognition, poetry that is meant to be socially useful to both the poets and the patrons their poetry celebrates. Shakespeare puts the rival poet or poets into the sonnets precisely in order to sketch, by force of contrast, the category of literary autonomy that he sees as necessary to document the aversive sexuality he feels in relation to the Young Man. Admitting that his own poems are not particularly flattering, Shakespeare grants that the Young Man might turn to other, more conventional poets:

> I grant thou wert not married to my Muse,
> And therefore mayst without attaint o'erlook
> The dedicated words which writers use
> Of their fair subject, blessing every book.
> Thou art as fair in knowledge as in hue,
> Finding thy worth a limit past my praise,
> And therefore art enforced to seek anew
> Some fresher stamp of the time-bettering days,
>
> (82)

Since Shakespeare's poetry is not up to the task of advertising the Young Man, he is entitled to seek "some fresher stamp of the time-bettering days." The real point of sonnet 82, however, is that when the Young Man seeks this fresher stamp he enters an entire symbolic economy of dedications and patronage in which writers and readers both use culture to get ahead socially. Indeed, the context of social ambition that is alluded to here is very much part of Petrarchan conventions as conventionally understood. William Kerrigan suggests that the open secret of conventional erotic poetry, at least at court, is that the poet really loves the patron, and that poetic descriptions of the beloved (her eyes are like the sun) are covert celebrations of the patron.[28] Lorna Hutson adds taste to this account of the social contract between ambitious patrons and their equally ambitious poets: the poet's work is valorized by being accepted by a patron whose taste is itself valorized by the poet.[29] These contractual stakes are, of course, the very stakes that Shakespeare must accept in the Dark Lady poems. Indeed, in the poems Shakespeare addresses to the Dark Lady he comes close to revealing the open secret that love poetry is about the real-world agendas of poets and patrons as much as it is about erotically pining lovers and chaste beloveds. After all, Shakespeare strongly hints that it is the Dark Lady herself who demands cutting-edge poetry and flattering images of herself, and this fact accounts for the breeziness between the two of them: the Dark Lady is a beloved woman who is also, or at least is *like,* a masculine patron eagerly consuming images of her own body.[30] And the kind of (disturbing) intimacy that Shakespeare feels in relation to the Dark Lady (he agrees to flatter her if she will flatter him) seems to be precisely the kind of relationship that the rival poets enter into with the Young Man. After all, when Shakespeare admits that the Young Man was not married to his muse, he hints that marriage *is* in the air when the rival poets turn up.

In fact, Shakespeare persistently highlights the fact that the competitive, worldly poetry that the rivals write for the Young Man defines an intense experience of intersubjective intimacy. One example is sonnet 79 in which Shakespeare makes a distinction between an earlier time when he alone wrote poems to the Young Man and the present time in which others have displaced Shakespeare because they are better poets:

> Whilst I alone did call upon thy aid
> My verse alone had all thy gentle grace;

But now my gracious numbers are decayed,
And my sick Muse doth give another place.
I grant, sweet love, thy lovely argument
Deserves the travail of worthier pen;
Yet what of thee thy poet doth invent
He robs thee of, and pays it thee again;
He lends thee virtue, and he stole that word
From thy behavior; beauty doth he give,
And found it in thy cheek; he can afford
No praise to thee, but what in thee doth live:
    Then thank him not for that which he doth say,
    Since what he owes thee, thou thyself dost pay.

Shakespeare again acknowledges that his own poems do not do much for the Young Man and that the Young Man "deserves the travail of worthier pen." But Shakespeare also hints that there is something socially dangerous about the mutually useful, flattering intimacy that the Young Man experiences with the rival poets, notably in the closing image of the servants who steal from their obliging master ("Then thank him not for that which he doth say, / Since what he owes thee, thou thyself dost pay"). As Alan Bray notes, when money moves across the class line, the social intimacy of friendship could come to look like sodomy.[31] It is a problem that Shakespeare knows all too well from the potentially sodomitical intimacy he feels in relation to the Dark Lady; but whereas in that context Shakespeare himself absorbs the hint of sodomy in order to release the Young Man as a sort of free particle, untainted by a dark and dangerous sexuality, in the case of the rivals, it is Shakespeare who is excluded by a social/antisocial bond that he witnesses in appalled but fascinated horror.

    This appalled but fascinated exclusion from the intimacy of the Young Man and rivals is also suggested in sonnet 86, in which Shakespeare claims that his verse has been astonished not through "fear" of the superiority of the rival poet's verse but rather because the rival has possessed the Young Man so completely that there is none of the Young Man left for Shakespeare to use:

I was not sick of any fear from thence.
But when your countenance filled up his line,
Then lacked I matter, that enfeebled mine.

Here Shakespeare sets up a zero-sum economy in which there is only
so much of the Young Man to go around, and when the Young Man
is filling the work of rival poets then there is none of him for Shakespeare's poetry to use. But the intense physicality of the sonnet, notably
including the notion that the Young Man can physically fill up another
poet's lines, contains a sexual charge: the exchanges of useful, worldly
poetry amount to a corporeal practice that excludes Shakespeare in a
way that is frightening—but which is perhaps also erotic. After all, the
speaker of the sonnets enjoys alienation, and when it comes to defining modes of alienation, Shakespeare is nothing if not inventive.[32]

Critical to the sequence as a whole is that the compensatory pleasure that Shakespeare feels in knowing his love to be different in kind
from the worldly, potentially sodomitical intimacy that binds the rivals
and the Young Man extends to the pleasure of knowing that his poetry,
too, is different from the worldly fruits of their "worthier pens." Indeed,
the importance of the rivals is precisely that they define cutting-edge,
modern poetry that is firmly implanted in the market of patronage at
court so that Shakespeare can ostentatiously distinguish his own verse
from theirs. It may be hard to accept that Shakespeare really felt his
poems to be anything other than cutting-edge and highly marketable,
but it is important to pay attention to what he says about them. "Why
is my verse so barren of new pride," Shakespeare asks in sonnet 76,
"So far from variation or quick change? / Why with the time do I
not glance aside / To new-found methods and to compounds strange."
There is a sense, here and elsewhere, of something like technological
change in poetry that Shakespeare is quite conspicuously not keeping
up with. And in sonnet 17 Shakespeare claims that if the Young Man
does not reproduce himself sexually, his poetry is destined to wither:

So should my papers (yellowed with their age)
Be scorned, like old men of less truth than tongue,

And your true rights be termed a poet's rage,
And stretched metre of antique song;
    But were some child of yours alive that time,
    You should live twice: in it, and in my rhyme.

To say that Shakespeare's poetry will only work to immortalize the Young Man if the Young Man reproduces himself sexually is to say that Shakespeare's poetry will not work to immortalize the Young Man. More to the point, since the Young Man seems quite opposed to the idea of reproducing sexually and is therefore quite unlikely to satisfy the condition of Shakespeare's if-then clause, Shakespeare is left to ponder a future in which his poetry will indeed be wrinkled and old and forgotten.

Even as he emphasizes how pathetic and outdated his verse is, Shakespeare is also capable of celebrating his poetry's strange power. The first, and exemplary, instance of this tendency is sonnet 18, which ends with the apparently decisive, "So long as men can breathe or eyes can see, / So long lives this, and this gives life to thee." But the reference to actual biological readers (equipped with lungs and eyes) introduces a certain vulnerability that is echoed in the tentativeness and even finally the emptiness of a poem that is all about Shakespeare's declining to compare the Young Man to a summer's day, or to anything else for that matter. Shakespeare says that the Young Man is better than a summer's day in one respect only: in addition to being lovely he is also unchanging. Any actual summer's day will eventually come to an end, thereby demonstrating its imperfection, but the Young Man's "eternal summer shall not fade." This argument seems to amount to a willful misunderstanding of the usual theory of encomiastic metaphors in which the value of the beloved is captured through a comparison to something at the height of fleeting beauty. But the poem says that the Young Man is unchanging (his only quality!) only to the extent that the poem in fact turns out to be eternal; after all, it is (only) "this" that "gives life to thee." Shakespeare essentially claims that he cannot compare the Young Man to a summer's day because he has just begun a poem that will make the Young Man better than a summer's day by making him eternal. This is not saying much *about* the Young Man, and, moreover, it returns us to those all-too-human readers with their all-too-human lungs and eyes in whose hands the future of the Young Man *and* this poem in fact lie. If this poem is haunting (or, at a minimum, memorable), then that is so only because it is finally so weirdly empty. It is not the only one. There are many weirdly empty sonnets in the sequence, particularly sonnet 105, in which Shakespeare apologizes that since his "verse [is] to constancy confined" all he can do is to repeat that the Young Man is "fair, kind and true"—and then repeats this phrase three times.

By finding a strange, empty power in poetry that pointedly departs from the norms of cutting-edge poetry spelled out to such effect in the work of the rival poets, Shakespeare is sketching the outlines of something like autonomous poetry, perhaps almost avant-garde poetry, whose status is confirmed in part by its systematic difference from what sells. Pierre Bourdieu, in *The Field of Cultural Production,* sees autonomous art defined by a logic of "loser wins": it is a reverse economy where all culture that sells is eschewed and all culture that doesn't sell is celebrated.[33] In nineteenth-century France, the context Bourdieu studies in that book, the culture that sells is popular fiction, which literally sells on the book market. In early sixteenth-century England, or within the world evoked in Shakespeare's sonnets, the culture that sells is poetry that floats on the patronage market, poetry that produces real-world status for both poet and patron. Pointedly locating his poetry apart from this market, Shakespeare writes, "I will not praise, that purpose not to sell" (21). This is a powerful move that makes the rival poets go from looking like excellent poets to mercenary poets in pursuit of nothing but filthy lucre.

Exposed as he was to the changing whims of the literary marketplace, Shakespeare must have been painfully aware of the speed with which tastes could change. For him to imagine eternal poetry would require more than imagining poetry that is successful in the here and now. In fact, it may be by imagining poetry that fails in the here and now that Shakespeare catches a glimpse of poetry that is eternal—not because it is recognized or valorized in any one moment in the long history of literary whim, but because it has fallen through a sort of crack in literary history. Like Wittgenstein's rabbit-duck (Figure 1), poetry that does not conform to the poetic whims of the current day, which are spelled out to such effect in the work of the rivals, can be looked at in two ways: from one standpoint it presents the image of total failure, the abject inability to get the job done, but from another standpoint, poetry so strongly differentiated from the changing canons of literary tastes presents the visage of eternity.

In the context of a book that has sought to chart the fate of a transitional, early modern discourse of sexuality, part of the payoff of the kind of poetic autonomy that Shakespeare sketches in the sonnets is that autonomous poetry gains an avant-gardist freedom *not* to be held to the normative standards (sexual and otherwise) that apply in other sectors of society.[34] Shakespeare's sonnets ultimately suggest the power of radically autonomous poetry to reimagine the basis of social ties from the ground up. This function is still very much at the heart of modern literature as Bersani, for example, conceives of it in his discussion of Gide in *Homos:*

> To me, the interest of the writers that I look at in *Homos*—especially Gide and Genet—is not that they are relevant to specific policy issues that we face today (for example, what the most effective AIDS activism might be)—they are not relevant to such issues—but rather, that they propose what are for the moment necessarily mythic reconfigurations of identity and of sociality. The problem with queer politics as we now define it is that, however broad its reach may be, it is still a micro politics

Figure 1

focused on numerous particular issues which there is no reason to believe will ever be exhausted if the fundamental types of community and relationality out of which such issues spring are not themselves questioned and attacked.[35]

For Bersani, the activity of imagining radically different modes of "relationality" has to be "at least for the moment, an activity of the intellectual imagination—one for which the micropoliticians often have no use or patience but which seems to me no less important an activity and no more of a luxury than our immediate and, of course, vital concrete struggles."[36] The plight of Bersani's intellectuals, who have left micropoliticians and the vital concrete struggles of day-to-day life behind, is in some sense anticipated by the Shakespeare we imagine as the speaker of the *Sonnets*. This Shakespeare uses his militantly autonomous sonnets—sonnets that fulfill no real-world functions, that announce themselves to be the work of a loser—to memorialize a weird, asocial experience whose felt reality is captured in depersonalized and depersonalizing emotions that connect bodies when a connection between socially legible persons has become impossible. It is a discourse of sexuality that is not part of any grand narrative, neither the rise of sexual identities nor the triumph of personality under the protective aegis of domestic intimacy. It amounts to nothing less than the impulse to push beyond society altogether. And if, from the standpoint of history, these sonnets and the sexuality they depict represent a dead end, then it is all the more true that they are today a resource for rethinking, reimagining, and reconfiguring the most basic forms of sociability on which the modernity we now inhabit stands.

Epilogue

The kind of sexual experience that Wyatt's poetry injects into sixteenth-century English literary history is, in some sense, a dead end. The literary discourse that celebrates theatrical emotions for their power to liberate the person and interpersonal interactions from the social world and its normative social grammars is the fruit of a transitional period, a hiatus, between a firmly consolidated feudal world and an equally well-consolidated modernity. The rise of the novel marks the emergence of a modern social formation as well as the ideal of romantic, intimate sexuality that affirms rich individual personalities built on fully psychological emotions. A novel like Richardson's *Pamela* (1749) still looks back to the earlier sexual terrain I have been examining, but only to mark its close. Richardson stages the social contradiction between a hereditary class system that sanctifies Mr. B and a middle-class value system that rewards the acquired gentility that Pamela's letters demonstrate, but only to *resolve* this social contradiction in favor of a seemingly neutral gentility that is emblematized by the sexual intimacy that transcends social background.[1]

Insofar as it solves the massive social contradiction between an aristocratic social imaginary and an inclusive, civilized social imaginary, *Pamela* represents something like a last chapter in the history of the asocial sexuality that I have traced in this study. From this point on, sexuality is firmly integrated into the struggle for intimacy between persons who encounter each other as richly individualized human beings, and henceforth it will be everyone's social dignity as a human person that will be at stake in sex: Pamela compliments Mr. B (and therefore herself as the putative author of the epistolary novel) on the delicacy with which he discusses their wedding night. Sexuality is integrated into social life only at the cost of being concealed delicately.[2] If alternative forms of erotic practice not governed by the social ideal of intimacy survive, they can do so only in sexual subcultures and along social margins, shadowing intimacy and sometimes invading its airy precincts, perhaps continuing in some sense to represent the truth of sexuality, but never more able to challenge it directly.

What is so distinctive about the great Renaissance experiment I trace in this book is the determination with which self-consciously serious literary writers from Wyatt to Shakespeare set out to systematically explore sexual and social futures other than Pamela's wedding night. Working at the cusp of modernity, these writers sought to fuse the contradictions of their society into something completely new, and if the asocial, theatrically emotional interpersonal grammar they elaborated had no broad future, if it was in some sense destined to die out in the cold fire of eighteenth-century intimacy, then it nonetheless survives today as a discourse in the literary texts they composed. So conceived, these texts essentially function as an archive, and a resource, for rethinking and reimagining the most basic norms and ideals by which social life today is waged. I began this book with the desire to make a contribution to the labor of imagining alternatives to the sexual and social modernity we now inhabit; in Wyatt, Sidney, Spenser, and Shakespeare I found not a set of case studies but a group of fellow thinkers.

NOTES

INTRODUCTION

1. Eve Kosofsky Sedgwick points to the way prestigious relationships between men are mediated by women who are given in marriage or used to produce heirs, but part of the point Sedgwick makes is that there is always a continuum between highly affectionate homosocial ties and erotic ties between men. Critics have followed Foucault in showing that the sexual culture of the period lacked the discursive mechanism that bundles desire into discrete sexual identities like heterosexuality and homosexuality, and they have argued that in this context sexuality could inhabit a whole range of social relationships not specifically designated as sexual. In a series of groundbreaking studies, for example, Alan Bray showed that sexuality could slip in and out of the privileged "friendships" between men upon which the unabashedly patriarchal early modern society rests without necessarily drawing attention to itself as sexuality. Laurie Shannon offers an important survey of the eroticism of sameness within the privileged context of early modern friendship, an experience she contextualizes richly within early modern thinking about interpersonal similarity and sameness. Important studies have also examined how the homosocial framework affects sexuality between women as well as cross-gender sexuality. Valerie Traub argues that same-sex desire between women could seem conventional or even pass unnoticed as long as it did not blur gender lines or impinge on women's destined role in reproduction. Moreover, as Jonathan Goldberg, Jeffrey Masten, Richard Rambuss, and Bruce Smith have shown, the ability of sexuality to slip in and out of a whole range of social bonds without drawing attention to itself as sexuality is also a central fact about the literary culture of the period, and it plays an important role in the construction of literary authority for both men and women. See Eve Kosofsky Sedgwick, *Between Men: English Literature and Male Homosocial Desire* (New York: Columbia University Press, 1985); Alan Bray, "Homosexuality and the Signs of Male Friendship in Elizabethan

England," in *Queering the Renaissance,* ed. Jonathan Goldberg (Durham, NC: Duke University Press, 2004); Bray, *Homosexuality in Renaissance England* (New York: Columbia University Press, 1982); Laurie Shannon, *Sovereign Amity: Figures of Friendship in Shakespearean Contexts* (Chicago: University of Chicago Press, 2002); Valerie Traub, "The (In)Significance of 'Lesbian' Desire in Early Modern England," in *Queering the Renaissance,* ed. Goldberg, reprinted with other essays in *The Renaissance of Lesbianism in Early Modern England* (New York: Cambridge University Press, 2002); Jonathan Goldberg, *Sodometries: Renaissance Texts, Modern Sexualities* (Stanford, CA: Stanford University Press, 1992); Jeffrey Masten, *Textual Intercourse: Collaboration, Authorship, and Sexualities in Renaissance Drama* (New York: Cambridge University Press, 1997); Richard Rambuss, *Spenser's Secret Career* (New York: Cambridge University Press, 1993); Bruce R. Smith, *Homosexual Desire in Shakespeare's England* (Chicago: University of Chicago Press, 1991). It is worth noting that several of these critics prefigure my own account here of the various ways that sexuality fails to be fully contained by social concerns. Goldberg, in *Sodometries,* has influenced me the most in this regard.

2. See note 2 in Jeff Nunokawa, "Eros and Isolation: The Anti-Social George Eliot," *ELH: English Literary History* 58, no. 2 (Summer 1991): 427–38.

3. I am thinking in particular of David Halperin's important early article, "Forgetting Foucault: Acts, Identities, and the History of Sexuality," *Representations* 63 (Summer 1998): 93–120, in which he discusses a variety of premodern discourses that seem to define specifically sexual experiences in the absence of a modern identitarian framework.

4. See Alan Bray, "Homosexuality and the Signs of Male Friendship in Elizabethan England," in *Queering the Renaissance,* ed. Goldberg, 40–61.

5. Traub identifies moments when desire between women becomes aware of itself as a recognizable morphology of desire, a kind of lesbianism before the word, and her book is called, significantly, *The Renaissance of Lesbianism.* In *Homosexual Desire in Shakespeare's England,* Smith offers a powerful discussion of the ways pastoral and classical mythological references could be used to point to the reality and the specificity of sexuality between men; the models he discusses interestingly scramble the expectations of the modern identitarian framework. See also Elizabeth Susan Wahl, *Invisible Relations: Representations of Female Intimacy in the Age of Enlightenment* (Stanford, CA: Stanford University Press, 1999).

6. In pursuing this research program I am motivated by the view that the early modern period is not interesting because it is the origin of all that is modern, as a defanged genealogical approach has often suggested; rather, it is interesting because it represents a last moment before much of the modern world that we still inhabit was consolidated.

7. Sexual minorities today struggle to gain access to the legal protections of

sanctioned domestic intimacy; for a powerful critique of this political program, see Michael Warner, *The Trouble with Normal: Sex, Politics, and the Ethics of Queer Life* (New York: Free Press, 1999).

8. See Norbert Elias, *The Civilizing Process,* trans. Edmund Jephcott (Cambridge, MA: Basil Blackwell, 1994); and Niklas Luhmann, *Love as Passion: The Codification of Intimacy,* trans. Jeremy Gaines and Doris L. Jones (Stanford, CA: Stanford University Press, 1998).

9. My interest in using early modern theories of emotion to recover the felt experience of early modern sexuality intersects with Smith's project of physiological and historical phenomenology, which tries to reconstruct the experience of the early modern world and to use this as a standpoint from which to approach interpretation of early modern texts. See his *The Acoustic World of Early Modern England: Attending to the O-Factor* (Chicago: University of Chicago Press, 1999). In particular I am attempting to recover the unsettling and depersonalizing force of powerful early modern emotions as a means to reinterpret sometimes conventional-sounding invocations of such emotions in sixteenth-century poetry, including Sir Thomas Wyatt's.

10. See Gail Kern Paster, *The Body Embarrassed: Drama and the Disciplines of Shame in Early Modern England* (Ithaca, NY: Cornell University Press, 1993); Michael Schoenfeldt, *Bodies and Selves in Early Modern England: Physiology and Inwardness in Spenser, Shakespeare, Herbert, and Milton* (New York: Cambridge University Press, 1999); Martha C. Nussbaum, *Upheavals of Thought: The Intelligence of Emotions* (New York: Cambridge University Press, 2001). For a philosophically rigorous approach to early modern thinking on the emotions, see Susan James, *Passion and Action: The Emotions in Seventeenth-Century Philosophy* (New York: Oxford University Press, 1997). See also Mary Floyd-Wilson's important account of the theory of humors in regional terms, a perspective she calls "geohumoralism," in *English Ethnicity and Race in Early Modern Drama* (New York: Cambridge University Press, 2003).

11. In other words, the sexuality I discuss is rooted in facts about the social world the self inhabits, but these social facts are violently transported into the heart of the self where they become the basis of a powerful *affective* experience of other persons. In this sense, emotions are used to define what Foucault calls "a limit experience" that opens the self to new forms of sociability. See David M. Halperin, *Saint Foucault: Towards a Gay Hagiography* (New York: Oxford University Press, 1995), 99–100.

12. In describing literary representations of emotions as a grammar of sexuality, I am drawing on Goldberg's investigation of "the syntax of desires not readily named" (*Sodometries,* 22).

13. See Leo Bersani, *The Freudian Body: Psychoanalysis and Art* (New York:

Columbia University Press, 1986), 39; Jean Laplanche, *Life and Death in Psychoanalysis,* trans. Jeffrey Mehlman (Baltimore, MD: Johns Hopkins University Press, 1976). For Bersani's important discussion of the political implications of a self-shattering sexuality, see "Is the Rectum a Grave?" *October* 43 (1987): 197–222. This article is reprinted in Goldberg, ed., *Queering the Renaissance.*

14. Masten, "Is the Fundament a Grave?" in *The Body in Parts,* ed. David Hillman and Carla Mazzio (New York: Routledge, 1997), 129–46; Cynthia Marshall, *The Shattering of the Self: Violence, Subjectivity, and Early Modern Texts* (Baltimore, MD: Johns Hopkins University Press, 2002). Marshall's extraordinarily valuable account situates mainstream early modern culture within an economy of unsettling pleasures that engulf speakers and characters, including nominally authoritative *masculine* ones. Marshall's account is also valuable for the way it situates early modern sexual pleasure within contested early modern discourses of the emotions. She draws on a Lacanian psycholinguistic theory to specify the erotic experience she describes; my account is different in that I aim to emphasize the role a concrete sociohistorical reality plays in producing the kinds of pleasurable interpersonal failures to which Marshall's account is so finely attuned.

15. This paradigm was obviously defined by Stephen Greenblatt's *Renaissance Self-Fashioning: From More to Shakespeare* (Chicago: Chicago University Press, 1980). Katharine Eisaman Maus offers a philosophically inflected variant of the self-fashioning model in *Inwardness and the Theater in the English Renaissance* (Chicago: University of Chicago Press, 1995).

16. And here my project intersects with the work of Michael Warner and Lauren Berlant who, together with Leo Bersani, have framed sexuality as a potentially transformative exploration of modes of interpersonal relations that simply depart from conventional social norms. Foucault first suggested this approach in a series of 1980s newspaper interviews discussing how the sexual subcultures of San Francisco defined new social experience and new forms of relationship. Halperin reprints excerpts in *Saint Foucault,* 99–100. See also Warner, *The Trouble with Normal,* and Lauren Berlant, *The Queen of America Goes to Washington City: Essays on Sex and Citizenship* (Durham, NC: Duke University Press, 1997). In sketching an experience of eroticism that stands apart from the socially regulated model of intimacy, I am also drawing on Candace Vogler's important article "Sex and Talk," which appeared in a special issue on intimacy, *Critical Inquiry* 24 (1998): 328–64. My interest in seeing early modern sexuality as projecting a certain alternative vision of social life is also influenced by Herbert Marcuse, *Eros and Civilization: A Philosophical Inquiry into Freud* (Boston: Beacon Press, 1966), though Marcuse relies on a repressive, Freudian model of desire that I do not share.

17. One of my central methodological claims is that literary texts stage the complex sociological reality of an emerging modernity in the highly abstract form

I describe here—as the encounter between incompatible social imaginaries that are fused into a fundamentally *asocial* sexuality.

18. Richard Helgerson, *Self-Crowned Laureates: Spenser, Jonson, Milton, and the Literary System* (Berkeley: University of California Press, 1983).

19. The writers I investigate here all share the fact that they *begin,* in one way or another, with the mode of courtly cultural politics but then seek to push beyond it toward something that, in retrospect, can only be called an autonomous literary realm. This is certainly true of such self-consciously courtly writers as Wyatt and Sidney, but it is also true of writers who inhabited the cusp or the margin of the court, including Spenser and Shakespeare, whose *Troilus and Cressida* (on which I focus in chapter 4) is perhaps one of his most self-conscious engagements with the realities of courtly life and whose sonnet sequence (discussed in chapter 5) takes up a self-consciously courtly form to chart the erotics of a relationship that has at least one foot in the world of aristocratic patronage.

20. Citing the formal experimentation of modernist texts, Bersani argues that art appropriates and elaborates the self-shattering pleasure of sexuality in productive ways; far from being a simple repression or even a sublimation of sexuality, Bersani sees art as a parallel expression of it, one that "might at least partially dissipate our savage sexuality" (*The Freudian Body,* 42). Though there certainly is some Renaissance literature that revels in self-conscious difficulty or that strategically fragments meaning and disorients readers (one example that comes to mind is *Troilus and Cressida,* a play that I discuss at length in chapter 4), the high modernist aesthetic that Bersani assumes is nevertheless anachronistic in the early modern context. Any discussion of the aesthetic effects of early modern art must take into account the early modern struggle for artistic or literary autonomy.

21. Richard Halpern's recent *Shakespeare's Perfume* is one valuable effort to measure the pressure that an emerging literary autonomy exerts in the early modern context, and he importantly connects the notion of autonomy with a sublimated sexuality. See *Shakespeare's Perfume: Sodomy and Sublimity in the Sonnets, Wilde, Freud, and Lacan* (Philadelphia: University of Pennsylvania Press, 2002). I also draw on Margaret W. Ferguson's important *Trials of Desire: Renaissance Defenses of Poetry* (New Haven, CT: Yale University Press, 1983).

1. THE SOCIAL STRUCTURE OF PASSION

1. Luhmann, *Love as Passion.*

2. Ibid., 15.

3. Ibid., 25.

4. On friendship, see Bray, "Homosexuality and the Signs of Male Friendship in Elizabethan England," in *Queering the Renaissance,* ed. Goldberg, 40–61.

5. Elias, *The Civilizing Process.*

6. Ibid., 331. In general this dimension of Elias's argument is more pronounced in *State Formation and Civilization,* the second volume of *The Civilizing Process* (originally published as two volumes in 1939).

7. Freud writes of his own research that "it was discovered that a person becomes neurotic because he cannot tolerate the amount of frustration which society imposes on him in the service of its cultural ideals, and it was inferred from this that the abolition or reduction of those demands would result in a return to possibilities of happiness." See *Civilization and Its Discontents,* ed. and trans. James Strachey (New York: W. W. Norton, 1961), 37–38. Elias sometimes uses this framework to suggest that his own work describes the strengthening of a Freudian superego set against the primal desire of the id. For example, he writes that "the pressure to restrain his impulses and the sociogenetic shame surrounding them— these are turned so completely into habits that [a person] cannot resist them even when alone, in the intimate sphere. Pleasure promising drives and pleasure denying taboos and prohibitions, socially generated feelings of shame and repugnance, come to battle within him. This, as has been mentioned, is clearly the state of affairs which Freud tries to express by such terms as the 'superego' and the 'unconscious'" (Elias, *The Civilizing Process,* 156).

8. Situating Erasmus's discourse of manners within the humanist pedagogy that both reaffirms traditional hierarchy and lays the foundation for a bourgeois order, Richard Halpern notes that what distinguishes Erasmus's notion of civility is his emphasis on imaginary identification with and imitation of other people. This emphasis on forming imaginary relationships with others is paralleled by Halpern's discussion of the humanists' efforts to inculcate a personalized style through imitation of models rather than memorization of linguistic rules. For Halpern, this plays an important role in what he sees as an emerging social system of regulated differences where the preeminent ideological effect is the sense of an individual identity. His concern with the rise of a sense of individualism concerns me less than a basic transformation in the way human relationships are structured. See Halpern, *The Poetics of Primitive Accumulation: English Renaissance Culture and the Genealogy of Capital* (Ithaca, NY: Cornell University Press, 1991), 32–33. For an account that sees civility as an unambiguous effort to increase the integration and discipline of the social body, see Jacques Revel, "The Uses of Civility," in *The Passions of the Renaissance,* ed. Roger Chartier, vol. 3 of *A History of Private Life,* ed. Phillipe Ariès and Georges Duby (Cambridge, MA: Harvard University Press, 1989).

9. In seeing increasing social interconnection as giving rise to a contested but nonetheless powerful notion of a shared humanity, I am drawing to some extent on Durkheim's argument that a functionally differentiated society gives rise to an

organic sense of solidarity that is also the root of religious experience. See Émile Durkheim, *The Division of Labor in Society,* trans. W. D. Halls (New York: Free Press, 1997) and *The Elementary Forms of the Religious Life,* trans. Joseph Ward Swain (New York: Free Press, 1965). In my characterization of modernity as defined by cultural interconnection, I am drawing on John Guillory, *Cultural Capital: The Problem of Literary Canon Formation* (Chicago: University of Chicago Press, 1993). Commenting on the impossibility of imagining any subcultural group's secession from the social totality, Guillory writes that "subcultural formations within the social condition of modernity obviously do form imagined communities with real consequences for many individuals, but their 'local, temporary, and conjunctural' acts of evaluation are the very cultural exhibits which prove the fact that 'values' are never produced by an actually exclusive 'local' consensus but always emerge in a determinate relation to the entire culture which holds in conflictual inter-relation every subcultural formation within it" (278–79). In describing moder-nity, Guillory draws on Althusser's idea of a structure in dominance articulated in "On the Materialist Dialectic" in *For Marx,* trans. Ben Brewster (New York: Verso, 1996).

10. For a powerful account of early modern discourses of governing popu-lations, including early variants of statistical thinking, see David Glimp, *Increase and Multiply: Governing Cultural Reproduction in Early Modern England* (Minneapolis: University of Minnesota Press, 2003).

11. The fact that the new cultural ideal of a fully humane relationship is rooted in a social world that is constituted only by struggle is expressed, in part, by the fact that the discourse of civility can never simply or fully list the requirements for a humane relationship. It is because the hypothetical human core identity, which all civil subjects theoretically share, is constructed and affirmed only through univer-sal social struggle that early modern conduct manuals are so often contradictory or ambiguous. Weberian (or Foucauldian) skepticism might lead one to conclude that such manuals are inculcating not specific rules but a technique of self-monitoring and self-disciplining. While I do not disagree, I prefer instead to see the emphasis on context sensitivity and the difficulty of spelling out what counts as "humane" as evidence of the way the project of civility points to a world orga-nized around continuing struggle to define the very terms of humane relationships.

12. For example, Elias quotes a fifteenth-century French knight on the plea-sures of war: "War is a joyous thing. We love each other so much in war. If we see that our cause is just and our kinsmen fight boldly, tears come to our eyes." And analyzing courtly paintings from the fifteenth century, Elias argues that low-class buffoonery is allowed into the paintings, rather than being discretely banished from them, because aristocrats viewed peasants as physical rather than social facts, more like rocks than like other people (*The Civilizing Process,* 160, 168–78).

13. Pierre Bourdieu sometimes casts the historical transition Elias describes as the origin of the striated cultural system whose role in reproducing class distinctions he studies. Considerable work would be required to establish the way the recognition of social interconnection in the ideal of a shared humanity is aligned with the rise of culture as a fundamental medium in which social status or class—group definition, in short—is worked out. But it is certainly true that insofar as it adds a cultural or behavioral component to social status, the discourse of civility introduces a version of class or status that is very different from the genealogical claim to possessing aristocratic blood; unlike hereditary distinction, cultural distinction is achieved only in relation to others within a contested social totality that must always be at least implicitly acknowledged as the precondition of culturally mediated social struggle. But by identifying the new cultural elites around the absolute monarchies as a *hereditary* vanguard that possesses its civility as if by birth, the discourse of civility props a symbolic distinction achieved only through successful struggle within a complex social totality onto a feudal ideology of hereditary aristocracy in which social status is defined, a priori, by blood alone. For some of Bourdieu's comments about early modern civility, see *Distinction: A Social Critique of the Judgement of Taste,* trans. Richard Nice (Cambridge, MA: Harvard University Press, 1984), 70–74.

14. The paradox of a culturally mediated form of social distinction that is pressed into the service of reaffirming a blood-borne version of social distinction is brought out by the courtly conduct books that sought to teach ambitious young men how to get ahead at court. Frank Whigham's *Ambition and Privilege* (Berkeley: University of California Press, 1984) makes clear how thoroughly these courtly conduct manuals are marked by the paradoxical pressure to adopt a cultural veneer that will simply *reveal* a social status that is not culturally mediated at all but which rides in the blood. In Castiglione's *Book of the Courtier,* trans. Charles S. Singleton (New York: Anchor Books, 1959), 43–45, the contradiction between undermining blood-borne status through an emphasis on acculturation and reinscribing heredity by claiming that good behavior comes naturally to courtly elites is registered (and to some extent covered over) by *sprezzatura,* the naturalness or effortlessness that makes good behavior seem inborn. *Sprezzatura* was, of course, itself only one strategy among others, a symbolic property that could be acquired through study and practice and self-discipline, but ambitious young men used the idea of "natural effortlessness" to finesse the contradiction between inborn status and a learnable status that can signify only within a contested, culturally mediated totality.

15. The two tendencies contained within the civilizing process, on the one hand generating universal standards of behavior and on the other hand using a restricted civility to mark a social elite, may be associated with two genres of

conduct literature, one aiming to teach universal civility and the other socially distinctive courtliness; while the universalizing tendency is represented by Erasmus's *Civility in Boys,* the restricting tendency is represented by Castiglione's *Book of the Courtier.* Bourdieu's notion of habitus (developed, for example, in *The Logic of Practice,* trans. Richard Nice [Stanford, CA: Stanford University Press, 1990]) helps to clarify the sociologically conflicted situation in which culture comes to seem inborn or natural. The concept of habitus refers to a set of cultural dispositions that suit an individual for life at a certain position in the social world; a habitus makes a certain kind of life seem obvious, and this obviousness spans from the clothes that seem natural to the cultural entertainments that seem interesting. In the mature social context that Bourdieu describes, habitus is a fundamental filter through which the social position of an individual is worked out; it is the condition for and the starting point of struggle about social status. And yet a habitus becomes legible only in the context of a whole culture, a whole system of habitus; in fact, as Bourdieu describes them, habitus carry with them a (tendentious) picture of the social whole, a cognitive map of society from a particular (usually class-specific) point of view. Part of what is so fascinating about Bourdieu's notion of habitus is that he emphasizes how deeply habitus is ingrained in the body; though it is learned, typically through the earliest experiences of family life, habitus is nevertheless experienced as *natural,* as a set of dispositions or tastes that do not seem learned or cultural at all. In the early modern context, the continuing pressure of a residual hereditary social imaginary threatens to make the *virtually* corporeal quality of habitus literal by making different kinds of culture seem to reside in different kinds of bodies. Whereas Bourdieu suggests that habitus are cognitive maps that are always defined in complex relation to other habitus positions, early modern habitus come to seem to define biological identities that deny any notion of a shared social world. Supplied with an aristocratic social imaginary, the cultural elites around the early modern state come to claim, often successfully, that they embody a degree of refinement that is permanently out of reach for other social agents; as such, these elites come to seem capable of seceding from a humane, universally civilized social world precisely in the name of the civility and humanity they possess as if by birth.

16. In making these claims I am also influenced by Julia Kristeva's psychoanalytic account of subjects whose desires are not about objects, traditionally viewed, but about abjection and aversiveness. See *Powers of Horror: An Essay on Abjection,* trans. Leon S. Roudiez (New York: Columbia University Press, 1982). In order to define this aversiveness in a social register, I transpose some of Althusser's ideas about historical "contradiction" (in the essay "Contradiction and Overdetermination," reprinted in *For Marx*). In standard Marxist usage, the term refers to the encounter of incompatible forces of production that drive history forward. For

example, within capitalism the central contradiction is between owners (who have an interest in private ownership of the means of production) and workers (who have an interest in communal ownership of the means of production). This contradiction is resolved by the transition to a communist society. Althusser suggests that this model of historical change is too simple. Analyzing the Russian Revolution, he suggests that a revolution was possible there not despite but because of the persistence of a feudal agrarian economy that complicated the pure encounter of workers and owners that is supposed to characterize capitalism. For Althusser, these archaic axes of social struggle fuse with components of modern social struggle to create an opening (in his terms, an "overdetermined" opening) through which the decisive historical event of the revolution was able to occur. In my discussion I also emphasize the fusing of incompatible social imaginaries, each of which also contains *internal* terms for social struggle. Thus, the struggle between feudal overlords and retainers in and of itself does not open the social breach that defines sexuality, but when overdetermined with the struggle between more and less refined courtiers, it does do so.

17. Bersani, "Is the Rectum a Grave?" esp. 215. For another important account of Bersani's thinking, which I discussed at greater length in the introduction to this book, see *The Freudian Body*.

18. Of course, there are moments (as in *Coriolanus*, for instance) when a recognizably Bersaniesque sexuality does emerge as a resistance to the pressure for self-fashioning.

19. Leo Bersani, "Is the Rectum a Grave?" 217.

20. Unlike MacKinnon and Dworkin, Bersani does not aim for what he calls a "redemptive reinvention of sex" that would make sex better, more politically progressive, or more egalitarian. Quite the opposite; for Bersani sexuality is valuable precisely because it inverts and upturns the norms and techniques for welding people together within social life. Ibid., 215.

21. Ibid., 222.

22. Looked at through the lens of Bersani's account of sexuality, such social breakdowns are also the engines of a special class of relationships that are sexual precisely to the extent that they are felt as the (pleasurable) violation of any available social norms. I argue that the early modern period stands in the midst of a massive transformation in the very terms of social life and that what passes for normative structures of relationship is therefore very much up for grabs. But if sexuality amounts to the enjoyment of the failure of whatever passes for normative structures of relationship, then in such a historical context a recognizably Bersaniesque sexuality will come to seem a *central,* rather than a marginal, feature of social life. In essence, I describe a historically contingent sexuality that accrues spontaneously to the interpersonal breakdowns generated when a modern vision

of universal humanity is shattered or abraded by a residual premodern social imaginary that sees heredity as the engine of properly social relationships.

23. Nussbaum, *Upheavals of Thought*. My own interest in the ways literary texts make use of concrete and specific emotional experiences is influenced by the editors' introduction to *Shame and Its Sisters: A Silvan Tomkins Reader*, ed. Eve Kosofsky Sedgwick and Adam Frank (Durham, NC: Duke University Press, 1995). Tomkins's thinking on emotions is in some ways quite anomalous, and Nussbaum's work better illustrates both mainstream psychology and key aspects of an unspoken consensus that implicitly inform much modern thinking about subjectivity.

24. Nussbaum, *Upheavals of Thought*, 22.

25. Edward Reynolds, *A Treatise of the Passions and Faculties of the Soule of Man* (1640), facsimile edition (Gainsville, FL: Scholars' Facsimiles and Reprints, 1971), 41–46.

26. Adela Pinch emphasizes the alien and unsettling quality of emotion in *Strange Fits of Passion: Epistemologies of Emotion, Hume to Austen* (Stanford, CA: Stanford University Press, 1996). I argue that, at least in the early modern context, the view that emotions are alien results from (presumably short-lived) turbulence between different theories of emotions.

27. There have been important critical accounts that track the implications of humoral thinking for our understanding of early modern culture. For one instance that sees humors as a bodily excess, see Paster, *The Body Embarrassed*. Paster's more recent work modifies this perspective by emphasizing the implications of humoral thinking for a theory of action, especially in drama. See "The Tragic Subject and Its Passions," in *The Cambridge Companion to Shakespearean Tragedy*, ed. Claire McEachern (New York: Cambridge University Press, 2002), 142–59. Michael Schoenfeldt offers a nuanced review of the role that humoral thinking plays in literary descriptions of selves and their connections to bodies. Schoenfeldt's account is valuable because of his emphasis on the importance of the stoical ideal of moderation and temperance of bodily affects. See *Bodies and Selves in Early Modern England*. For a historical account of Galen and the influence of his thought in Europe, see Oswei Tempkin, *Galenism: Rise and Decline of a Medical Philosophy* (Ithaca, NY: Cornell University Press, 1973). See also Galen's *On the Passions and Errors of the Soul*, trans. Paul W. Harkins (Columbus: Ohio State University Press, 1963). For an important account of humors in regional terms, see Mary Floyd-Wilson, *English Ethnicity and Race in Early Modern Drama*.

28. The cognitivist bias in modern thinking on emotions occasionally sparks a reactive overvaluation of the physical or material component of emotion. One famous instance is William James, *The Principles of Psychology* (New York: Dover, 1950).

29. It is worth noting that in Jonson's *Every Man Out of His Humor* (1599),

once the characters are dishumored they literally disappear from the stage, as if there were nothing left of an individual once a defining humor is cured.

30. I discuss this moment at greater length in chapter 3. The fact that early modern authors celebrate overwhelming, somatic emotions as the very terrain of sexual intersubjectivity suggests that they produce what Foucault terms an *ars erotica*. Foucault himself undertakes such an approach to classical culture in the second volume of his history of sexuality, *The Use of Pleasure,* trans. Robert Hurley (New York: Vintage Books, 1990). For a discussion of Foucault's interest in sado-masochistic eroticism as a kind of limit experience that might push beyond the norms of liberal society, see Halperin, *Saint Foucault,* 85–99.

31. In *The Freudian Body* Bersani argues that all sexuality derives from infant masochism cultivated as a defense against the perceived danger of being overwhelmed by the physical world. In developing this view he draws on Laplanche, *Life and Death in Psychoanalysis.*

32. Judith Butler's views follow from her emphasis on the performativity of gender. See *Gender Trouble: Feminism and the Subversion of Identity* (New York: Routledge, 1990), 128–41.

33. All Wyatt poems are quoted from *Sir Thomas Wyatt: The Complete Poems,* ed. R. A. Rebholz (New Haven, CT: Yale University Press, 1981). Subsequent references are internal.

34. Many critics of Wyatt's poetry see it as a site where a powerful sense of self emerges. See, for one instance, Anne Ferry, *The "Inward" Language: Sonnets of Wyatt, Sidney, Shakespeare* (Chicago: University of Chicago Press, 1983). Stephen Greenblatt argues that Wyatt's poetry registers a kind of true self only in the space between the series of masks that he adopts to deal with the shifting political ground in the court of Henry VIII. See the paradigm-defining *Renaissance Self-Fashioning,* chapter 3. My response to Wyatt has been deeply influenced by Jonathan Crewe's brilliant discussion in *Trials of Authorship: Anterior Forms and Poetic Reconstruction from Wyatt to Shakespeare* (Berkeley: University of California Press, 1990). In his discussion of Wyatt and Surrey, Crewe is attentive to the payoff these poets hope for (in terms of authority or pleasure) from assuming extremely risky, self-abasing positions; for Crewe, the logic of their poems is the loser wins. I contextualize this mode of risk taking within the asocial sexuality I examine in this book.

35. Thomas Greene also sees Wyatt's poetry as a rejection of an emerging modernity, though Greene defines modernity in a negative way as the loss of traditional stability. See *The Light at Troy: Imitation and Discovery in Renaissance Poetry* (New Haven, CT: Yale University Press, 1982), chap. 3. Some commentators have sought to contextualize Wyatt's world-weariness within nascent capitalism. In this regard, see Raymond Southall, *Literature and the Rise of Capitalism: Critical Essays*

Mainly on the Sixteenth and Seventeenth Centuries (London: Lawrence & Wishart, 1973).

36. Judith Butler discusses a similar turn against the self in *The Psychic Life of Power: Theories in Subjection* (Stanford, CA: Stanford University Press, 1997). For her, this turn against the self is, paradoxically, the origin of the modern subject that remains a potentially destabilizing force when it reappears as desire. As Butler puts it, "desire will aim at unraveling the subject, but will be thwarted by precisely the subject in whose name it operates" (9).

37. For Joan Kelly, the emphasis on gender difference in Petrarchan poetry (both Italian and English) represents a major departure from the earlier medieval romance tradition. Kelly argues that the medieval tradition of courtly love was, in fact, premised on the aristocratic similarity of the lover and his beloved lady. Courtly love represents the transfer of the political theory of vassalage onto an extramarital love relation; the freedom to enter into such a bond attested to a shared aristocratic status. One of the main points Kelly makes is that feudal male homosociality is so intensely focused on reproduction that it actually allows aristocratic women considerable freedom to define extramarital sexual bonds as long as those bonds do not interfere with familial reproduction. Kelly argues that the Italian Renaissance inheritors of the courtly love tradition begin to emphasize gender dissimilarity because of changes in how elite men relate to one another. In Renaissance courts elite men no longer relate to their superiors as aristocratic equals but as dependents, and Kelly argues that this new and disturbingly unequal relationship between rulers and courtiers is worked out, in part, by imagining countless courtships of a chaste and inaccessible beloved. See "Did Women Have a Renaissance?" in *Women, History, and Theory: The Essays of Joan Kelly* (Chicago: University of Chicago Press, 1984). For a powerful account of how humanists used gender to manage their asymmetrical relationships with their aristocratic patrons, see Barbara Correll, *The End of Conduct: "Grobianus" and the Renaissance Text of the Subject* (Ithaca, NY: Cornell University Press, 1996), chap. 2. Alan Stewart, in *Close Readers: Humanism and Sodomy in Early Modern England* (Princeton, NJ: Princeton University Press, 1997), offers detailed assessments of the private spaces shared by socially advancing humanists and noblemen.

38. Drawing on Lacanian psychoanalysis to emphasize the way language splits the subject, Cynthia Marshall writes that "Petrarchanism actually delivers jouissance *through* language, or more specifically through linguistic failure," in *The Shattering of the Self,* 59. Marshall's account offers an extremely valuable reassessment of the Petrarchan tradition by contextualizing the obviously sexist dynamic of feminine objectification in an economy of unsettling pleasures that frequently engulf nominally authoritative masculine speakers. As I suggested in my discussion of Bersani, I decline an appeal to a foundational psycholinguistic theory in favor

of emphasizing the role a concrete sociohistorical reality plays in producing the kinds of pleasurable interpersonal failures that fill the Petrarchan tradition. Wyatt simply makes strategic use of Petrarchan conventions to point to a basic fissure in the fabric of his social world that exists outside of those literary conventions and that contains a real sexual charge. Other early modern authors share Wyatt's interest in using Petrarchan discourse to point to the erotic experiences that inhabit the fissures that run through the early modern social world, but they deploy these conventions in different ways. Whereas Wyatt tends to emphasize the culturally alien force of the beloved and is often explicit about the presence of other men in the Petrarchan situation, in Spenser's *Amoretti* sequence, which I discuss in chapter 2, Spenser treats the beloved as occupying a stable place near the apex of the social hierarchy in order to paint himself as abjectly lowborn in relation to her. Shakespeare's sonnets represent a more complex use of the Petrarchan framework. As I discuss in chapter 5, in Shakespeare's sequence the beloved Young Man oscillates between being an elite aristocrat and a poor upstart, and it is the ensuing uncertainty about how Shakespeare, as a poet, should approach him that opens the door to a specifically sexual tie between these men.

39. Wyatt was rumored to have had an affair with Anne Boleyn, whose execution he may have seen while imprisoned in the Tower of London, an experience that may be recorded in "Who List His Wealth and Ease Retain." Eric Ives reviews the historical evidence for their affair in *Anne Boleyn* (Cambridge, MA: Blackwell, 1986), esp. 83–85. Heather Dubrow observes that the poem pulls in multiple interpretive directions and that this ambiguity is especially pronounced in the word "wild," which can mean either "resistant" or "shy." This undecidability will become relevant to my discussion later. See *Echoes of Desire: English Petrarchism and Its Counterdiscourses* (Ithaca, NY: Cornell University Press, 1995), 95–97.

40. Stephen Merriam Foley, *Sir Thomas Wyatt* (Boston: Twayne, 1990), 104.

41. In his discussion of the connection between Petrarchan rhetoric and European colonialism, Roland Greene also argues that the lady of "They Flee from Me" invokes European discourses about New World populations. See his *Unrequited Conquests: Love and Empire in the Colonial Americas* (Chicago: University of Chicago Press, 1999), 163–66. While Barbara L. Estrin does not connect the beloved woman of this poem to colonial discourses, she tellingly describes her unsettling power. For Estrin, the beloved here actually morphs into a man who "penetrates and controls" the speaker. See *Laura: Uncovering Gender and Genre in Wyatt, Donne, and Marvell* (Durham, NC: Duke University Press, 1994), 129.

42. See *Petrarch's Lyric Poems,* trans. Robert M. Durling (Cambridge, MA: Harvard University Press, 1976), 443. H. A. Mason argues that Wyatt's poem refers to Thomas Cromwell. See *Sir Thomas Wyatt: A Literary Portrait* (Bristol, England: Bristol Classics Press, 1986), 250–56.

43. The translation of a male superior into a female beloved is made possible by seeing in the chastity of the beloved the (very masculine) power to keep a (perhaps dependent) man off balance.

44. Wyatt's poems illustrate paths to the sexualization of male-male and male-female bonds. The case of relationships between women is harder to fit into the model I explore here. The thoroughness of early modern patriarchy leads to opportunities for female-female sexuality but also makes it difficult to define these as specifically sexual. Elizabeth Susan Wahl does examine ways that sexual relations between women might become visible *as such*. See her *Invisible Relations: Representations of Female Intimacy in the Age of Enlightenment*, especially chapter 4 in which Wahl argues that Katherine Philips comes close to articulating something like a lesbian identity. But rarely are such relationships invested with the massive social difference that defines the discourse of sexuality I describe in this book.

2. INTIMACY AND THE EROTICISM OF SOCIAL DISTANCE

1. I have also suggested that this sexuality is a historical rival to the modern notion of intimacy. Like intimacy, the early modern experience of asocial sexuality I examine here is a sexualized experience of others that stands apart from social life, though unlike modern intimacy, it is not institutionalized in a private, domestic sphere.

2. Helgerson argues that Spenser invented the idea of the poetic career by "abandoning all social identity except that conferred by his elected vocation" (Helgerson, *Self-Crowned Laureates*, 63).

3. Arthur Marotti, "'Love Is Not Love': Elizabethan Sonnet Sequences and the Social Order," *ELH* 49 (1982): 396–428. I locate Sidney's sonnets in the context of courtly culture in which art still had to legitimate itself by appealing to an external social hierarchy. In the context of courtly culture, poetry could seem like a way of pursuing extraliterary goals by literary means, and if Sidney is the greatest practitioner of this courtly mode of cultural politics, then George Puttenham is its greatest theorist. For Puttenham, every literary ambition is also a political or social ambition, a perspective that has been very much enshrined in New Historicist criticism. See, for example, Louis Montrose, "Of Gentlemen and Shepherds: The Politics of Elizabethan Pastoral Form," *ELH* 50 (1983): 415–59. It is worth noting that Puttenham himself occasionally offers views about literature that push toward autonomy, not least his famous claim that the poet "is a pleader of pleasant and lovely causes, and nothing perilous." See *The Arte of English Poesie* (1589; repr. Kent, OH: Kent State University Press, 1974), 160.

4. Sidney's sonnets are cited from the edition by William A. Ringler Jr. (Oxford, England: Clarendon Press, 1962). Subsequent references are given internally.

5. Quoted in Alan Stewart, *Philip Sidney: A Double Life* (New York: St. Martin's Press, 2000), 35.

6. Ibid., 34.

7. *On Good Manners in Boys,* trans. Brian McGregor, in *The Collected Works of Erasmus,* ed. J. K. Sowards (Toronto: University of Toronto Press, 1985), 25: 273. For a discussion of the ways humanist tutors elicited from their noble charges a discipline directed at humanists themselves, see Correll, "Malleable Material, Models of Power: Woman in Erasmus's 'Marriage Group' and Good Manners in Boys," in *The End of Conduct,* first published in *ELH* 57 (1990): 241–62.

8. This elision is, of course, a strategy used by humanists themselves as a way to insinuate lowborn men into elevated circles.

9. For an account of how Petrarch's own poetry was used in Italy to combine projects of erotic and linguistic refinement, see Gordon Braden, "Applied Petrarchism: The Loves of Pietro Bembo," *MLQ: Modern Language Quarterly* 57, no. 3 (1996): 397–423.

10. Puttenham, *The Arte of English Poesie,* 60.

11. For an important account of why poetry was so frequently viewed as shameful or even viceful, see Halpern's "A Mint of Phrases: Ideology and Style Production in Tudor England," in *The Poetics of Primitive.* Halpern offers the brilliant argument that the social anxieties generated by the humanist education program's impulse to supplement an older class system with specialized forms of linguistic competence were displaced onto vernacular poetry.

12. The locus classicus for the view that print was considered shameful by courtly poets is J. W. Saunders's "'The Stigma of Print': A Note on the Social Bases of Tudor Poetry," *Essays in Criticism* 1 (1951). For more recent treatments of the relationship between print and manuscript cultures, see Helgerson, *Self-Crowned Laureates;* Arthur F. Marotti, *Manuscript, Print, and the English Renaissance Lyric* (Ithaca, NY: Cornell University Press, 1995); and Wendy Wall's important *The Imprint of Gender: Authorship and Publication in the English Renaissance* (Ithaca, NY: Cornell University Press, 1993). In "Disclosures in Print: The 'Violent Enlargement' of the Renaissance Voyeuristic Text," *SEL: Studies in English Literature, 1500–1900* 29 (Winter 1989): 35–59, Wall argues that publication is problematic for early modern writers primarily because it spills private matters into the public domain. In the context of Sidney, I would substitute for "private" a restricted culture that seeks to express class, and while I do not believe that Sidney really meant to disavow his own poetry, I do believe that the pose is part of a project of asserting a kind of cultural authority not easily translatable into modern conceptions of literary authority.

13. For an account of the way manuscript collections and the printed miscellanies based on them evince an aesthetic not of originality but of similarity or

repetition, see Randall Louis Anderson, "'The Merit of a Manuscript Poem': The Case for Bodleian MS Rawlinson Poet. 85," in *Print, Manuscript, and Performance: The Changing Relation of the Media in Early Modern England,* ed. Arthur F. Marotti and Michael Bristol (Columbus: Ohio State University Press, 2000), 127–53.

14. See Sally Minogue, "A Woman's Touch: Astrophil, Stella, and 'Queen Vertue's Court,'" *ELH* 63 (Fall 1996): 555–70. Minogue argues against Marotti's love-is-not-love paradigm by drawing attention to what she sees as an explicitly erotic subtext in *Astrophil and Stella* addressed to Queen Elizabeth herself. Within the context of my argument, this looks like an expansion of the restricted erotic community to include the queen.

15. See Dubrow, *Echoes of Desire.*

16. "Stella" was, of course, a married woman, and as such Sidney's desired relationship with her would have been adulterous, making Sidney's claim to the "virtue" of erotic consummation seem odd. But while adultery was not exactly licit, it may have been an aristocratic privilege, and within the context of Sidney's cultural production adultery is certainly compatible with the expression of elevated social rank. While the range and extent of structural modifications of the illicit/licit distinction within a cultural politics of class-based refinement remains to be described in greater detail, one must be wary of simply designating as "scandalous" poetic representations of adultery, same-sex relations, or gender-role inversions (or incest, for that matter) without assessing the project of the representation within a complex cultural terrain. For a discussion that treats incest as the real secret of *Astrophil and Stella* (and reflects on the process of decoding Renaissance literature for secrets in the first place), see Jonathan V. Crewe's superb "Countercurrents," in *Hidden Designs: The Critical Profession and Renaissance Literature* (New York: Methuen, 1986).

17. Sidney's complaint that all representation debases the love that it would represent is seen by Wendy Wall as typical of Elizabethan sonnet sequences generally. Commenting on Samuel Daniel's *Delia,* Wall writes that "the index of the speaker's love is the silence of the poems. . . . Some of Daniel's poems mourn the inability of language to capture his true feelings, while others grieve at hidden emotions involuntarily made visible." See *The Imprint of Gender,* 46. Arguing against the claim that emotion is in some privileged sense inward or hard to represent, Jacqueline T. Miller argues that "representation precedes and produces the passion," and situates this argument in early modern discourses of the emotions including Thomas Wright's *Passions of the Minde in Generall.* See "The Passion Signified: Imitation and the Construction of Emotions in Sidney and Wroth," *Criticism* 43, no. 4 (2001): 406–21, 406. In my view, Sidney's claim that something inexpressible remains behind the sonnets points less to a private subject who resists self-exposure than to the wish to point to a form of socially restricted eroticism.

18. Clark Hulse also picks up the impulse toward a private language in these sonnets, though he sees the private audience as consisting of Sidney and Rich only and thus frames the impulse in a romantic rather than a sociological light. At the same time, he reads a secret subtext of political rebellion in the sonnets. See "Stella's Wit: Penelope Rich as Reader of Sidney's Sonnets," in *Rewriting the Renaissance: The Discourses of Sexual Difference in Early Modern Europe*, ed. Margaret W. Ferguson, Maureen Quilligan, and Nancy J. Vickers (Chicago: University of Chicago Press, 1986), 272–86.

19. *The Faerie Queene*, 12.1.9; this phrase is also the title of Jonathan Goldberg's indispensable study of Spenser's narrative strategies. See *Endlesse Worke: Spenser and the Structures of Discourse* (Baltimore, MD: Johns Hopkins University Press, 1981).

20. Paul Alpers argues that the late minor poetry is not minor at all but that it constitutes an "alternative body of major poetry to Spenser's epic endeavors." See his "Spenser's Late Pastorals," *ELH* 56 (1989): 797–817. Several critics have discussed the relationship between the epic and the late minor poetry. In *Spenser's Secret Career*, especially chapter 3, "'In Sundrie Hands': The 1590 Faerie Queene and Spenser's Complaints," Rambuss sees the late Spenser reacting to a lack of patronage by aggressively "disclosing" the secrets of the great and of the court in general; Louis Montrose, "Spenser's Domestic Domain: Poetry, Property, and the Early Modern Subject," in *Subject and Object in Renaissance Culture*, ed. Margreta de Grazia, Maureen Quilligan, and Peter Stallybrass (New York: Cambridge University Press, 1996), sees Spenser's poetry as intellectual property that compensates for lack of "real" property, and reads the *Epithalamion* and *Colin Clout's Come Home Again* as attaching the metaphor of the poetic domain to Spenser's own marriage and the fairly large estate he was granted in Ireland in exchange for his work as a colonial administrator; Donald Cheney, "Spenser's Fortieth Birthday and Related Fictions," *Spenser Studies* 4 (1983): 3–31, sees the *Amoretti* as an aggressive validation of an overtly erotic relationship over the Neoplatonic sublimation favored at court.

21. Little is known about the historical Elizabeth Boyle. Though she probably enjoyed no particularly elevated social rank, she was related to Richard Boyle, later Earl of Cork, whom Spenser might have considered a valuable contact. Many reconstructions of Boyle's life and career depend on the supposed evidence of the *Amoretti* themselves. After reading the poems, the editors of the Variorum edition (Edwin Greenlaw et. al., eds. [Baltimore: Johns Hopkins University Press, 1934]) find it easy to imagine a "beautiful, dignified, golden-haired English woman, who possessed both character and education, and who was related to the noble Althorp family whom Spenser so revered, and hence was at least a distant kinswoman of Spenser himself. Her most notable achievement, from our point of view, was serving as inspiration for some of the finest love poetry in the English language" (11: 175). I should note that by making Boyle "high" in relation to himself but low in

relation to the queen, Spenser is taking advantage of a quirk in Petrarchan conventions in which gender difference is a form of status difference that may stand at an oblique angle to class positioning. For Spenser, the Petrarchan lady is a kind of switching point between a gender hierarchy that always places the lady on top and a class hierarchy that may assign her to a less exalted social position.

22. Spenser was taken on at the Merchant Taylor's school under Richard Mulcaster on charity and held a "sizarship" for poor students while at Pembroke Hall, Cambridge. The marks of Spenser's social disadvantage are reviewed by Montrose, "Spenser's Domestic Domain," 83–84. The most useful recent discussion of Spenser's life is Richard Rambuss's "Spenser's Life and Career," in *The Cambridge Companion to Spenser,* ed. Andrew Hadfield (New York: Cambridge University Press, 2001).

23. Gordon Braden suggests that in the *Amoretti* the lady's pride is both attacked and praised, and that this is part of the dynamic of courtship the sonnets chart. Perhaps less convincing is Braden's claim that this is due to Spenser's certainty that his suit will eventually be accepted. See "Pride, Humility, and the Petrarchan Happy Ending," *Spenser Studies* 18: 123–42.

24. Carol Kaske notes the extraordinary vindictiveness of the sonnet's wish that the beloved be made to "bow to a baser mate / That I may love in equal sort / As she doth laugh at me, making my pain her sport." Kaske goes on to argue that Spenser must mean someone far lower on the social ladder than himself, which discounts Spenser's theatrical emphasis on his own baseness. Kaske's article illuminates the ways the *Amoretti* are indebted to the biblical psalms both thematically and metrically. See "Spenser's Amoretti and Epithalamion: A Psalter of Love," in *Centered on the Word: Literature, Scripture, and the Tudor-Stuart Middle Way,* ed. Daniel W. Doerksen and Christopher Hodgkins (Newark: University of Delaware Press, 2004), 28–49.

25. Sonnet 30 explicitly attaches the perverse economy of endless pain to the class difference with which this affective experience (like every affective experience in the *Amoretti*) begins, for there the lady's perverse hardening in response to blows is seen as evidence for her gentility: "Such is the powre of love in gentle mind / That it can alter all the course of kind." Elizabeth's hardening in response to blows is evidence of "love," and perversity is the form that love takes in "noble mind."

26. A reading that followed the dysfunctional erotic relationship between Spenser and Boyle into the *Epithalamion* would take note of the self-consciousness with which poetry is there presented as a means of supplementing the relational lowliness that Spenser's representation of Boyle's elevation entails. Spenser concludes the *Epithalamion* by claiming that it is a "song made in lieu of many ornaments, / With which my love should duly have bene dect" and invites his poem

to "Be unto her a goodly ornament, / And for short time an endless moniment" (stanza 24). Spenser thus highlights his own alleged poverty and consequent unworthiness (he has no real ornaments to give Boyle), and claims for his symbolic work a limited power to add social prestige to the poet.

27. Helgerson, *Self-Crowned Laureates,* 63.

28. In his *Forms of Nationhood: The Elizabethan Writing of England* (Chicago: University of Chicago Press, 1992), Richard Helgerson argues that Spenser's epic participates in the project of forging a national culture. For Helgerson, however, this national culture mediates between members of an empowered elite who recognize themselves as a "nation" by excluding commoners whose interests are not identical to the interests of the state. Helgerson thus treats the nation that reads epics as an expanded version of Sidney's coterie audience unified by bonds of strong (and well-policed) identification.

3. CIVILITY AND THE EMOTIONAL TOPOGRAPHY OF *THE FAIRIE QUEENE*

1. All passages from *The Faerie Queene* are cited from J. C. Smith and E. de Selincourt, *Spenser: Poetical Words* (New York: Oxford University Press, 1977).

2. See Elias, *The Civilizing Process,* 44–47. Elias notes that the shock that modern readers sometimes feel at the explicitness of dicta contained in early modern conduct literature is a sign of our being further along in the same historical development he traces. However, I emphasize that insofar as they assume almost nothing about their reader's state of preparedness, the explicitness of dicta in Renaissance civility handbooks suggests a powerful impulse toward universalizing the notion of good behavior.

3. Spenser always insists that he is not, himself, a member of this courtly elite and therefore has trouble understanding its ways. The recurring claim of exclusion from the court and courtly elites, or of puzzlement about what passes for good behavior in those precincts, is partly rooted in Spenser's biography. Whatever his father's profession, Spenser got to Cambridge only on a fellowship for poor boys, and throughout all of his writing Spenser treats the notion of being a poor boy as a kind of prized, personal trope. For a discussion of the stances of exclusion that Spenser adopted throughout his career, see Louis Montrose's "Spenser's Domestic Domain: Poetry, Property, and the Early Modern Subject," in *Subject and Object in Renaissance Culture,* ed. de Grazia et al. Montrose argues that Spenser uses his poetry as a way of advancing his social ambition. I disagree with this view for reasons I will explain later. For a useful discussion of the role of biography in accounts of Spenser's work, see Richard Rambuss, "Spenser's Loves, Spenser's Career," in *Spenser's Life and the Subject of Biography,* ed. Judith Anderson,

Donald Cheney, and David A. Richardson (Amherst: University of Massachusetts Press, 1996), 1–17.

4. Elias attempts to sort out this conflict by trying to distinguish between "civility" (the norms that ought, in principle, to govern all interpersonal relationships) and "courtesy" or "courtliness" (the special refinement and elegance that distinguishes the courtly elite). In fact, the discourse of civility oscillates between, on the one hand, providing a universal grammar of social interactions built around a hypothetically universal human essence and, on the other hand, reaffirming the separateness of a courtly elite by endorsing the notion that they possess a kind of hereditary cultural sophistication that is permanently out of reach for others. Spenser highlights and heightens this contradiction at the heart of the discourse of civility.

5. I am influenced here by John Guillory's account of the force of symbolic capital today. See *Cultural Capital*. Guillory argues that the notion that some literary texts belong to or represent certain social groups is based on a denial of the fundamental fact of group interconnection within the social formation of modernity.

6. Ernst Robert Curtius, *European Literature and the Latin Middle Ages,* trans. Willard R. Trask (Princeton, NJ: Princeton University Press, 1983), 159–62. Originally published in 1948.

7. John Guillory describes the continuing importance of an appeal to divine inspiration throughout the Renaissance and the difficulty with which the secularized notion of the imagination is developed in *Poetic Authority: Spenser, Milton, and Literary History* (New York: Columbia University Press, 1983).

8. In some ways, Dorothy Stephens's discussion of the Cave of Lust episode parallels my discussion of Spenser's inability to imagine a satisfying relationship with Raleigh except in a space of shared debasement. She too describes alternative social possibilities that emerge in a space that is at some significant remove from the dominant mechanisms of the social. See her chapters on *The Faerie Queene* in *The Limits of Eroticism in Post-Petrarchan Narrative: Conditional Pleasure from Spenser to Marvell* (New York: Cambridge University Press, 1998).

9. Martha J. Craig reviews the parallels between Raleigh's biography, including the Throckmorton affair, and the Timias/Belphebe episode. She frames Timias's submission and degradation as socially functional parts of a political system of absolutism. "The Protocol of Submission: Raleigh as Timias," *Genre 29,* no. 3 (Fall 1996): 325–40.

10. In her study of classical sources in Spenser, Theresa Krier notes that Timias's mistaking Belphebe for an angel as well as her blush are borrowed from analogous episodes in Ovid. In both Spenser and Ovid, Krier sees blushing as evidence that a secret core of the self has been made visible, which renders the

blusher open to intimacy. She comments that "to observe the rising blood in the face is to observe the most deeply internal being made external and visible against the will." See Krier's *Gazing on Secret Sights: Spenser, Classical Imitation, and the Decorums of Vision* (Ithaca, NY: Cornell University Press, 1990), 168. For Krier's discussion of intimacy and civility, see p. 155.

11. Sheila T. Cavanagh also notes that "since her genealogy is dramatically indeterminate, Belphoebe's social and political status defies categorization," and that this unsettled social and political status has an effect on how she is experienced sexually since it "situates Belphoebe outside the rules and boundaries of ordinary sexual exchange." See *Wanton Eyes and Chaste Desires: Female Sexuality in The Faerie Queene* (Bloomington: Indiana University Press, 1994), 130–31.

12. For another account of the pressure Elizabeth's genealogy exerts on pastoral poetry, see Montrose, "Of Gentlemen and Shepherds."

13. In his comments on this episode, Reed Way Dasenbrock argues that the relationship between Timias and Belphebe is based on a double bind resulting from a switch from a temporal to a spiritual status disparity between lover and beloved. Dasenbrock argues that because of their social position, squires, including Timias, are especially exposed to the painful experience of a Petrarchan courtship; he sees Spenser as criticizing the Petrarchan ideal because of the asymmetry it introduces into intimate relationships. I argue that Spenser finds the asymmetries introduced by the Petrarchan model exciting. Dasenbrock is useful in pointing to the need to shift from a character-based analysis that is invited by the allegorical discipline of books 1 and 2 to an emphasis on groups of characters and their relationships in books 3 and 4. See his "Escaping the Squire's Double Bind in Books III and IV of *The Faerie Queene,*" *SEL* 26 (1986): 25–45. For a study that tries to read books 3 and 4 by emphasizing spiritual categories allegorically implanted into individual characters, see Thomas P. Roche, *The Kindly Flame: A Study of the Third and Fourth Books of "The Faerie Queene"* (Princeton, NJ: Princeton University Press, 1964).

14. See their introduction to *Shame and Its Sisters,* ed. Sedgwick and Frank, 5.

15. Ibid., 135.

16. I derive the notion of overdetermination here from Louis Althusser. My account of the social totality as composed of multiple, contradictory sets of terms for relationships owes a general debt to Althusser, though I tend to read social relationship in the personal register as well as the register of the sociologically (and economically) defined groups that Althusser insists on. The notion of a series of contradictions fusing into an overdetermined (i.e., radically unstable) whole is also derived from Althusser, though in place of the revolutionary rupture (along with a revolutionary consciousness) that he describes, I find affects that point toward a mode of sociability that stands at an oblique angle to the dominant mechanisms

of the social world. See Althusser, especially the essays "Contradiction and Over-determination" and "On the Materialist Dialectic," in *For Marx*. Judith Butler appropriates the notion of overdetermination for questions of identity in *Excitable Speech: A Politics of the Performative* (New York: Routledge, 1997).

17. The eroticism in this quasi-religious encounter is reminiscent of the moments discussed by Richard Rambuss in his important *Closet Devotions* (Durham, NC: Duke University Press, 1998).

18. Nietzsche suggests one way of understanding why individuals might choose powerful affective charges even when they seem painful: to deaden the greater pain of social weakness and thus, for Nietzsche, to affirm the will to power and the life instincts. See *The Genealogy of Morals,* trans. Walter Kaufmann and R. J. Hollingdale (New York: Vintage Books, 1989), 87–88.

19. Moreover, in the concluding stanzas of the passage Belphebe is converted into the rose of *The Romance of the Rose*. By self-consciously recalling the medieval romance tradition here, Spenser may be writing a bit of literary history, suggesting that allegorical romances are an important literary precursor for his epic insofar as they share his interest in offering archives of human affective competencies. For the most part, Spenser declines the allegorical mode of representing the affects in favor of the rich, physiological blazons of affect that I go on to discuss. One partial exception is Britomart's rescue of Amoret from the enchanter Busirane. Some commentators have seen in this episode a critique that reveals that the Petrarchan writer (represented here by Busirane, who writes with living blood) is finally uninterested in establishing an intersubjective link with the beloved lady whom he so ardently woos. From this standpoint, Amoret chained to the pillar of iron is a symbol of the Petrarchan beloved reduced to a mere token in the game of masculine poetic authority. Drawing attention to the obvious, physical component of the image, Elizabeth J. Bellamy has recently noted that Busirane does not try to win over Amoret at all but rather seeks to preserve "a magus-like distance from the object of his own sadism." Yet having identified distance as constitutive of the Amoret-Busirane relationship (rather than a mark of its failure), Bellamy goes on to see Busirane's sadism as standing in "the precarious space of married chastity, that scarcely emergent component of the still-evolving institution known as bourgeois marriage." For Bellamy, Spenser solves the problem generated by modern, married sexuality's resistance "to accommodation into literary representation" by replacing it with the picture of Busirane's torture of Amoret. See "Waiting for Hymen: Literary History as 'Symptom' in Spenser and Milton," *ELH* 64 (1997): 391–414, 406–7. I do not see Spenser anticipating the modern notion of married sexuality so much as pointing to historical rivals.

20. If something like a wish (or even an aggressive prediction) of social disgrace is expressed, however fleetingly, in these lines, then Spenser's wish came true,

for in 1592 Raleigh was indeed disgraced and exiled from the court after his unsanctioned marriage to one of Elizabeth's maids-in-waiting became public. The second half of the Belphoebe and Timias story, in which Timias loses all of the marks of his social existence, is an allegory of Raleigh's fall from court.

21. Arthur's nonrecognition of the impassioned Timias encapsulates a complex historical transition in the terms for social relationships between men. When Timias decides to pursue Florimel's attacker rather than Florimel herself at the beginning of book 3, he disrupts the service bond between lord and squire. This disruption is now confirmed through the insertion of Belphebe—allegorically, a version of the absolute monarch—as a kind of third term in their relationship. Belphebe has her own attendants, the damsels who finally catch up to her and Timias in stanza 37, and by the time the story of Timias and Belphebe finally ends in book 4, Timias will essentially join these damsels. By inserting Timias into this story with Belphebe, Spenser traces a long arc from the position of servant to the mythologically feudal Arthur to servant (in a very different sense) of the absolute monarch; in between stands the body deprived of the inherited, blood-borne social identity that old-style aristocratic service depends on.

22. Britomart is a lady dressed as a knight and on a quest to find Arthegall, with whom she is to found the kingly line that leads to Queen Elizabeth. Her destabilized gender position seems to open her to a number of sexualized encounters throughout book 3, her encounter with Malecasta among them. Kathryn Schwartz also points to the role of Britomart's complex gender position in wreaking havoc with the codes of chivalry. Discussing the Castle Joyeous episode, for example, Schwartz points to the way Britomart articulates the norms of courtesy outside the castle but fails to specify her role (whether as feminine beloved or as masculine protector). This is an important supplement to my own account of the sexually productive conflict between competing modes of courtesy or civility. See *Tough Love: Amazon Encounters in the English Renaissance* (Durham, NC: Duke University Press, 2000), 165. Commenting on Britomart's overall allegorical trajectory, Heather Dubrow notes that her experience of Arthegall itself oscillates between recognizing the social significance of the union, a perspective emphasized by her nurse Glauce, and seeing a relationship with him as fundamentally inconceivable in a way that makes it look more like the sexuality that ties her to Malecasta. See *Echoes of Desire,* 257–58.

23. Helgerson, "Two Versions of Gothic," in *Forms of Nationhood.*

24. C. S. Lewis, *The Allegory of Love: A Study in Medieval Tradition* (New York: Oxford University Press, 1936), 338–44.

25. See Helgerson, "The New Poet Presents Himself," in *Self-Crowned Laureates.* To a certain extent the notion of a professional poet seems to require the existence of a literary market. I am thinking here of Bourdieu's theoretical account

in *The Field of Cultural Production,* ed. and trans. Randal Johnson (New York: Columbia University Press, 1993). In a sense, therefore, Helgerson ends up pointing to a hiatus in literary history; while writers a generation after Spenser could increasingly turn to the commercial market to provide an alternative source of literary authority, a development that Helgerson's model of careerism anticipates, Spenser could only negate, more or less theatrically, more or less overtly, a notion of courtly service that he nonetheless had to acknowledge as the only clear career track open to him.

26. Ian Frederick Moulton attends to the possibility of an "erotics of a literary career" in his chapter on Ben Jonson in *Before Pornography: Erotic Writing in Early Modern England* (New York: Oxford University Press, 2000). In noting the difficulty of defining pornography before there is a discourse of pornography, Moulton celebrates the way eroticism spills through many discourses.

27. It is certainly worth pointing out, however, that Queen Elizabeth's sexuality, at least, is not tangential to her social world but a central component of her core ideology, which she used to manage competition between her courtiers. For one account of this mode of politics, see Philippa Berry, *Of Chastity and Power: Elizabethan Literature and the Unmarried Queen* (New York: Routledge, 1989). In regard to the role sexuality plays in mediating Spenser's relationship to the court, see also Greenblatt, "To Fashion a Gentleman," in *Renaissance Self-Fashioning.* Greenblatt argues that Spenser treats sexuality as a dangerous site that requires constant vigilance and more generally that Spenser worships power, which is indubitably true though I see this worship in a rather more perverse light than Greenblatt does.

28. Other writers exhibit an analogously exorbitant ambition. For a persuasive discussion of the unsettled and unsettling quality of John Donne's ambition, see John Carey, *John Donne: Life, Mind, and Art* (Boston: Faber and Faber, 1990).

29. See Goldberg, "Spenser's Familiar Letters," in *Sodometries.*

30. For the Elizabethans, friendship was a charged and somewhat overdetermined category. See Alan Bray, "Homosexuality and the Signs of Male Friendship in Elizabethan England," in *Queering the Renaissance,* ed. Goldberg. Rambuss offers an indispensable account of the use Spenser makes of homosocial ties, including the socially ambiguous role of secretary to a great man, in articulating the terms of his literary career. See *Spenser's Secret Career.*

31. *The Faerie Queene,* 12.1.9. I follow Goldberg's vital *Endlesse Worke* in taking the phrase "endless work" as an emblem of Spenser's relationship to his own writing. I am suggesting that for Spenser, the compulsive writing that lies behind his curious career amounts to a way of exploring and documenting other forms of relationality, other mechanisms of social bonding, what Goldberg has referred to as "another social scene," just beyond the dominant mechanisms of sociability.

See his introduction to *Queering the Renaissance,* 5. Disappointment with the re-sources of his social world lends some of Spenser's later writings a satirical edge; elements of book 4 of *The Faerie Queene,* for example, give us the beginning of an organized critique of the normal mechanisms of social bonding that underpin Elizabethan society.

32. John Guillory, *Poetic Authority,* 28.

4. AT THE LIMITS OF THE SOCIAL WORLD

1. Using the notion of homosocial ties as a yardstick of normativity, critics often frame dramatic representations of desire as either functionally social or anti-social. Desire functions socially when it leads to useful marriages or produces heirs, or even when it generates deep ties of affection between men that can then be consolidated through a tactical marriage that binds families. By contrast, desire seems antisocial when it attacks sex-gender norms, for example, by leading women to rebel against the authority of parents as in *Romeo and Juliet* or by running against the class hierarchy, as it famously does in Marlowe's *Edward II.* Drawing on Stephen Greenblatt's "subversion-containment" framework, critics often make both sides of the argument simultaneously. To cite a sophisticated example, in *Desire and Anxiety: Circulations of Sexuality in Shakespearean Drama* (New York: Routledge, 1992), Valerie Traub argues that plays both construct a historically nas-cent sexual ideology of romantic love and countersign a sociosexual order that sees such a romantic and individualistic sexuality as anarchic. In the last chapter of that study, however, Traub points to an important methodological innovation in the study of theatrical representations of sexuality by arguing that early mod-ern theatrical cross-dressing provides a "basis upon which homoeroticism can be safely explored" (118), an argument that anticipates her important later account of the "insignificance" of lesbian desire in "The (In)Significance of 'Lesbian' Desire in Early Modern England," in *Queering the Renaissance,* ed. Goldberg. Mario DiGangi examines how socially functional same-sex relations are depicted in different dra-matic genres in *The Homoerotics of Early Modern Drama* (New York: Cambridge University Press, 1997). In a rich discussion of the invisibility of early modern eroticism on the stage, Celia R. Daileader argues that early modern drama approaches sexuality and eroticism by self-consciously pointing to and theorizing an "offstage" space that houses those things that cannot be brought onto the stage, often endowing them with a transcendent potential. See *Eroticism on the Renais-sance Stage: Transcendence, Desire, and the Limits of the Visible* (New York: Cambridge University Press, 1998).

2. My discussion of the social function of sexuality in a patriarchal society obviously draws on Sedgwick, *Between Men,* as well as Gayle Rubin's notion of

sex-gender systems in "The Traffic in Women," in *Toward an Anthropology of Women,* ed. Rayna Reiter (New York: Monthly Review Press, 1975).

3. One symptom of Shakespeare's vision of a special form of sexual intersubjectivity that coexists alongside the functional norms of Renaissance society without attacking *or* affirming them is the two-world structure characteristic of many plays, especially comedies such as *As You Like It* and *A Midsummer Night's Dream.* At one level, these plays register the norms of Renaissance patriarchy and use these norms to project a dramatic resolution that reaffirms the structures of the Renaissance sex-gender system; at another level, however, these plays systematically explore forms of desire and interpersonal bonding that simply do not fit into the dominant mechanisms of early modern social life. *A Midsummer Night's Dream,* for example, begins by projecting a frankly patriarchal outcome in which Hermia's desires must give way to the social need to use marriage to establish functional alliances between families, but Shakespeare uses the space of the play itself, and a detour through the second world of the woods, to explore forms of desire that seem incompatible with this homosocial order. Critics have tended to emphasize one side of this equation or the other, either seizing on the way the narrative arc ultimately reaffirms dominant social structures or, alternatively, framing the desires that well up in the interval as radical challenges to the sex-gender status quo. I suggest that the two-world structure really points to the *simultaneous* coexistence in the plays of a social system of gender and sexuality that reflects the repressive norms of Shakespeare's own society *and* an experience of sexual bonding that is radically, even perversely, indifferent to the needs or requirements of the early modern sex-gender system. To some extent, the structure that Shakespeare uses to think about sexuality is characteristic of much humanist writing, and the two-world motif is discussed in Harry Berger's classic essay "The Renaissance Imagination: Second World and Green World," in *Second World and Green World: Studies in Renaissance Fiction-Making,* Harry Berger Jr. (Berkeley: University of California Press, 1988), 3–40.

4. See Eric S. Mallin, "Emulous Factions and the Collapse of Chivalry," in *Inscribing the Time* (Berkeley: University of California Press, 1995). Identifying (sequentially) Achilles and Hector as the Earl of Essex, Mallin identifies the Greek camp and the Trojan-Greek struggle as representing the death throes of Elizabeth's central strategy of power, namely, encouraging nobles at court to emulate and compete with each other. In *Troilus and Cressida,* this competition eclipses the queen herself. Though Mallin's account does not consistently distinguish between homosocial and homosexual relationships, it has the virtue of foregrounding the emerging symbolic economy (organized around what he terms "chivalry") as a complex, potentially totalizing terrain in which social conflict is played out according to an autonomous social and cultural logic. Mallin essentially reads the

play as offering a prescription for a successful social economy (his article ends by invoking the future), whereas I see Shakespeare making strategic use of a fundamentally immature symbolic economy to designate social breakdowns that the play then identifies as properly sexual. Heather James reviews the connection between the play and the Essex rebellion in her chapter on Troilus and Cressida, "Tricks We Play on the Dead: Making History in *Troilus and Cressida*," in *Shakespeare's Troy: Drama, Politics, and the Translation of Empire* (New York: Cambridge University Press, 1997).

5. See the Arden edition of the play edited by David Bevington (Walton-on-Thames, UK: Thomas Nelson and Sons, 1998), 120. All quotations from the play follow this edition. This preface addresses an "eternal reader" to tell him that "you have here a new play, never staled with the stage, never clapper-clawed with the palms of the vulgar." It therefore casts the public theaters as a scene of vulgar culture that should be avoided by those with pretensions to refined taste, and it imagines that the text of the play might serve to affirm a community of readers with elite taste because it has never been contaminated by the community of vulgar theatergoers.

6. For a careful description of the eighteenth-century symbolic economy in which culture is used to mediate social position, see Jonathan Brody Kramnick, *Making the English Canon* (New York: Cambridge University Press: 1998). I see Shakespeare as engaged in a complex moment in which elements of the sociological regime of systematically regulated access to cultural goods that Kramnick describes are emerging but have not yet been consolidated. In this historical hiatus a number of alternative models of poetry are imagined, models that include Shakespeare's impulse to archive human affects as a means of documenting an alternative social scene.

7. Pandarus makes the comparison frequently; for example, at 1.1.75–77 he says of his niece, "and she were not kin to me, she would be as fair o' Friday as Helen is o' Sunday."

8. Traub notes that in this play all women seem like "foreigners" (*Desire and Anxiety*, 77). Traub situates the play within the early modern discourse of syphilis and identifies women as potent sources of political as well as sexual infection. Traub goes on to make the suggestive claim that under the pressure of the discourse of syphilis, *Troilus and Cressida* makes all sexual relationships seem diseased. In his survey of the trope of disease in the play, Jonathan Gil Harris suggestively comments that the play seems like it might have begun as a comedy of humors. See "'The Enterprise is Sick': Pathologies of Value and Transnationality in *Troilus and Cressida*," *Renaissance Drama* 29 (2000): 3–37.

9. In an effort to reinvigorate the apparently exhausted homosocial roots of the war, Hector challenges the Greeks to fight for the honor of their women. The

wording of the challenge, which is delivered by Aeneas, suggests that heterosexuality simply spells out the terms of social competition between men. He dares the Greeks to fight for their beloveds, or else "he'll say in Troy, when he retires, / The Grecian dames are sunburnt and not worth / The splinter of a lance" (1.3.281–83). Insofar as Helen is one notable "Grecian dame," this amounts to threatening to do the work of the Greeks for them by convincing the Trojans to let Helen go— something Hector does in fact try to do in the Trojan war council scene. But in Hector's challenge to the Greeks, women are only an excuse for a rivalry between men. For a historically rooted but theoretical account of this mode of social competition, see Whiggham, *Ambition and Privilege*. Whiggham's account tends to deemphasize the sexual politics that, together with the cultural politics he describes, define the gestalt of "normal procedures" of social life against which Shakespeare rebels in the interest of making sexual relationships socially legible. For an account that attempts to connect cultural and sexual politics at the court of Elizabeth, see Berry, *Of Chastity and Power*.

10. In a striking discussion, David Foley McCandless argues that Shakespeare presents the Trojan War as a process of emasculation, though he argues that Troilus refuses to embrace masochism as a form of sexual gratification. McCandless also notes Cressida's disavowal of sexuality, something I also go on to discuss. See "Troilus and Cressida," in *Gender and Performance in Shakespeare's Problem Comedies* (Bloomington: Indiana University Press, 1997).

11. Because patriarchal society subsumes male-female bonds beneath the male-male bonds on which social (as opposed to biological) reproduction depends, the fact that Troilus fails to see Cressida as a token in social exchanges with men, and instead sees her as the object of specifically sexual attention, opens him to the risk of being feminized. Similarly, because male-male bonds lie at the very heart of patriarchal society, suspending the social consequences of such relationships can be redescribed as an attack on society itself. This redescription is often accomplished by deploying the feared category of sodomy, something I will go on to discuss. But I see both the accusation of feminization and the accusation of sodomy as ways of disavowing the specifically sexual relationship that is characterized not by its danger to the social world but by its indifference to it. Specifically sexual relationships are endangered when social consequences, whether bad or good, are reattached to them; the specific ways that social consequences can be reattached to sexual bonds will be one of the key differences in how men and women experience the sexual turn in Shakespeare's play.

12. Shakespeare's interest in defining sexual relationships in a way that bypasses the intimacy mediated by shared emotions is paralleled by Vogler's discussion of marital sexuality, "Sex and Talk," as a place in which the social norms that govern domestic life are temporarily violated.

13. Troilus is, of course, a prince of Troy. The point is that in order to define the relationship as sexual, Troilus disavows a real social status in order to invest his relationship with Cressida with the radical social impossibility that alone is erotic. This tactical renunciation of real social status is also expressed by his virtual demotion to the status of a woman. Declining Pandarus's entreaties to enter battle, for example, Troilus responds, "I am weaker than a woman's tear" (1.1.9).

14. Commenting on the epilogue in which Pandarus announces both that he has become infected with venereal disease and that the theater audience will become infected, Traub argues that the audience is here forced to acknowledge that it is "in" a kind of sexual relationship. See *Desire and Anxiety*, 80. As I go on to discuss, I agree that there is a kind of analogy between sexual relationships and the cultural consumption of theater, but I do not believe that this fact is meant to elicit audience anxiety.

15. See Kenneth Palmer, ed., *Troilus and Cressida* (New York: Routledge, 1994), 303.

16. See René Girard, "The Politics of Desire in *Troilus and Cressida*," in *Shakespeare and the Question of Theory*, ed. Patricia Parker and Geoffrey Hartman (New York: Methuen, 1985), 188–209, 198.

17. Linda Charnes, too, sees the play as a struggle to restore homosociability; as she puts it, the abduction of Helen is important only "insofar as it enables several kinds of 'commerce' between Greek and Trojan men." See "'So Unsecret to Ourselves': Notorious Identity and the Material Subject in Shakespeare's *Troilus and Cressida*," *Shakespeare Quarterly* 40 (Winter 1989): 413–40, 424. A version of this essay also appears in her *Notorious Identity: Materializing the Subject in Shakespeare* (Cambridge, MA: Harvard University Press, 1993). Charnes's account is valuable because she attempts to insert the traffic-in-women model into the social and psychic dynamic of attaining social status. She writes, "through the holding of Helen, difference is established, and with difference (in the language of the play, 'distinction') 'reputation' is built and confirmed" (424). Charnes sees what she terms "aggressive homoeroticism" as a part of homosocial relationships. My own account describes the social logic of distinction as a potent way of disrupting a homosocial model that depends on the traffic in women but includes, or can include, sex between men.

18. Troilus's way of salvaging sexuality by ascribing biological superiority to the Greeks along with Cressida suggests a complex link between homosocial struggle and the relational impossibility that opens the sexual domain. On the one hand, once Cressida is handed over to the Greeks, seeing her becomes physically dangerous, a fact that fits in perfectly with Troilus's conception of sexual desire. When Cressida reminds Troilus that it will be incredibly perilous for him to visit her in the Greek camp, Troilus excitedly embraces this risk: "I'll grow friend with

danger" (4.4.69). On the other hand, however, there is a sense that once she has been removed to the Greek camp, Cressida becomes off-limits for Troilus in a new way that threatens the specificity of the sexual connection between them despite his efforts to preserve it. After all, in the Greek camp Cressida is possessed by men, by her father Calchas (whose blood she tries unsuccessfully to disavow: "I have forgot my father. / I know no touch of consanguinity" [4.2.97]) but also by Diomedes on whose protection Calchas evidently relies and to whom he has evidently turned over his daughter.

19. Here I reflect Jonathan Dollimore's suggestive claim that "Cressida internalizes the contradiction of the war itself"; but whereas Dollimore connects this fact to the split in Cressida's subjectivity that Troilus registers when he says, "this is and is not Cressid" (5.2.144), I examine the way it authorizes a special mode of sexual intersubjectivity that persists as a potential even if it is not actualized in the imagined world of the play. See *Radical Tragedy: Religion, Ideology, and Power in the Drama of Shakespeare and His Contemporaries* (Brighton, UK: Harvester Press, 1984), 48.

20. Thersites compares Menelaus and Troilus at 5.2.200.

21. David Hillman sees the use of digestive metaphors as a defining feature of the play as a whole; he argues that *Troilus and Cressida* aims to "enact a restoration of words, and of the ideals created out of them, in their sources inside the body." "The Gastric Epic: *Troilus and Cressida,*" *Shakespeare Quarterly* 48, no. 3 (Autumn 1997): 295–313, 296.

22. See William Empson, *Some Versions of Pastoral* (New York: New Directions, 1960), 87–89.

23. Stanley Cavell's views on *Othello* are relevant to my discussion here. In "Othello and the Stake of the Other," in *Disowning Knowledge* (New York: Cambridge University Press, 1987), 125–42, Cavell argues that Othello's jealousy amounts to a skepticism about the possibility of knowing Desdemona. As the title of Cavell's book already suggests, Cavell sees Othello's skepticism as a willful forgetting of what Othello already knows about Desdemona. Within Cavell's application of Wittgenstein's language philosophy, this skepticism is equivalent to the turn to metaphysics; the only way out of the impasse that this metaphysical question generates is to return to "ordinary language" and to the "natural forms of life" that ordinary language points to. In my own reading of *Othello,* by contrast, I focus on Othello's impulse to reject precisely the "natural forms of life" figured by the bourgeois bliss that Desdemona threatens to reduce him to. In this regard, Othello's relationship with Iago is valuable because it systematically colonizes the offensively ordinary relationship with Desdemona. But I see in this alternative relationship (as well as in the powerful affects that it liberates) social alternatives that lie dormant within the heart of the "natural forms of life" that a happy marriage would supposedly countersign. Shakespeare's interest in these alternatives does not

seem so much like a lapse into the "metaphysics" that invokes the apparently time-less (and insoluble) encounter of the self and the other, as an impulse to revolu-tionize the "natural forms of life" embodied in ordinary language.

24. Gregory Bredbeck, *Sodomy and Interpretation: Marlowe to Milton* (Ithaca, NY: Cornell University Press, 1991), 33–48. A version of Bredbeck's comments on the play also appeared in "Constructing Patroclus: The High and Low Discourses of Renaissance Sodomy," in *The Performance of Power,* ed. Sue Ellen Case and Janelle Reinert (Iowa City: University of Iowa Press, 1991). Bredbeck sees Thersites' somewhat hysterical comments as participating in a Renaissance discourse of sodomy that is designed to reinforce normative social categories and hierarchies. Describing the way sodomy also organizes Ulysses' oration on social order, Bred-beck comments that "the sodomitical allusions within the play do not specify sexual difference so much as they open up a vast and complicated network of political meanings" (45). Bredbeck's discussion allows me to make the point that when Shakespeare makes sexual relationships publicly significant by locating them in spaces of social dysfunction, he differentiates them from the kind of antisocial-ity identified by the discourse of sodomy.

25. Anger at the murder of his friend finally drives Achilles back onto the battlefield and thus sets the classical story of the Trojan War back on course to its fateful denouement. This allows Ulysses to declare a victory not against the Tro-jans but against Achilles: "O, courage, courage, princes! Great Achilles/ Is arming, weeping, cursing, vowing vengeance./ Patroclus' wounds have roused his drowsy blood" (5.5.30–32). This seems like a moment in which social consequences accrue to a specifically sexual bond, just as Nestor hopes, although what Achilles ends up doing on the battlefield (murdering Hector in a spectacular violation of chivalry) seems not to be exactly what Ulysses had in mind for him.

26. Insofar as it simply keeps him from his social duties, the relationship with Patroclus is analogous to the relationship Achilles is said to have with the Trojan princess Polyxena. But while Achilles' relationship with Patroclus elicits the charge of sodomy, Achilles' relationship with Polyxena elicits the charge of feminization. When Ulysses remarks that "better would it fit Achilles much, / To throw down Hector than Polyxena" (3.3.209–10), Patroclus himself draws the conclusion: "To this effect, Achilles, have I moved you./ A woman impudent and mannish grown/ Is not more loathed than an effeminate man / In time of action" (3.3.218–21).

27. Affects have both a "feeling" component and an "expression" component; while fear is a feeling that belongs to a particular person at a particular time, it is also a characteristic tensing of the facial muscles that is as available to observers as it is to the one who feels fear. For one account, see the work of Silvan Tomkins reprinted in *Shame and Its Sisters,* ed. Sedgwick and Frank. While modern observers are often struck most strongly by the feeling component of affects and only come

to recognize the importance of the expression component through reflection, the reverse appears to have been true for early modern observers. Part of the explanation lies in the commitment of early modern observers to a humoral theory in which affective states are thought of as ratios of blood, water, black bile, and yellow bile. In Shakespeare's play, the expressive component of affects is so strongly emphasized that Achilles' pride is significant to other characters trying to enter into a relationship with him. Early modern affects essentially define states of the body that place it in definite relations to other bodies. In developing this account I have obviously drawn on important recent work on early modern affects, especially Paster, *The Body Embarrassed;* and Schoenfeldt, *Bodies and Selves in Early Modern England.* I have also benefited from Gail Kern Paster's useful account of Shakespeare's dramatic assumption that passions change the bodies of his characters and vice versa in a context before psychology and physiology had yet divorced. See "The Tragic Subject and Its Passions," in *The Cambridge Companion to Shakespearean Tragedy,* ed. McEachern.

28. For the inexpressibility topos, see Curtius, *European Literature and the Latin Middle Ages,* 159–62. The inexpressibility topos is frequently invoked in lyric poetry, often in the face of the beauties of a beloved lady, as it is by Troilus when he encounters Cressida and says that he has lost his powers of speech. Here the inexpressibility topos is applied to a social situation that is then redirected by Patroclus to energize a personal relationship that is analogous to the Troilus–Cressida bond. The emphasis on the theater's ability to represent registers of social life that it cannot actually bring before the audience is a recurring feature of Shakespeare's plays, most often deployed when it comes to representing the doings of the court to which regular theatergoers presumably had no access. In *1 Henry IV,* for example, when Falstaff and Hal playact the encounter between Hal and his father, it is the difference between the throne that is represented and the bar stool that is at hand that constitutes the pleasure of the theater for Mistress Quickly. Mistress Quickly is thus quite self-conscious about consuming *representations* of social distance, and the fact that she is consuming representations is crucial to her sense of where cultural pleasure comes from.

29. Charnes and Mallin both note that an actor playing the part of Ulysses would likely heighten the comedy of the complaint about Patroclus's comic theater by engaging in the very "slanderous imitation" that Ulysses also decries. If so, even as Ulysses complains about Achilles' nonrelationship with the Greek state, he (inadvertently?) opens a comparable relationship with the Greek state; just as Patroclus and Achilles draw the state into the bedroom for the purposes of pleasure, so their bedroom is drawn back into the state.

30. Using theater and theatricality to cement a sexual tie that has its roots in very real social contradictions but leaves those real social contradictions behind is

an important recurring feature in Shakespeare's plays. In *As You Like It,* to cite just one example, Rosalind adopts the disguise of a boy as a tactical means of responding to a very real problem in her social life; once she has assumed this disguise, however, the pleasures of theatricality quickly unhinge her from her strategic goals and social interests, and her disguise becomes a vehicle for a range of powerfully unconventional experiences of sexuality that can only be fit back into social life by means of a highly artificial deus ex machina conclusion. What joins theatricality and sexuality, in *As You Like It* as much as in *Troilus and Cressida,* is a shared attitude of indifference, distance, or even perverse detachment from conventions and norms of early modern social life that enables it to harness real social contradictions and use them to provoke sexuality.

31. Louis Montrose, *The Purpose of Playing: Shakespeare and the Cultural Politics of the Elizabethan Theater* (Chicago: University of Chicago Press, 1996), 34. In his striking study of the place of the theater, Steven Mullaney argues that the theater exploited a social contradiction between the court and the city authorities to emerge "as a cultural institution only by materially embodying that contradiction, dislocating itself from the confines of the existing social order and taking up a place on the margins of society." See *The Place of the Stage: License, Play, and Power in Renaissance England* (Chicago: University of Chicago Press, 1988), vii. Jean-Christophe Agnew offers a much more functionalist account of the special status of the theater as an institution apart from the social world in *Worlds Apart: The Market and the Theater in Anglo-American Thought, 1550–1750* (New York: Cambridge University Press, 1986).

32. In a powerful discussion of *Titus Andronicus,* Cynthia Marshall rightly suggests that Shakespeare was well aware of the pleasures of watching (and imagining being subjected to) violence; revealing the roots of the play's depictions of torture in early modern accounts of the suffering of martyrs, Marshall concludes that "the play deploys physical violence in disturbingly revelatory ways, troubling the familiar claims of audiences and critics to oppose violence, challenging the humanist aesthetic that sees suffering and pleasure as inherently unrelated" (*The Shattering of the Self,* 137). Though it is unclear whether the humanist aesthetic to which Marshall refers was yet consolidated in the early modern context, her vision of a form of aesthetic pleasure that is inherently or structurally inhumane is compelling, and I draw on it here in describing the private theater of Patroclus as a model for a socially dysfunctional theater.

33. For a general review of the anxiety surrounding theatricality in the early modern context, see Jonas Barish, *The Antitheatrical Prejudice* (Berkeley: University of California Press, 1981). I draw the idea of an imagined community from Benedict Anderson, *Imagined Communities: Reflections on the Origin and Spread of Nationalism* (New York: Verso, 1991). Jean Howard usefully frames early modern

attacks on the theater as attacks on social groups. See *The Stage and Social Struggle in Early Modern England* (New York: Routledge, 1994), especially chapter 2, "'Sathans Synagogue': The Theater as Constructed by Its Enemies." It is worth pointing out that responses to early modern antitheatrical attacks often argue that the theater serves other social interests than those the Puritans serve. Robert Weimann, for example, recovers the deep roots the institution of the theater has in the rituals and pleasures of a traditional, rural form of life Shakespeare himself presumably experienced in his country youth, and he therefore argues that Shakespeare's plays defend a vision of community that declines the puritan work ethic and celebrates pleasure as a fundamental goal of human life. What is striking about this defense is that Weimann endorses the assumption of the Puritan antitheatrical critics that the theater *ought* to serve social communities in some way and that it can be evaluated according to how well it carries out this function. What Shakespeare seems to suggest in *Troilus and Cressida,* by contrast, is that the theater is not a technology for forging or supporting functional communities of the kind Ulysses likes to imagine, but that it stands apart from conventional social life in a way that anticipates the procedures of a fully autonomous culture. In essence, Shakespeare responds to the charge of the antitheatrical critics not with the claim that the theater has beneficial social consequences after all (the strategy pioneered by Aristotle against Plato but also deployed by Sidney against Gosson), but that the theater has no functional social consequences at all. It is a vision ironically seconded by panic-stricken Puritan accounts of the Elizabethan playhouses as the scenes of lively, sexualized forms of collective life defined by heterogeneity and noncoincidence of interests, a form of life that seems no less real for being incapable of being consolidated into an imagined community that might survive the place and time of performance. Commenting specifically on *Troilus and Cressida,* Laura Levine argues that the play offers a theoretical defense against some of the anxieties of the antitheatrical critics only to feed that anxiety all the more assiduously, both in the internal scenes of theater and in relation to the audience. See *Men in Women's Clothing: Anti-Theatricality and Effeminization, 1579–1642* (New York: Cambridge University Press, 1994).

34. Perhaps we should say that from Shakespeare's standpoint there is no cultural relationship in precisely the way that, to invoke the Lacanian slogan, there is no sexual relationship. Lacan uses this slogan to capture the interpersonal incommensurability that he takes to be fundamental to sexuality. See Jacques Lacan, *Feminine Sexuality: Jacques Lacan and the Ecole Freudienne,* ed. Juliet Mitchell and ed. and trans. Jacqueline Rose (New York: Macmillan, 1982). This Lacanian slogan has also recently been galvanized toward an anticommunitarian politics in Judith Butler, Ernesto Laclau, and Slavoj Žižek, *Contingency, Hegemony, Universality: Contemporary Dialogues on the Left* (London: Verso, 2000).

35. The sadomasochism I allude to here raises the question of the connection between affects and pain. Affects always orient an individual toward the world (i.e., the person, thing, animal, object, or concrete thought that inspires the affect), and in this regard affects (even painful ones) seem to differ from pain. In *The Body in Pain* (New York: Oxford University Press, 1985), Elaine Scarry describes pain as tending to push patients into a solipsistic state that can be bridged only through specialized techniques (for example, the medical questionnaires designed to elicit information about the specific qualities of pain and thus to return pain to the public world). Affects, by contrast, appear to integrate the individual into the world, and in particular into the social world. It is for this reason that the pride of Achilles, for example, names a specific mode of integration into the social world and becomes significant to other characters trying to define a social relationship with him.

36. In "Fragments of Nationalism in *Troilus and Cressida,*" *Shakespeare Quarterly* 51, no. 2 (Summer 2000): 181–200, Matthew A. Greenfield suggestively argues that "if Shakespeare's histories maintain an investment in some idea of national community, *Troilus and Cressida* works programmatically to reveal the nation as a collection of frictions" (181).

37. Here I am drawing on Leo Bersani's claim that one of the basic functions of literature and art is to engage in what he terms "mythic reconfigurations" of basic modes of relationality. See Tim Dean, Hal Foster, and Kaja Silverman, "A Conversation with Leo Bersani," *October* 82 (Spring 1998): 3–16, 4. For a practical application of this account to Jean Genet, among others writers, see Bersani's *Homos* (Cambridge, MA: Harvard University Press, 1995).

5. POETIC AUTONOMY AND THE HISTORY OF SEXUALITY IN SHAKESPEARE'S *SONNETS*

1. See Joseph Pequigney, *Such Is My Love: A Study of Shakespeare's Sonnets* (Chicago: University of Chicago Press, 1985), which argues that "the psychological dynamics of the poet's relations with the friend comply in large measure with Freud's authoritative discussions of homosexuality" (1). Pequigney's readings were important in their moment, but he tends to rely on an indefensible literalism in relation to both literature and psychoanalysis. His basic point that the reality of sexual desire between men is captured by the sonnets is incontrovertible and is an axiom of my own discussion.

2. On the history of editors confronting the homoeroticism of the sonnets, see Peter Stallybrass, "Editing as Cultural Formation: The Sexing of Shakespeare's Sonnets," *Modern Language Quarterly* 54, no. 1 (Spring 1993): 91–103. Stallybrass draws attention to the insistence with which early editors confronted and corrected

the image of Shakespeare as sodomite; for him, the feared and repeatedly refuted notion of Shakespeare's homosexuality paradoxically lies at the heart of the eighteenth-century project of casting Shakespeare as the national poet. Besides editorial rewriting—changing gender pronouns or giving misleading titles—editors have sought to contain the relationship by historicizing it into an intense but ultimately platonic Elizabethan friendship. This strategy is still available to Douglas Bush and Alfred Harbage, the editors of the 1970 Penguin edition of the sonnets. In their introduction they admit the possibility of homoeroticism in the sonnets only to dismiss it: "Since modern readers are unused to such ardor in masculine friendship and are likely to leap at the notion of homosexuality (a notion sufficiently refuted by the sonnets themselves), we may remember that such an ideal . . . could exist in real life." See William Shakespeare, *The Sonnets,* ed. Douglas Bush and Alfred Harbage (New York: Penguin Books, 1970), 13. In her thoughtful discussion, Margreta de Grazia is somewhat skeptical of the amount of modern attention that has been paid to Benson's changes, noting that his revisions are not as thoroughgoing as is sometimes supposed. She makes the important claim that the modern tendency to emphasize the supposed scandal of same-gender eroticism has come at the expense of paying attention to the (for her, real) scandal of cross-class eroticism. See Margreta de Grazia, "The Scandal of Shakespeare's Sonnets," in *Shakespeare's Sonnets: Critical Essays,* ed. James Schiffer (New York: Garland Publishers, 1999).

3. Richard Barnfield, *The Complete Poems,* ed. George Klawitter (Selinsgrove, PA: Susquehanna University Press, 1990). I am drawing on Smith, *Homosexual Desire in Shakespeare's England,* 99–115.

4. In *Homosexual Desire in Shakespeare's England,* Smith takes note of the enormous number of forms of relationship that Shakespeare reviews but that all seem unable to capture the specificity of the relationship between Shakespeare and the Young Man: Smith identifies references in the sonnets to the relationship of friends, of a knight and his lady, of a father and his son, and of a husband and his wife, among others. I think Smith correctly diagnoses Shakespeare's impulse in the sonnets to render a same-sex relationship legible as sexual, but for Smith Shakespeare solves the problem only by resorting to an identitarian framework. Arguing against the Foucauldian slogan that there were no homosexuals in Elizabethan England, Smith essentially claims that Shakespeare was the first one. "It will not do," he concludes, "to say that Shakespeare's sonnets cannot be about homosexual desire since no one else in early modern England addressed homosexual desire in just these terms. Using a new imaginative vocabulary to talk about an old subject brings Shakespeare to a conclusion altogether different from that of poets in other sequences of sonnets" (265). Smith sees in the sonnets a "way of putting sex into discourse" that is a version of Foucault's *scientia sexualis* in which the self is

interrogated about its sexual desires. This interrogation is what the sonnets allow us readers to do: "the persona speaks to himself" and "we are privileged to 'overhear' . . . we share with the speaker a privacy and secrecy different in degree and in kind from the much more public performance that goes on in pastoral monologues" (232).

5. Smith, "I, you, he, she, and we: On the Sexual Politics of Shakespeare's Sonnets," in *Shakespeare's Sonnets: Critical Essays,* ed. Schiffer, 172.

6. I also suggest, somewhat speculatively, that by entrusting men who love each other and who are set apart from the social world because of it with the responsibility of shepherding the alternative social energy that emerges in Wyatt's Petrarch translations, Shakespeare may be pointing to a future in which sexual minority communities are invested with the power to recast and reimagine the most basic forms of sociability by which society is structured.

7. Fineman famously claims that in his sonnets Shakespeare invents heterosexuality. See *Shakespeare's Perjured Eye: Poetic Subjectivity in the Sonnets* (Berkeley: University of California Press, 1986). For an important book-length study of the sonnets that transposes Fineman's psychoanalytic claims into an early modern theological vocabulary, see Lisa Freinkel, *Reading Shakespeare's Will: The Theology of Figure from Augustine to the Sonnets* (New York: Columbia University Press, 2002). Freinkel also offers an acute discussion of anti-Semitism in *The Merchant of Venice* that attends to the social role of melancholy.

8. Smith, *Homosexual Desire in Shakespeare's England,* 257.

9. All citations of Shakespeare's *Sonnets* are from Katherine Duncan-Jones's new Arden edition (New York: Thomas Nelson and Sons, 1997). I have also consulted Stephen Booth's *Shakespeare's Sonnets* (New Haven, CT: Yale University Press, 1977) throughout for his useful analytic commentary.

10. Joel Fineman has taken the line "perjured eye" as indicative of a new kind of subjectivity that is explicitly Lacanian (split internally) and engaged in what Fineman takes to be definitive of heterosexual relationships (defined by knowledge about the impossibility of knowing the other). He sees this as a turn against a long tradition of erotic poetry in which the poet identifies with the perfections of the beloved. I will offer some criticism of Fineman's claims.

11. See Jonathan Goldberg, "Romeo and Juliet's Open R's," in *Queering the Renaissance,* ed. Goldberg. In "The Scandal of Shakespeare's Sonnets," de Grazia makes a similar point.

12. See Valerie Traub, "Sex without Issue: Sodomy, Reproduction, and Signification in Shakespeare's Sonnets," in *Shakespeare's Sonnets,* ed. Schiffer. For Traub, panic at the thought of heterosexuality is the necessary consequence of the sonnets' having resorted to an ideology of sexual reproduction to "authorize" male-male desire through an explicit focus (in the early sonnets) on producing an heir.

One important question that this approach raises is whether a sexualized rela-tionship between men would need to be "authorized" by a reproductive ideology in the first place.

13. The important idea of a "sex-gender system" is from Gayle Rubin, "The Traffic in Women," in *Toward an Anthropology of Women*, ed. Reiter.

14. See Sedgwick, *Between Men*, especially chapter 2, "Swan in Love: The Example of Shakespeare's Sonnets." References are cited internally.

15. See William Empson's virtuoso reading of "They That Have Power to Hurt and Will Do None" in *Some Versions of Pastoral*, 88. Empson suggestively expands his reading of the sonnets into a discussion of the Henriad by seeing Hal as a version of the Young Man. In discussing *1 Henry IV*, Empson rightly diagnoses a deep streak of masochism in Shakespeare's account of desire. My point here is to specify that masochism in a historically concrete social context. Discussing the same poem, Lynne Magnusson ("'Power to Hurt': Language and Service in Sid-ney's Household Letters and Shakespeare's Sonnets," *ELH* 65 [1998]: 799–824) also emphasizes the ambiguities of the service relationship Shakespeare seems to imag-ine with his beloved.

16. De Grazia rightly considers it likely that Shakespeare would "experience the Young Man's aristocratic otherness before the Dark Lady's bourgeois same-ness" (De Grazia, "The Scandal of Shakespeare's Sonnets," 101). I add only that Shakespeare himself defines the world of the sonnets in such a way as to ensure that aristocratic status is a sign of fundamental alterity that forecloses the possi-bility of a successful interpersonal bond.

17. John F. Reichert argues that one source for the reproduction sonnets gen-erally, but sonnet 20 in particular, is Erasmus's "Epistle to Persuade a Young Man to Marriage," from Erasmus's epistolary manual. See "Sonnet XX and Erasmus's 'Epistle to Perswade a Yong Gentleman to Marriage,'" *Shakespeare Quarterly* 16 (1965): 238–40. For Reichert, citing this source is, of course, a way of disavowing an erotic connection. This Erasmian source, however, suggests a complex position for Shakespeare that is analogous to the position of humanist tutors to aristocrats. Barbara Correll argues that humanists negotiate their position to the aristocrats they both teach and serve by imagining themselves in the position of a woman who teaches her husband how to control her. See "Malleable Material, Models of Power: Woman in Erasmus's 'Marriage Group' and *Good Manners in Boys*," in *The End of Conduct*. Insofar as Shakespeare adopts the stance of the humanist tutor in order to argue that the Young Man should turn away from his tutor altogether, he intensifies the dynamic Correll describes.

18. Lorna Hutson also suggests that the Young Man's social status is identified as not needing cultural inflation. She writes, "The inward worth which did not need painting [i.e., poetry] is revealed to inhere not in the interpretive relation,

the encounter with the text, but in the husbandry which appeared to have been superseded, the lines of life which produce noble bloods: 'And their gross painting might be better us'd, / Where cheeks need blood.'" See "Why the Lady's Eyes Are Nothing Like the Sun," in *Women, Texts, and Histories, 1575–1760,* ed. Clare Brant and Diane Purkiss (New York: Routledge, 1993), 20.

19. Equally at stake, of course, is a relationship that is not socially legible, that goes beyond the kind of ties that can join men in functionally social ways in the early modern world. In sonnet 72 ("O, lest the world should task you to recite / What merit lived in me that you should love") Shakespeare worries that the world will turn to the Young Man for an obituary after Shakespeare's death, thus endowing their relationship with a social legitimacy that Shakespeare seeks everywhere to sidestep.

20. See Laplanche, *Life and Death in Psychoanalysis.*

21. Shakespeare identifies with the Young Man and feels whole, and yet this identification is inseparable from looking forward to inevitable, self-shattering rejection. Perhaps the most extreme manifestation of this conjunction comes in sonnet 31 in which Shakespeare claims that having the Young Man restores all the friends and lovers who have died along the way: "Thy bosom is endeared with all hearts / Which I by lacking, have supposed dead." Yet even as Shakespeare fantasizes about feeling magically reunited with lost friends, he is compelled to imagine the Young Man as a Frankenstein-like monster whose body is stitched together from pieces of Shakespeare's dead friends. Technically, Shakespeare claims that the Young Man gets all the love that Shakespeare has owed to many different people because the Young Man restores to Shakespeare all those he has lost, but the image of the Young Man as a grave where buried love lives finally provides only a rather ghoulish reminder of loss, emptiness, and incompleteness. This is one of very few poems where Shakespeare imagines having the young Man for himself, but while he has him Shakespeare finds that he has something that is full of death.

22. For a powerful discussion of the sense of loss that runs through so much Renaissance literature and that represents a context for my own reading of the moments of intense melancholy in the *Sonnets,* see Lynn Enterline, *The Tears of Narcissus: Melancholia and Masculinity in Early Modern Writing* (Stanford, CA: Stanford University Press, 1995). For a discussion of the role of melancholy in the context of the modern subject's experience of the structures of power that subjugate it but on which it nonetheless depends for its very existence, see Butler, *The Psychic Life of Power,* especially chapter 6, "Psychic Inceptions: Melancholy, Ambivalence, Rage."

23. For a countervailing account of the *Sonnets* that emphasizes the danger of indulging in the passions, see Schoenfeldt, "The Matter of Inwardness: Shakespeare's Sonnets," in *Bodies and Selves in Early Modern England.*

24. Sedgwick makes a similar observation in *Between Men,* 44–45.

25. Though the quarto indubitably reads "eyes" in line 10, Booth notes that most editors have doubted that Shakespeare intended the word twice in two lines. The most frequently adopted alternative is "brows." See Booth, *Shakespeare's Sonnets,* 435.

26. In a fascinating discussion of the historical connection between sexuality and the aesthetic category of the sublime, Richard Halpern argues that Shakespeare's *Sonnets* aestheticize the notion of sodomy to produce a characteristically Shakespearean homosexuality. See *Shakespeare's Perfume,* 21.

27. See Arthur Marotti, "'Love Is Not Love.'"

28. See Kerrigan's introduction to his edition of *The Sonnets and a Lover's Complaint* (New York: Penguin, 1988). Kerrigan frames his discussion in terms of the philosophical problem of whether it is possible to represent the beloved Young Man truthfully. Kerrigan notes that metaphorical comparisons make the beloved the place of an imagined competition between reader and author. Shakespeare declines to insert the Young Man into this kind of competition by withholding metaphors in his poems about the Young Man.

29. See Hutson, "Why the Ladies' Eyes Are Nothing Like the Sun."

30. The painful ease with which Shakespeare can be modern is also glanced at, I think, in sonnet 111 where Shakespeare bemoans (perhaps ironically) the fact that he must work to make money.

31. Bray notes that within the Elizabethan discourse of friendship, the moment a relationship seems antisocial is often aligned with the moment in which a relationship between patron and servant comes to appear driven by economic self-interest rather than the disinterested "service" that is supported by a clearly shared aristocratic status. See Bray, "Homosexuality and the Signs of Male Friendship in Elizabethan England," in *Queering the Renaissance,* ed. Goldberg.

32. Witnessing the intimacy that ties the Young Man to the rival poets essentially provokes a kind of panic that recharges the sexuality of great social distance. A crucial point is that Shakespeare does not position the sexuality that connects him and the Young Man within the intense mode of intimacy that shades into a kind of sex practice that induces panic; rather, Shakespearean sexuality derives from the panic that polices his own continuing exclusion from whatever the Young Man and the rival poets are up to.

33. For a thorough discussion of the structure and genesis of autonomy in literature, see Bourdieu, *The Field of Cultural Production,* especially chapter 1, "The Field of Cultural Production, or The Economic World Reversed."

34. Thus, for Oscar Wilde, the celebration of art for art's sake gave him a license for rediscovering the same-sex "truth" of the sonnets. See Wilde's literary detective novel, *The Portrait of Mr. W. H.,* in *Complete Shorter Fiction,* ed. Isobel Murray (New York: Oxford University Press, 1979).

35. Dean et al., "An Interview with Leo Bersani," 11.
36. Ibid.

EPILOGUE

1. In her virtuoso reading of Richardson's novel, Nancy Armstrong makes clear how the sexual intimacy Pamela finally achieves with Mr. B was explicitly conceived as a delegitimizing attack on an inherited class structure that privileged the aristocracy over the emerging middle class. In other words, Richardson sketches a *form* of relationship that is a weapon in the middle-class war on aristocratic privilege as well as the aristocratic homosocial bonding that becomes something of a running gag in eighteenth-century novels, as it is, for example, in *Tom Jones;* it is only because *Pamela* (and its author) are so firmly rooted in bourgeois militancy that the victory of Pamela's middle-class sensibility over a rival class position, and the intimate sexuality that she advocates so tirelessly, is represented as the end of class and the victory of a set of universally binding norms for fully humane relationships. See Nancy Armstrong, *Desire and Domestic Fiction: A Political History of the Novel* (New York: Oxford University Press, 1987), 108–34.

2. But once it has been pushed behind the domestic veil, the intimate sexuality Mr. B and Pamela initiate becomes a silent emblem of the most highly developed form of human sociability. As Jürgen Habermas's account makes clear, the bourgeois fantasy of the public sphere is premised on a sort of fantasy of universalizing the intimate sociability of the private sphere. For Habermas, the institutions of the public sphere "preserved a kind of social status that, far from presupposing the equality of status, disregarded status altogether. The tendency replaced the celebration of rank with the tact befitting equals. The parity on whose basis alone the authority of the better argument could assert itself against that of social hierarchy and in the end carry the day meant, in the thought of the day, the parity of 'common humanity,'" and this "common humanity" is most fully developed in the private relations imagined by early novels like *Pamela*. See *The Structural Transformation of the Public Sphere: An Inquiry into a Category of Bourgeois Society,* trans. Frederick Burger and Frederick Lawrence (Cambridge, MA: MIT Press, 1989), 36.

INDEX

Daniel Juan Gil is assistant professor of English at TCU in Fort Worth, Texas.